McGraw-Hill
ENGLISH

Authors

Elizabeth Sulzby
The University of Michigan
Marvin Klein
Western Washington University
William Teale
University of Texas at San Antonio
James Hoffman
University of Texas at Austin

Literature Consultant

Sylvia Peña
University of Houston

Contributing Authors

Lois Easton
Arizona Department of Education
Henrietta Grooms
Tyler ISD, Texas
Miles Olson
University of Colorado
Arnold Webb
Research for Better Schools, Philadelphia, Pennsylvania

McGraw-Hill School Division

New York   Oklahoma City   St. Louis   San Francisco   Dallas   Atlanta

Cover Photograph: © George Obremski/Image Bank

Grateful acknowledgment for permission to reprint copyrighted material, illustrations and photographs appearing in this book is made on page 448 of this book, which is hereby made a part of this copyright page.

ISBN 0-07-047057-X

McGraw-Hill School Division
1200 Northwest 63rd Street
Oklahoma City, Oklahoma 73116-5712

3 4 5 6 7 8 9 0   8 9 7 6 5 4 3 2 1 0 9

McGraw-Hill
ENGLISH

CONTENTS

UNIT 2

Composition · How-to Paragraph

Grammar · Nouns

UNIT 3

Composition • Book Report

Grammar • Verbs I

UNIT
4

Composition · Writing Directions

Grammar · Verbs II

UNIT 6

Composition · Research Report

Grammar · Adjectives

PART FOUR · Other Times and Other Places

UNIT 8

Composition · Story

Grammar · Sentences II

A Letter to the Student

You are beginning a new school year. You are meeting new people, including your teacher and classmates. This book is also new—at least to you.

As the authors of this book, we want you to know why we wrote it as we did. We planned this book so that you can make the best possible use of your time.

We are sure you will learn to write better this year. In this book, you will follow a clear, step-by-step plan as you write. You will also learn how knowledge of grammar makes you a better writer.

To help you get the most from this book, you will need to keep three types of journals or logs:

* **a personal journal**—in which you will write down your thoughts and feelings on many subjects during the year. You may use these notes to find ideas for your writing. This journal is for your eyes only.
* **a spelling log**—in which you will list the words you spell wrong in your writing. Keep it in a special place and go over the words before you do any new writing.
* **a learning log**—in which you will write about skills you found difficult and how you learned them, or skills you understood easily. By going over your learning log, you can do better next time.

Remember that we thought about you while writing this book. Let us know if we have helped you to improve your writing.

The Writing Process

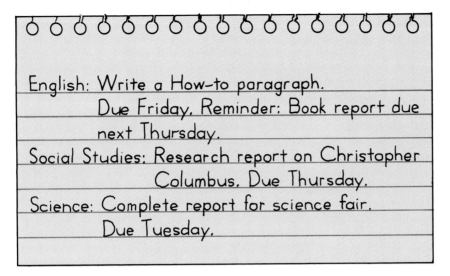

English: Write a How-to paragraph.
        Due Friday. Reminder: Book report due
        next Thursday.
Social Studies: Research report on Christopher
        Columbus. Due Thursday.
Science: Complete report for science fair.
        Due Tuesday.

Do you write a lot in your class? This book will help you write reports, stories, and letters. However, good writing takes planning. It starts long before you put pencil to paper.

In each unit, you will complete your own work by following a step-by-step plan called the *writing process*. Here, briefly, are the steps:

Planning

- First, you must know the features of the kind of writing you will do. You will read a literature model of that type.
- Next, you must know your purpose and audience for writing.
- Choose, a topic that interests you and that you know about.
- Then, take notes, make lists, draw a chart, or plan an outline to help you organize your ideas.

Choose a topic you *care* about.

Composing

- Use your notes to write a first draft. Include any new ideas you get, too.

> Every word does not have to be right. You can always make changes later.

Revising

- Have a partner read your draft. Discuss how you can make your ideas clearer or more interesting. Make changes in the content.
- Revise for style or organization. Decide where to combine sentences or move them around so they will read better. Add details or take out extra words.

> Now is the time to make your draft say *exactly* what you want it to say. Focus on your message.

Proofreading/Writing a Final Copy

- Read over your draft for mistakes in punctuation, capitalization, and spelling.
- Write a final copy, making all your changes.

> It takes a little time to check mistakes, but it's *important*. Tiny errors can get in the reader's way.

Presenting

- Find interesting ways to share your work with other people.

> Make your writing *fun* to read!

The more you practice the writing process, the easier it will be for you to write each time. Your work will improve steadily throughout the year.

Our Approach to Grammar

Some students like to study grammar. Others do not. We wrote this book for both kinds of students. We will explain how we did it.

First we asked ourselves this question: What is easy about grammar for students your age, and what is not? We tested students around the country. The results helped us plan the grammar parts of this book.

Every grammar lesson has a section called Strategy. It gives you a hint to help you understand a hard part of the grammar skill.

The instruction and exercises are divided into **A** and **B** sections. Use the **A** part of the instruction to help you with the **A** part of the exercises; do the same with the **B** parts.

You may sometimes wonder if there is a good reason to study grammar. In this book, we show how grammar can improve your writing.

We hope you will find this English book interesting and helpful. We worked hard to make it just right for you!

PART ONE

Builders
and Dreamers

Hold fast to dreams
For if dreams die
Life is a broken-winged bird
That cannot fly.

Hold fast to dreams
For when dreams go
Life is a barren field
Frozen with snow.

"Dreams"
by Langston Hughes

◆

   Dreaming and building something can be fun. If
our dreams are big enough, anything is possible. In
these two units, think about your dreams and the
special things you want to do.

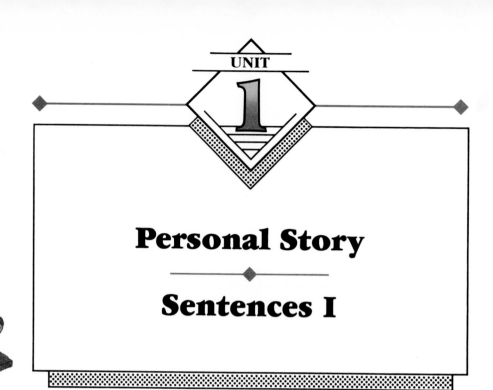

Personal Story

Sentences I

What Do You Know?

"What have you been doing lately?"

When a friend asks you this question, what do you say? You may tell stories about places you've been or people you've met. Your story might be about a project or hobby, such as starting a club or setting up a model train set. Whenever you tell someone about yourself, you are telling a **personal story**. A personal story tells what you feel and think about an experience.

There are many different ways to tell a personal story. You might tell a story to a friend in the playground or on the telephone. You also write personal stories in letters to friends or relatives.

Thinking About Personal Stories

What is a Personal Story?

A **personal story** is a story with these features:

- It tells a story that involved the writer. The story can be true or made up by the writer.
- The writer uses the words *I*, *me*, or *my* in the story.
- It tells about the time, place, and people in the story.
- It may tell about the events in the order in which they happened.
- It shows the writer's feelings about the experience.

People write and tell personal stories for different reasons. They tell funny stories to make others laugh. Some stories are about a special time or about a person who is important to us. Other stories are about an important lesson that the storyteller has learned and wants to share.

Storytellers have told personal stories throughout history. Today, you can read personal stories about the lives of famous people in magazines, newspapers, and books. Even many television shows and movies are based on personal stories.

Discussion

1. What are some stories about yourself that you like to tell again and again?
2. What makes a story interesting?
3. Which do you like better, writing a story or telling it to someone?

Reading a Personal Story

Now that you have learned about the special features of a personal story, read this personal story.

Sails in the Sky
by Laura Schenone

It is kite season now. That's what my friend Lani calls the fall—kite season. We go up to her roof every day to build kites. Her grandfather is teaching us how to make them the Chinese way, the way he learned when he was a boy.

If it wasn't for Lani and her grandfather I never would have known anything about kites. When I used to think about flying I would think of planes: loud engines and people in rows of seats with tiny windows. I would imagine flying to Puerto Rico, where my family is from. Now when I think of flying, I think of kites.

Lani and I got to be friends last year. We used to do things together after school. This year she seemed to be busy a lot. She would say she had to get right home when school was out. When I asked her why, she would just smile and say she was working on something with her grandfather.

One day Lani asked me to come home with her after school. She said she had something to show me. When we got to her apartment, we climbed six flights to the top of her building. Lani's grandfather was waiting for us on the roof. He was attaching a string to a beautiful kite—a Chinese hawk that he and Lani had built.

"So now you know what I've been doing after school," Lani said.

Lani's grandfather showed us the kites he had built. There was a butterfly kite, a fish kite, and bird kites for all kinds of wind. The kite he was most proud of was his dragon kite. It had a long tail made of many round pieces he had

The writer uses the word *I*.

Events are told in order.

21

strung together and painted green and red. I really hope that someday I can see that dragon kite fly. I would like to see that long tail twist through the air. Lani's grandfather said it is very difficult. It needs a lot of wind and many people. I asked if Lani and I could help him fly it. He said, "We'll see."

"Do you want to help me get the hawk into the air?" Lani asked. When I said yes she gave me the kite to hold. Then she stood a few feet away with the string. When the wind came I let go and she pulled the string tighter and tighter until the kite lifted up into the sky above Chinatown.

Now Lani and I are both making bird kites. I will paint mine blue when it is finished. It is a small bird with a light spine for light wind.

When we finish our kites, we will take them to the park. Or we will just fly them up here on the roof with Lani's grandfather.

The writer tells about her feelings.

To me the best way to fly is not in an airplane, but with a kite. I can feel the wind in my arms when I hold the string. I can make my kite dive. I can see the blue wings that I painted lift higher and higher into the air. It will be like my own small sail in the sky.

22

Understanding What You've Read

Write your answers on a separate piece of paper.

1. What time of year is it when the personal story is being told?
2. What characters are in the story?
3. How can you tell that the story is being told by the person who experienced it?
4. How does the writer feel about flying kites?
5. Why do you think this story is important to the person telling it?

Writing Assignment

Imagine that you've made a new friend. What story would you tell that new friend about yourself? In the next few lessons, you will learn to write a personal story, step by step. You will also see how another student, Gary, develops his personal story.

Your **audience** will be your class. Your **purpose** will be to describe a personal experience and your feelings about it.

Choose a Topic

Think of three general topics that you would like to write about in a personal story. Choose topics from the list below, or think of some of your own.

sports	class projects	pets
vacations	hobbies	clubs

Save your work for the next lesson.

Narrowing a Topic

Gary looked at his list of topics. He thought that the topic of school projects would be interesting to write about. But there were too many. Gary decided to choose just one, his school newspaper.

A personal story should tell about a single experience or event that is interesting to you. When a story tells about more than one event, it can be confusing to the reader, or audience.

Here are parts of two stories about school. As you read them, think about how they are different.

I like the third grade. Last month, I acted in the class play. Many people watched. Yesterday, we learned how to make paper animals. I have made a lot of new friends.	Being in class plays is exciting. The first time I got on stage, I was nervous. But after I said my first line, I knew that everything would go well.

In the paragraph at the left, the topic of school is too general, or broad. The paragraph tells about many experiences, but it does not tell enough about any one of them. To tell enough, you must limit your topic or subject. You must write about a smaller, *narrower* topic. The paragraph at the right is narrowed to one school experience, the class play. The topic is narrowed further because the writer tells about being on stage for the first time.

Notice how the broad topic of school has been narrowed to a specific topic.

Broad Topic	Narrowed Topic	Narrower Topic
school	science class	the time my teacher made a volcano
school	school trips	the class trip to the state science fair

24

Practice

A. Rewrite each list of topics. List the topics in order from broadest to narrowest.

1. baseball
sports
my first game

2. hobbies
building a model airplane
making models

3. class trips
trips
the class trip to the museum

B. For each of these broad topics, write a more narrow topic.

4. books
5. animals
6. fairs
7. cities
8. food
9. camp

Narrow Your Topic

Look at the list of topics that you made in the last lesson. Use what you have learned in this lesson to help you narrow each topic. Then choose a topic that is small enough to write about in a paragraph. Make sure your topic is interesting. Save your choice for the next lesson.

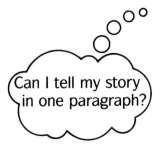

Can I tell my story in one paragraph?

Main Idea and Topic Sentence

A paragraph is usually about one main idea. The **main idea** is the most important idea about the topic. Look at the example below.

Topic: A Trip to Washington
Main Idea: saw a lot of famous people and places
Topic Sentence: During my trip to Washington, I saw a lot of famous people and places.

In some paragraphs, there is a sentence that states the main idea. This sentence is called a **topic sentence**. When you write your personal story, you will use a topic sentence. Your topic sentence will help you to decide what to tell about in the paragraph.

The topic sentence often begins the paragraph. It should be as interesting as possible. This sentence should make the reader want to read the rest of your story.

Here are two sentences that Gary thought could introduce his personal story. Which sentence do you think Gary used?

Topic Sentence: Last week, I learned some things about finding news.
Topic Sentence: Last week, I learned that news often pops up where you least expect it.

The second sentence is more interesting. It makes the reader want to find out what the news was and where Gary found it. He decided to use it.

Practice

A. Read each topic sentence and main idea. Write a topic sentence that tells the main idea.

    1. Topic: The Day I Cleaned Out My Attic

        Main Idea: I found a lot of interesting pictures

    2. Topic: Building Our Clubhouse

        Main Idea: we made a lot of funny mistakes

    3. Topic: Yesterday's Big Snowstorm

        Main Idea: it made each trip outside into an adventure

B. Read each pair of sentences. Choose the sentence that would be a more interesting topic sentence, and write it.

    4. a. I put on a magic show for my friends.

        b. My friends won't let me forget the time I put on a magic show.

    5. a. A week on Uncle Edgar's farm taught me to keep on my toes.

        b. I liked spending a week on Uncle Edgar's farm.

    6. a. I had a good time at the zoo.

        b. My trip to the zoo was as wild as a trip to the jungle.

APPLY STEP BY STEP

Write Your Topic Sentence

Look at the topic that you chose in the last lesson. Write a topic sentence that states your main idea. Save your work for the next lesson.

Using Supporting Details

The topic sentence tells the main idea of a paragraph. The other sentences add details that support the topic sentence. **Details** are facts or pieces of information that tell more about the main idea. Details that do not help the reader understand the main idea should not be in the paragraph.

Details in a paragraph can be organized in different ways. For a personal story, you could put the details in the order in which they happened.

Gary thought about his topic sentence: Last week, I learned that news often pops up where you least expect it. Then, he wrote some details to support the main idea. Here are notes he made for the details.

    ---ask neighbors for news
    ---Mr. Morris/Roberta have nothing to tell me
    ---Ms. Wilson talks about garden
    ---firemen get our cat out of tree
    ---my grandfather reads a lot of newpapers

After Gary listed his details, he realized that something was wrong. The details were listed in the order in which they happened. But the last detail did not support the main idea. The main idea was about finding news. The fact that Gary's grandfather reads a lot of newspapers did not tell more about the main idea. So, Gary crossed the last detail off the list.

Practice

A. Read the topic sentence and details below. Write the details that tell about the main idea. Leave out the details that do not tell about the main idea.
Topic Sentence: My first magic show was almost my last.
I got lost and was late starting the show.
During my first trick, my table fell over.
Last year, I saw a famous magician.
Then, I did a coin trick that everyone liked.
I also made animals out of balloons.
At the end of my show, all the people clapped.
I practice a lot.

B. Read the topic sentence and the details below. Then write the details in the order in which they happened.
Topic Sentence: Running a lemonade stand was more trouble than I bargained for.
Rain began right after I set up the stand.
Then, everyone already had lemonade.
I had to take everything back into the house.
Later, Joe told me where they got the lemonade.
After the rain, I set up the stand again.
He said that another stand was around the corner.

Write Your Details

Look at the topic sentence you wrote for your story. Then think about details that tell about your main idea. Make notes on the details. Put the details in order. Save your work for the next lesson.

Writing a First Draft

Read the first draft of the personal story below. The writer wasn't worried about making it perfect. It will be changed later.

Last week, I learned that news pops up where you least expect it first. I asked some neighbors if they could tell me anything for my school newspaper. Mr. Morris had no news. Roberta had no news. Next, Ms. Wilson talked about her garden for an hour I walkked to the school, but nothing was going on. Then, I got worryed. Would I ever find something to write about I went home. i saw firefighters rescueing our cat from a tree. I asked the firefighters a lot of Questions. The next time I search for news, I'll start by looking in my own backyard.

Write Your First Draft

Tell your ideas to your teacher. Begin with a topic sentence that tells the main idea. Make sure the topic sentence tells your feelings about the experience.

Use your list of details to help you put the events in order. Be sure to include the characters, time, and place of the experience. Write on every other line of the page. Save your work.

Discussing a First Draft

One way to improve your first draft is to discuss it with a classmate.

Discussion Strategy

Begin your discussion by saying something nice about your partner's work. This will make your partner feel more comfortable talking to you.

Use this checklist to discuss with your class the personal story on the previous page.

Content Checklist
- ✔ Does the story tell about the characters, time, and place of the experience?
- ✔ Are the events told in the correct order?
- ✔ Does the story show the writer's feelings about the experience?

Revise Your First Draft for Content

To the Reader: Exchange papers with a classmate. Cover up your partner's topic sentence. Then, read the rest of the story. Guess what the main idea is. If your guess is different from the topic sentence, discuss ways to make the main idea clearer. Use the Content Checklist for help.

To the Writer: Listen to your partner's comments. Then, revise your draft for content. Save your work.

Combining Sentences for Style

Gary's partner, Betty, noticed that some sentences repeated the same words and should be combined.

You can use the word *and* to combine sentences that have the same naming parts.

I asked questions. I took notes.
I asked questions <u>and</u> took notes.

You can also use the word *and* to combine sentences that have the same telling parts.

Hank walked to the park. Jan walked to the park.
Hank <u>and</u> Jan walked to the park.

Here is how Gary combined sentences in his draft.

These sentences have the same telling part.

These sentences have the same naming part.

Last week, I learned that news pops up where you least expect it first. I asked some neighbors if they could tell me anything for my school newspaper. Mr. Morris had no news. Roberta had no news. Next, Ms. Wilson talked about her garden for an hour I walkked to the school, but nothing was going on. Then, I got worryed. Would I ever find something to write about I went home. I saw firefighters rescueing our cat from a tree. I asked the firefighters a lot of Questions. The next time I search for news, I'll start by looking in my own backyard.

Practice

Read each pair of sentences. Combine either the naming parts or telling parts of the sentences to make a new sentence. Write a new sentence on another piece of paper.

1. Maria helped plan the class party.
   I helped plan the class party.
2. Joe folded the colored paper.
   Tanya folded the colored paper.
3. Our classmates laughed.
   Our classmates danced.
4. Everyone liked the songs.
   Everyone liked the talent show.
5. Friends from other classes joined us.
   Teachers from other classes joined us.
6. Later, everyone cleaned the tables.
   Later, everyone swept the floor.

Revising Checklist
   ✔ Have I included all of the features of a personal story?
   ✔ Where can I combine naming parts or telling parts of sentences to make new sentences?

Revise Your First Draft For Style

   Use the checklist above to help you revise your story. Use the proofreading marks to make changes on your first draft. Combine naming parts or telling parts.

Writing Sentences

Gary read his personal story again to make sure it was correct. He found the rules for paragraph form and punctuation in a grammar book. Here are the rules that Gary found.

Rule	Example
Indent the first sentence in a paragraph.	Last week, I learned that news pops up where you least expect it.
Begin each sentence with a capital letter.	When I got home, I saw firefighters.
A statement is a sentence that tells something. A statement ends with a period.	Firefighters were rescuing our cat from a tree.
A command is a sentence that gives an order or instruction. A command ends with a period.	Move away from the tree. Please clean the room.
An exclamation is a sentence that shows strong feeling or surprise. An exclamation ends with an exclamation mark.	I was excited! Please hurry! What a scary show!
A question is a sentence that asks something. It ends with a question mark.	Would I ever find something to write about?

Practice

Write the sentences below on another piece of paper. Use capital letters where necessary. Add the correct end marks. Indent the first sentence.

(1) i like to listen to the radio (2) last Friday, I turned on the radio in the middle of a news show (3) a reporter was talking about spaceships coming down. (4) that man really sounded scared (5) What was going on (6)finally, I found out that it was just a story (7) Wow, I would like to make shows like that when I grow up

Proofreading Checklist
✔ Did I indent the first sentence of the paragraph?
✔ Did I begin each sentence with a capital letter?
✔ Did I put the correct end mark at the end of each sentence?

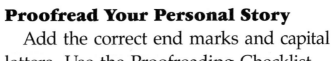

APPLY STEP BY STEP

Proofread Your Personal Story

Add the correct end marks and capital letters. Use the Proofreading Checklist. Make corrections on your draft. Save your work.

Checking Spelling/Writing a Final Copy

Spelling Strategy

When you proofread, keep a spelling notebook of misspelled words. Write them correctly in the book. Here is Gary's revised and proofread story.

> ¶ Last week, I learned that news pops up where you least expect it first. I asked some neighbors if they could tell me anything for my school newspaper. Mr. Morris had ~~no news.~~ Roberta had no news. Next, Ms. Wilson talked about her garden for an hour. I walked (walkked) to the school, but nothing was going on. Then, I got worried (worryed). Would I ever find something to write about I went home. and I saw firefighters rescuing (rescueing) our cat from a tree. I asked the firefighters a lot of Questions. The next time I search for news, I'll start by looking in my own backyard.

APPLY STEP BY STEP

Check Your Spelling

Use the proofreading marks to correct spelling mistakes.

Write a Final Copy

Write a neat, final copy of your personal story. Proofread your work.

Sharing Your Personal Story

Speaking/Listening Strategy

When telling your story in front of a group, speak loudly and clearly. Try to remember exactly how you felt during the events that you are telling about. If you are part of the audience, listen closely to learn the character, time, and place of the story, as well as the order of the events.

Choosing a Way to Share

Here are a few ways you can share your story.

Reading Aloud Read your personal story to the class. If you feel nervous, pretend that you are on the telephone talking to a friend.

Presenting a Play While you read your story, have students act out the events that you are describing.

Making a Class Reader Collect your classmates' personal stories, and put them in a book titled *Our Stories*. Put it on the class bulletin board.

Share Your Personal Story

Choose a way to share your personal story. Present your story, and find out your audience's feelings about it.

Begin a Learning Log

- What do I like most about my personal story?
- What part of writing the story was most fun?
- If I were assigned another personal story, what would I write about?

The Literature Connection: Sentences

Are words important? You bet they are! Without them, we could not talk or write to others. We need words to share our thoughts and ideas.

We can put our words together in sentences. A **sentence** can tell about anything. It can describe a pet or ask how to build a kite. It can tell why you feel happy or sad. A sentence can say anything you want.

Every word in a sentence means something. Sometimes you can make up your own words, too. Find the imaginary word the writer uses in this poem.

Blum
by
Dorothy Aldis

Dog means dog. And cat
  means cat.
And there are lots of
  words like that.
A cart's a cart to pull
  or push.
A leaf's a leaf on tree
  or bush.
But there's another word
  I say
When I am left alone to
  play.

The word is Blum. Blum
  is a word
That very few have ever
  heard.
It is very nice to
  hum.
Or you can shout it:
  BLUM BLUM BLUM.
But shout or whisper,
  hum or sing,
It doesn't mean a
  single thing.

Discussion

1. Do you like the word *blum*? Explain why.
2. What does *blum* mean to you?
3. What would happen if every word in a sentence were an imaginary word like *blum*?

The Writing Connection:
Sentences

Before you write a sentence, think about the exact idea you want to say. Each word you use will help you share the idea with others. Even if your sentence has an imaginary word like *blum*, readers may be able to figure out what the word means.

Here is an example.

The story was so blum that I laughed out loud. What does *blum* mean in the sentence? Since the story made the person laugh, *blum* could mean *funny*.

Activity

Make up a word of your own. You will use the word to tell about something from the picture above.

♦ Write the word on a piece of paper.
♦ Make up a meaning for your word. Write a good definition next to the word.
♦ On another paper, use your word in a sentence.

The sentence should tell something about the picture and give clues to the meaning of your word. Share your sentence with your classmates. Have your classmates write a definition for your word.

What Is a Sentence?

A **sentence** is a group of words that tells a complete thought.

A. A sentence must always tell a complete thought.

> Who swims well?
> A fish? My brother?
> A beaver?

A beaver swims well.

A group of words that is not a complete sentence confuses the reader. It makes no sense.

Swims well.

B. A sentence starts with a capital letter and ends with an end mark.

Beavers build dams.
The animals use sticks and rocks.
Mud holds the dams together.

Strategy

After you write a sentence, make sure the meaning is clear. Read it aloud. Does it make sense? Give it to a friend. Does your friend understand what you mean? Have you written a complete thought?

Check Your Understanding

A. Write the letter that tells whether each group of words is a *sentence* or *not a sentence*.
  1. Cuts down trees.
      a. sentence   **b.** not a sentence
  2. Beavers cut down trees.
      a. sentence   **b.** not a sentence

B. Write the letter that tells whether each group of words is a correct sentence.

3. beavers eat leaves and twigs **a.** yes **b.** no
4. Beavers eat leaves and twigs. **a.** yes **b.** no

Practice

A. Write whether each group of words is a *sentence* or *not a sentence*.

5. The busy animals.
6. Beavers drag large branches.
7. The animals make dams from wood.
8. The playful young beavers.

B. Add a capital letter and an end mark to make each group of words a sentence. Then, write the sentence.

9. beavers build houses
10. a beaver family lives in a house
11. tunnels lead in and out
12. the animals store food nearby

C. Mixed Practice Write each group of words that is a complete thought. Add capital letters and end marks.

13. Builds houses in ponds.
14. beavers work very hard
15. a beaver slaps the pond with its tail
16. many other animals
17. animals work
18. Late at night in the house of the beaver.

Apply: Journal

Suppose you could build a house all your own. What would it be like? Write three sentences describing it.

41

Statements and Questions

◆

A. One kind of sentence is a statement.

A **statement** is a sentence that tells something. A statement gives the reader information. Put a period at the end of a statement.

> The children visit the Brooklyn Bridge.
> John Roebling designed the bridge.

B. Another kind of sentence is a question.

A **question** is a sentence that asks for information. Put a question mark at the end of a question.

> Have you seen the Brooklyn Bridge?
> Who built the bridge?

Strategy

It's easy to forget end marks when you write. Go back and check each sentence. Make sure you have used an end mark. End marks tell the reader what kind of sentence you have written.

Check Your Understanding

A. Write the letter that tells whether each sentence is a statement or a question.
   1. The Brooklyn Bridge had a birthday party.
      a. statement   **b.** question
   2. Workers completed the bridge 100 years ago.
      a. statement   **b.** question

B. Use the directions for Check Your Understanding A.

    3. Who went to the party?

        a. statement   **b.** question

    4. Do you like birthday parties?

        a. statement   **b.** question

Practice

A. Write *statement* if the sentence is a statement. Write *not a statement* if it is not a statement.

    5. Who built the first bridge?

    6. Maybe a log fell across a stream.

    7. A person walked across the log.

    8. The log made a bridge.

B. Write *question* if the sentence is a question. Write *not a question* if it is not a question.

    9. Another person fell off the log.

    10. What did that person do?

    11. The person put a second log next to the first one.

    12. How did the second log help?

C. Mixed Practice Write each sentence with the correct end mark. Write if it is a statement or question.

    13. What did other people invent?

    14. Some people built tall buildings.

    15. What do very tall buildings need?

    16. A tall building needs elevators.

    17. How do inventors think of new ideas?

    18. A steel bridge is stronger than a wooden one.

    19. People wonder who built the very first bridge.

Apply: Work with a Partner

Write two riddles. Make each riddle a question. Ask a friend to write statements that answer the riddles.

43

Commands and Exclamations

You have already learned about statements and questions. There are two other kinds of sentences.

A. The third kind of sentence is a command.

A **command** is a sentence that tells somebody to do something. Put a period at the end of a command.

Please come here.   Get me a hammer.
Find some nails.   Please measure the board.

B. The fourth kind of sentence is an exclamation.

An **exclamation** is a sentence that shows strong feeling or surprise. Put an exclamation mark (**!**) at the end of an exclamation.

What a good plan Alice drew!
How happy the children feel!
Fred bought so much lumber!

Strategy

Sometimes it's hard to tell whether a sentence is an exclamation or a statement. The writer decides. When you write, decide if the sentence shows strong feeling or surprise. If it does, use an exclamation mark.

Check Your Understanding

A. Write the letter that tells whether each sentence is a command or an exclamation.
1. Pass Bill the plans.
   a. command   **b.** exclamation
2. Please get Susan a ruler.
   a. command   **b.** exclamation

B. Use the directions for Check Your Understanding A.

   3. What a long board José carries!

      a. command   **b.** exclamation

   4. How heavy the board is!

      a. command   **b.** exclamation

Practice

A. Write *command* if the sentence is a command. Write *not a command* if it is not a command.

   5. Please cut this board.

   6. Stack the boards over there.

   7. How great the clubhouse looks!

   8. Did you sand this board?

B. Write *exclamation* if the sentence is an exclamation. Write *not an exclamation* if it is not an exclamation.

   9. An adult helps the children.

   10. Paint the outside first.

   11. What a bright color Lisa chose!

   12. How the children enjoy the clubhouse!

C. Mixed Practice Write each sentence with the correct end mark. Write if it is a *command* or an *exclamation*.

   13. Please move the bricks

   14. How hard the children work

   15. Please work harder, Michiko and Susan

   16. Wow, is this door heavy

   17. Hurry

   18. Did you ever see such a great clubhouse

Apply: Learning Log

What was the hardest part of this lesson? Describe it in your learning log. Tell what you still need to know about commands and exclamations.

Sentence Parts

A sentence has two main parts. They are called the **complete subject** and the **complete predicate**.

A. The **complete subject** of a sentence tells whom or what the sentence is about.

> Ferdinand Magellan planned a sea voyage.

> The long trip proved something important.

B. The **complete predicate** of a sentence tells what the subject does.

> The Spanish king gave Magellan five ships.

> The ships left Spain in 1519.

Strategy

Use the chart to help you write complete sentences.

Subject	+	Predicate	=	Sentence
Who or what the sentence is about	+	What the subject does	=	Complete thought

Check Your Understanding

A. Write the letter that names the underlined part of each sentence.

   1. The captain led the voyage.
      a. subject   **b.** predicate
   2. Brave sailors steered the ships.
      a. subject   **b.** predicate

B. Use the directions for Check Your Understanding A.

   3. One ship sprang a leak.
      a. subject   **b.** predicate
   4. A storm sank the ship.
      a. subject   **b.** predicate

Practice

A. Write each sentence. Tell whether the underlined words are the complete subject or the complete predicate.

    5. <u>Another ship</u> returned to Spain.

    6. <u>The explorers</u> sailed around South America.

    7. <u>The little ships</u> crossed the Pacific Ocean.

    8. <u>The sailors</u> ran out of food.

B. Use the directions for Practice A.

    9. The crew <u>found food at last</u>.

   10. Magellan <u>died during the long trip</u>.

   11. Another captain <u>led the crew</u>.

   12. The men <u>continued the voyage</u>.

C. Mixed Practice Write each sentence. Tell whether the underlined words are the complete subject or the complete predicate.

   13. Pirates <u>attacked the ship</u>.

   14. <u>Only one ship</u> returned to Spain.

   15. The men <u>came home after three years</u>.

   16. Many people <u>greeted the tired sailors</u>.

   17. <u>The king</u> listened to their adventures.

   18. Magellan <u>proved something important</u>.

   19. The world <u>is round</u>.

   20. <u>Merchants and settlers</u> visited many new lands.

Apply: Test a Partner

Write two complete subjects and two complete predicates. See if your partner can complete each sentence by writing the missing part. Check to be sure that each sentence makes sense.

Complete Subjects

The **complete subject** of a sentence tells whom or what the sentence is about.

A. Sometimes the complete subject is only one word. The complete subject is shown in red in the sentences below.

Sharon read about birds.

Bluebirds made a nest next door.

Swifts build nests in chimneys.

B. The complete subject can be a group of several words. All the words tell whom or what the sentence is about.

The lazy cowbird borrows a nest.

The bright red cardinal brings straw.

Several children tell about birds.

Strategy

Check the beginning of the sentence when you look for the complete subject. Most complete subjects come at the start of the sentence, before the action word.

Check Your Understanding

A. Write the letter of the complete subject.
1. Woodpeckers drill holes in trees.
    a. Woodpeckers   **b.** drill   **c.** holes   **d.** trees
2. Ken sees a woodpecker in the park.
    a. Ken   **b.** sees   **c.** woodpecker   **d.** park

B. Use the directions for Check Your Understanding A.

   3. A noisy bluejay flew into the tree.

      a. noisy   **b.** A noisy bluejay   **c.** into the tree

   4. Groups of birds travel together.

      a. Groups of birds   **b.** birds   **c.** travel

      d. together

Practice

A. Write each sentence. Underline the complete subject.

   5. Birds live in nests.

   6. Swallows put mud on walls.

   7. Chicks hatch from eggs in the spring.

B. Use the directions for Practice A.

   8. The busy parents bring food to the chicks.

   9. The tiny babies peep loudly.

  10. Several school children found a nest.

  11. The tiny nest hangs from a branch.

C. Mixed Practice Write each sentence. Underline the complete subject.

  12. Parrots perch in a cage.

  13. Many birds fly south in winter.

  14. People build houses for birds.

  15. Several students read about birdhouses.

  16. A flock of birds lands on the roof.

  17. The hungry birds eat seeds and flowers.

  18. All the boys and girls watch the birds.

  19. Chickadees and martins live in the birdhouse.

Apply: Work with a Group

Work with some classmates to write sentences. Each person adds a word until the sentence is complete.

Complete Predicates

The **complete predicate** of a sentence tells what the subject does.

A. Sometimes the complete predicate is one word. The complete predicate is shown in blue in the sentences below.

The wind howled.

The sky darkened.

The storm arrived.

B. Often the complete predicate is a group of several words. All these words tell what the subject does.

Aunt Em ran to the cellar.

The dog hid under the bed.

Dorothy chased her little dog.

Strategy

To find the complete predicate of a sentence, first look for the complete subject. The predicate usually comes after the complete subject. Remember that the complete predicate often has more than one word.

Check Your Understanding

A. Write the letter of the complete predicate of each sentence.
1. The house shook.
    a. house   **b.** the house   **c.** shook
2. Poor Dorothy fell.
    a. Poor Dorothy   **b.** fell   **c.** Dorothy fell

B. Use the directions for Check Your Understanding A.

3. The house flew through the air.
   a. The house   **b.** flew through the air
4. Dorothy traveled to Oz.
   a. Dorothy   **b.** traveled to Oz

Practice

A. Write each sentence. Draw one line under the complete predicate.

5. The big house landed.
6. Dorothy jumped.
7. The little dog whined.
8. The door opened.

B. Use the directions for Practice A.

9. Dorothy stepped outside.
10. The Munchkins welcomed the girl.
11. The little people sang for Dorothy.
12. Dorothy met a sad scarecrow.

C. Mixed Practice Write each sentence. Underline the complete predicate.

13. The scarecrow asked for a brain.
14. A tin man creaked.
15. A frightened lion cried.
16. Dorothy made many friends in Oz.
17. The friends found the Emerald City.
18. Toto followed Dorothy everywhere.
19. Dorothy and Toto followed a yellow brick road.
20. Dorothy woke up and saw Aunt Em.

Apply: Exploring Language

Name four things you like to eat. Write a sentence about each. Underline the complete predicate.

Dictionary: Alphabetical Order

Alphabetical order means the order of the letters in the alphabet.

```
A B C D E F G H I J K L M
N O P Q R S T U V W X Y Z
```

A. Words in a dictionary are listed in alphabetical order to make them easy to find. All words that start with the letter *a* come first. Next come all words starting with *b*, and so on.

First letter: a̲ble   b̲aby   c̲abin   z̲oo

B. Many words start with the same letter. They are put in alphabetical order by their second letter.

Second letter: ab̲le   ac̲t   ad̲d

If the first two letters are the same, the third letter is used to put the words in order.

Third letter: abl̲e   aba̲ord   abs̲ent

Strategy

You can use alphabetical order to find words quickly in other books, too. Encyclopedias and telephone books are examples. Can you think of others?

Check Your Understanding

A. Write the letter of the word in each group that would appear first in a dictionary.

   1. a. dark   **b.** house   **c.** milk   **d.** fill
   2. a. wet   **b.** old   **c.** silk   **d.** quilt

B. Use the directions for Check Your Understanding A.

3. **a.** churn
   b. cent
   c. circus
   d. comb

4. **a.** majesty
   b. man
   c. market
   d. mail

Practice

A. Write each group of words in alphabetical order.

5. enjoy
   sign
   computer

6. puppet
   force
   ill

7. hotel
   sew
   dial

8. frown
   puddle
   rocket

B. Write each group of words in alphabetical order.

9. shine
   spirit
   steam

10. even
    electric
    expert

11. mood
    moment
    monkey

12. rack
    rapid
    rage

C. Mixed Practice   Write each group of words in alphabetical order.

13. prize
    explain
    noodle

15. hound
    hotel
    home

17. sun
    suit
    sweet

19. zero
    whale
    very

14. color
    burn
    bunny

16. indoor
    insist
    infant

18. branch
    bring
    barrel
    brick

20. witch
    within
    which
    whine

Apply: Work with a Group

Divide the class into groups of three. List the first names of the group members in alphabetical order. Then list the last names of the members in alphabetical order. Compare the two lists.

Dictionary: Guide Words

sir / sizzle

sir (sėr) *noun* **1** polite title for speaking or writing to a man. **2** the title given to a knight.

site (sīt) *noun* place or location: *Here is the site for the new library.*

sit·ter (sit'ər) *noun* a baby-sitter.

A. One way to find words easily in a dictionary is to use the guide words. **Guide words** are pairs of words that appear at the top of a dictionary page. They show the first and last words on the page.

B. On the sample page above, the guide words are *sir* and *sizzle*. *Sir* is the first word on the page and *sizzle* is the last. All the other words on the page come between these two words in alphabetical order. For example, the words *sister* and *six* would appear on the page. *Seed* and *slow* would not.

Strategy

When you want to look up a word, use guide words to find the page where it appears.

Check Your Understanding

A. Write the letter of the word or words that correctly complete each sentence.
  1. Each dictionary page has ___.
     a. one guide word   **b.** two guide words
  2. Guide words appear at the ___ of the page.
     a. top   **b.** bottom   **c.** side

B. Use the directions for Check Your Understanding A.

   3. The word ___ would *not* appear on the sample page.
       a. sit **b.** simple **c.** size **d.** sister

   4. The word ___ *would* appear on the sample page.
       a. sixty **b.** side **c.** skate **d.** sip

Practice

A. Write the sentences. Fill in the missing words.

   5. Guide words tell you the ___ and ___ words on a dictionary page.

   6. Guide words are found at the ___ of the page.

   7. Guide words help you ___ words easily.

B. Write the guide words. Then write the word that would appear on the same dictionary page.

   8. sock/soil   sail soda slow

   9. practice/program   price prune put

   10. record/regular   refuse raid rein

   11. call/castle   chart cart cat

C. Mixed Practice Write each word. Write the guide words that would appear on the same dictionary page. Choose from the guide words in the box.

12. tag	**15.** tail	**18.** tunnel
13. tennis	**16.** talent	**19.** theater
14. truck	**17.** trip	**20.** turn

> **table/tame**
>
> **team/theme**
>
> **trap/turtle**

Apply: Work with a Partner

Write three words on a sheet of paper. Trade papers with a partner. In a dictionary, find guide words for the page where each word appears.

Dictionary: Word Meanings

mug·gy (mug′ē) *adjective* warm and damp. *It was a muggy day.*

mul·ber·ry (mul′ber′ē) *noun* **1** tree with small, berrylike fruit. **2** purple fruit of the mulberry.

mule (myül) *noun* **1** animal that is a mixture of a donkey and a horse. **2** stubborn person.

mumps (mumps) *noun* disease that causes fever and swelling of the face, and is spread from person to person.

munch (munch) *verb* chew noisily: *The rabbit munched its carrot.*

mur·al (myür′əl) *noun* picture painted on a wall.

A. A dictionary tells the meanings of words. Find the word *muggy* on this dictionary page. What does *muggy* mean?

A dictionary may also give an **example sentence** to show how a word is used. Read the example sentence after the meaning of *muggy*.

B. Some words have more than one meaning. Each meaning has a number before it. How many meanings does the word *mulberry* have?

Strategy

When you look up a word, read all the meanings. Which one fits the sentence you read?

Check Your Understanding

A. Use the dictionary page to answer the questions.

   1. Which word means a kind of disease?

   a. mule   **b.** mumps   **c.** muggy   **d.** mural

   2. Which word has an example sentence?

   a. mural   **b.** mule   **c.** muggy   **d.** mulberry

B. Use the dictionary page to answer the questions.

    3. How many meanings does <u>mule</u> have?

        a. one   **b.** two   **c.** three   **d.** four

    4. Which meaning of <u>mule</u> is about an animal?

        a. first   **b.** second   **c.** first and second

Practice

A. Use the dictionary page to answer the questions.

    5. What is the meaning of <u>mural</u>?

    6. What is the example sentence for <u>munch</u>?

    7. What does mumps cause?

B. Write the correct meaning of the underlined word in each sentence. Use the dictionary page.

    8. A <u>mule</u> pulled the wagon.

    9. We planted a <u>mulberry</u> in the yard.

  10. George is a <u>mule</u>, and he won't give up.

C. Mixed Practice Use the dictionary page to answer the questions.

  11. What is the meaning of <u>munch</u>?

  12. Which word means a tree or a fruit?

  13. Which word describes weather?

  14. Which meaning of <u>mulberry</u> fits this sentence?

       We picked mulberries for lunch.

  15. Write another example sentence for <u>munch</u>.

Apply: Work with a Partner

Find a word in the dictionary that has more than one meaning. Write two different meanings of the word. Have your partner write an example sentence for each meaning.

LANGUAGE IN ACTION

Using the Telephone

Suppose the phone rings, but your dad is busy. Do you know how to answer the phone correctly?

♦ Never give a stranger your phone number.
♦ Be polite. When you answer, say, "Hello," then ask the caller's name. You might wait until you know who the caller is before you say your name. Ask your parents about this.
♦ Never say that your parents aren't home or that you are alone. Just say that they can't come to the phone.
♦ If the call is not for you, take a message. Write down the caller's name and phone number. Write down the name of the person the message is for.
♦ Keep important phone numbers by each phone.

Practice

Imagine that you are listening to this phone conversation. Write three things that are wrong with it.

Art: Hello, Jackson residence. Arthur speaking.
Deb: Put Louis on the phone.
Art: Who's calling, please?
Deb: None of your business. Get Louis.
Art: There's no one home. May I take a message?
Deb: Never mind.

Apply

Work with a partner. Take turns pretending to answer the phone when your partner calls. Take messages.

HISTORY OF LANGUAGE

First Names in Different Languages

The teacher called out names in gym class. "John, Jean, Juan, Johannes, Ian," he read from his list. Then he started to laugh. "You all have the same name," he said. How could that be?

The teacher meant that all the boys' names had the same origin. They are spelled and pronounced differently because they come from different languages. All the names on the list come from the name *Jochanan* in the Hebrew language. Here is how Jochanan is spelled in other languages. Notice that many letters are the same in the different spellings.

French . . . **Jean**   German . . . **Joha**nnes
Spanish . . . **Juan**   Scottisch . . . **Ian**

Ann wanted to know about her name. What is its origin? How is it spelled in other languages? Ann looked in a book of names. She learned that her name came from the Hebrew name *Chana*. Here is how Chana is spelled in other languages.

French . . . **An**ne   German . . . **Ha**nn**ah**
Spanish . . . **Ana**   Italian . . . **Anna**

Activity

Write the three names in each line with the same origin. Look for names with many of the same letters.
1. Pierre, Phillip, Peter, Pedro, Paul
2. Judy, Joan, Jeanne, Jill, Juana
3. Mary, Mabel, Marie, Maria, Madeleine
4. Amos, Anton, Alex, Anthony, Antoine

UNIT REVIEW

Personal Story   *(page 19)*
1. On your paper, list three features of a personal story.

Main Idea and Topic Sentence/Using Supporting Details   *(pages 26-29)*
2. Read the topic sentence below. Then read the details that follow. Write the details that tell more about the topic sentence. *Topic sentence*: Writing my first song was not easy at all.
  a. I had to decide whether to make up the tune first or the words first.
  b. My favorite song is "Do Re Mi."
  c. I had trouble getting my lines to rhyme.

Combining Sentences/Punctuating Sentences
(pages 32-35)
Combine the naming parts or telling parts of each sentence pair below. Write each new sentence on another piece of paper.
  3. a. My brother ran in a race.   **b.** My aunt ran in a race.
  4. a. Paul watched the runners.   **b.** Paul cheered loudly.

Write these sentences correctly on another piece of paper. Use capital letters and end marks where needed.
  5. do you know how to make paper airplanes
  6. last week i made my first plane

What Is a Sentence?   *(pages 40-41)*
Write each group of words that is a complete thought. Add capital letters and end marks where they are needed.
  7. a zebra eats grass
  8. the young playful zebras
  9. zebras leap
  10. races across the field
  11. one large animal
  12. a baby zebra kicks
  13. some animals trot
  14. drinks from a stream

Statements, Questions, Commands, and Exclamations   *(pages 42-45)*

Write each sentence with the correct end mark. Write whether it is a *statement*, *question*, *command*, or *exclamation*.

15. Look at the polar bear
16. Please come here
17. When do the seals eat
18. The monkeys chatter
19. Which frog jumps best
20. How loud that bird is

Complete Subjects and Complete Predicates
(pages 46-51)

Write each sentence. Put one line under the complete subject. Put two lines under the complete predicate.

21. The first cars ran on steam.
22. One early car used three wheels.
23. Henry Ford built a famous car.
24. Cars traveled faster than horses.
25. People liked the strange new invention.

Dictionary Skills   *(pages 52-57)*

Write each group of words in alphabetical order.

26. sled   bus   motor
27. lady   label   lace
28. each   ever   eight

---

head (hed) *noun* **1** top part of the human body, or front part of an animal. **2** top part of a thing. **3** leader, person in charge: *The mayor is head of the city*.

Use the dictionary entry to answer the questions.

29. How many meanings are given for the word *head*?
30. What is the example sentence for *head*?
31. Which meaning of *head* would tell about a pin or a nail?
32. Write an example sentence for the first meaning of *head*.
33. Which guide words would be on the same page as *head*?
    hand/hinge   heart/high   have/hear

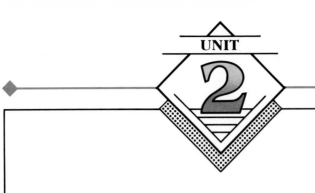

How-to Paragraph

Nouns

What Do You Know?

"How do I do this?"

Have you ever told someone how to play a game? Have you ever followed written instructions that explained how to build or cook something? Giving and following instructions is part of everyday life.

Have you ever built a model without following directions or by using directions that were unclear? When you were finished, the model probably did not look right. To be useful, instructions have to be clear. Each step must be easy to understand and follow. The steps must be in correct order, too. Instructions must also be complete. If even one step is missing, a task becomes difficult or even impossible to complete.

Thinking About How-to Paragraphs

What Is a How-to Paragraph?

A **how-to paragraph** has these features:

- A topic sentence introduces the job to be done.
- It names the materials needed.
- It explains the steps for doing or making something.
- Detail sentences tell each step to be followed.
- The steps are presented in their correct order.

Instructions can be found in many different places. The back of a package of food may contain cooking instructions. A game usually contains instructions on how to play it. Kits for building model cars, boats, and airplanes include instructions so that you know how to put the pieces of the models together correctly.

You can use instruction paragraphs to learn to do many things. You can also write instruction paragraphs to teach others what you already know.

Discussion

1. What instructions have you given to friends or relatives lately?
2. What instructions have you followed lately?
3. What often makes instructions hard to follow?

Reading a How-to Paragraph

Galileo was one of the greatest scientists who ever lived. Read this selection about one of his most important experiments.

In about 1590, Galileo tested another idea. Until that time, people believed that objects of different weights fell to earth at different speeds. They thought that a heavy object fell much more quickly than a lighter one. It seems as if that would be true, doesn't it? But Galileo was not so sure. So he tried dropping two objects of unequal weights. Both objects landed on the ground at almost the same time.

The topic sentence tells what is to be done.
The paragraph names the materials you'll need.
The steps are given in correct order.

You can test the "law of falling bodies" for yourself. First, get a paper clip or a hairpin. Then take a heavier object such as a coin, a pencil, or even a sneaker. Then, hold both objects, one in each hand, high above your head. Finally, drop both objects at the same time. See whether they land at the same time.

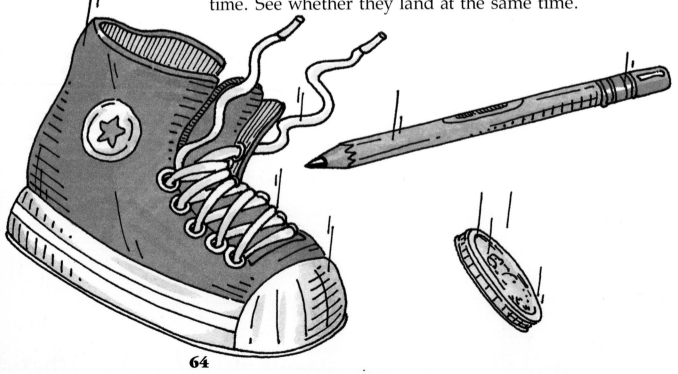

Understanding What You've Read

Answer these questions about the how-to paragraph.

1. What light object does the author suggest that you use in the experiment?

2. After you get the objects, what do you do with them?

3. Why is it important to drop both objects at the same time?

4. Why do you think it is important for the objects to be of different weights?

5. What else can you learn from the experiment?

Writing Assignment

An expert is someone who knows a great deal about some special thing. What are you an expert at? Think about the things you know how to do well. How would you tell other people how to do one of these activities?

In this unit, you will learn to write a how-to paragraph, step by step. You will also see how another student, Victor, writes his instructions. Your **audience** will be your classmates. Your **purpose** will be to give instructions that are clear enough for your classmates to follow.

Choose a Topic

Choose one of these topics for your paragraph. Or, make up one of your own. It's your choice.

- ◆ how to play a game
- ◆ how to set a table
- ◆ how to cook something
- ◆ how to build a model

Write down your choice. Save your work.

Writing Steps in Correct Order

The sentences in a how-to paragraph have to be in the right order. The first step should be listed first. The second step must be given next, and so on. If the steps are in the correct order, a person can follow them easily.

Sequence words help keep the order of the steps clear. Some sequence words are *first*, *next*, *then*, and *finally*.

Victor's class is creating a crafts book. Each student will write a set of instructions that tells how to make something. Victor has decided to write a paragraph that tells how to make a pencil holder.

Victor begins by listing these steps:

> - Trace the milk carton on a piece of paper.
> - Cut the top and part of the sides off a small milk carton.
> - Glue each piece of paper to a side of the carton.
> - Decorate the carton with stickers glitter or cutouts that you glue to the paper.

Victor soon notices that his steps are not in order. The second step should really be listed first. So, he changes its position on the list. He also realizes that he has left out this step:

> - Cut out what you have traced.

Can you see where it goes on the list?

Practice

These steps for growing a sunflower are mixed up. In addition, one step is missing. Write the steps in correct order in paragraph form. Add the missing step. Begin with the topic sentence.

- Then, fill the flowerpot with dark, moist soil.
- Growing a sunflower is easy and fun.
- In about two weeks, the seed will sprout.
- By the end of the summer, your sunflower might be 10 feet tall.
- After planting the seed, place the pot in a sunny spot.
- First, get a large, clean flowerpot.
- Keep the plant well watered all the time.
- Plant a sunflower seed in the soil.

Make a List

Look at the activity you chose in the last lesson. Narrow the topic, if necessary. (p. 24) For example, name the game you will tell how to play. Or, tell which toy you will describe how to make. List the steps that you need to complete your how-to paragraph. If you cannot list these steps, choose another activity that you know how to do. Remember to include any materials that are needed. Save your work for the next lesson.

Do I know all of the steps for the activity I have chosen?

Writing a First Draft

Read the first draft of Victor's how-to paragraph. He wasn't worried about making it perfect. It will be changed later.

> Pencel holders are easy to make. First cut the top and part of the sides off a small milk carton Next trace the milk carton on a piece of paper. then cut out what you have traced. Glue each peece of paper to a side of the carton. Finally, decorate the carton with stickers glitter or cutouts that you glue to the carton

APPLY STEP BY STEP

Write Your First Draft

You may want to talk about your ideas for a how-to paragraph with your teacher or a classmate. Or, you may want to work alone. Be sure to begin your paragraph with a topic sentence. List all the steps in order. Try to make your how-to paragraph as clear as possible. Write on every other line. Save your work.

Discussing a First Draft

Show your work to a classmate. See if he or she has any ideas for how to make it better.

Discussion Strategy

Everyone knows that it is easy to make mistakes. When you give suggestions, show your partner that it is easy to correct the mistakes. For example, don't say, "These steps are all mixed-up!" Instead, suggest, "Shouldn't this third step really be listed first?"

Use the Content Checklist to discuss Victor's draft with your class.

Content Checklist
- ✔ Does the paragraph begin with a topic sentence?
- ✔ Does it name the necessary materials?
- ✔ Do the detail sentences tell each step?
- ✔ Are the steps presented in their correct order?

Revise Your First Draft for Content

To the Reader: Read your partner's draft. Imagine you were trying to follow the steps in the paragraph. Can you think of any problems you might have? If you can, explain them to your partner. Use the Content Checklist to help.

To the Writer: Take notes on your partner's suggestions. Use them to revise your draft. Save your work for later.

Giving Exact Information

To be useful, instructions must give clear information. Exact amounts, distances, and directions are often helpful. Each set of instructions below tells how to open a combination lock. Which set gives more exact information?

Turn the dial past 0 to 33. Then turn to 45. Finally, turn past 0 twice and stop at 6.	Turn the dial clockwise past 0 to 33. Then turn counterclockwise to 45. Finally, turn clockwise past 0 twice and stop at 6.

The paragraph at the right gives more exact information. It tells *what direction* to turn the dial.

Read the instructions below for using a dishwasher. Which piece of information should be more exact?

Load the dishwasher. Then put soap in the proper area. Turn the dishwasher on full cycle.

The instructions do not tell how much soap to use. There should be a *measurement* such as "3 tablespoons of soap."

Here is how Victor made his directions more exact.

Pencel holders are easy to make. First cut the top and part of the

$a \frac{1}{2}$ inch

sides off a small milk carton. Next trace *each side of* the milk carton on a piece of

paper. then cut out what you have traced. Glue each peece of paper

to a side of the carton. Finally, decorate the carton with stickers

glitter or cutouts that you glue to the carton

Practice

Read each pair of sentences. Tell which one gives the most complete or exact information. Then write what information was missing from the other sentence.

1. "Sardines" is an enjoyable hiding game for four or more players.
   If you like "Hide-and-seek," you'll love "Sardines."
2. Everyone waits while the player who is "it" hides.
   One player hides while the others close their eyes and count to 100.
3. Each player searches for the hiding player alone.
   Everyone looks all over for the hiding player.
4. When a player finds the hiding place, he or she quietly hides with the person who is "it."
   You shouldn't shout or anything when you find where "it" is hiding.
5. The game ends when everyone finds the hiding place.
   Everyone hides until the game is finished.

Revising Checklist

✔ Have I included all the features of a how-to paragraph? (p. 63)
✔ Can I combine any subjects or predicates to make new sentences? (p. 32)
✔ Have I given exact information?

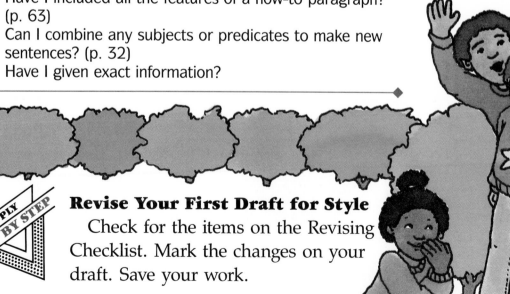

APPLY STEP BY STEP

Revise Your First Draft for Style
Check for the items on the Revising Checklist. Mark the changes on your draft. Save your work.

Using Commas

When you talk, you often pause, or stop briefly. When you write, a comma is a way to show a pause. Commas help to make the meaning of your sentences clear.

After Victor revised his paragraph, he looked up the rules for using commas. The chart shows some rules that Victor found.

Rule	Example
Use a comma (,) after a time order word when it begins a sentence.	First, fold the paper in half. Next, draw a line between the two corners.
Use a comma (,) after the words *yes, no,* and *well,* when they begin a sentence.	Yes, I like the crafts book. Well, we worked hard on it.
Use a comma (,) to set off the name of a person directly spoken to in a sentence.	Victor, I liked your suggestion. Thank you for helping, Rosemary.
Use a comma (,) to separate each item in a series. A series names three or more objects.	Victor, Rosemary, and Dan made pencil holders. Each pencil holder is made with a milk carton, paper, and stickers.
Use a comma before *and* when you join two complete thoughts.	Victor got the paper, and Dan found the milk cartons.

Practice

The commas are missing from the sentences below. Write each sentence. Add commas where necessary.

1. Randy are you going to vote for me?
2. No I plan to vote for Jimmy Dunn.
3. Is Jimmy making buttons posters or pinwheels to help him get votes?
4. He's making a giant kite and he'll fly it above the school tomorrow.
5. Jimmy Kevin and I are making the kite today.
6. First we thought we'd print "Have Fun with Dunn" on it.
7. Finally we decided on "Dunn Is the One!"
8. Well I hope it's a windy day tomorrow.
9. No I don't want your kite to fly well.
10. I've just made 40 pinwheels and I need the wind to make them spin.

Proofreading Marks	
∧	add
⌇	take away
¶	indent
≡	capitalize
/	small letter
◯	check spelling
∿	transpose

Proofreading Checklist

✔ Did I indent the first sentence of each paragraph? (p. 34)
✔ Did I begin each sentence with a capital letter? (p. 34)
✔ Did I put the correct end mark at the end of each sentence? (p. 34)
✔ Did I follow the rules for using commas correctly?
✔ Do all my sentences express complete thoughts?

APPLY STEP BY STEP

Proofread Your How-to Paragraph

Use the checklist above to proofread your work. Check to make sure you used capital letters and punctuation marks correctly. Make all corrections on your draft. Save your work for later.

Checking Spelling/Writing a Final Copy

Look at a word several times. Seeing the word helps you spell it. Picture the word in your mind. What is the order of the letters?

Here is Victor's revised and proofread paragraph.

> Pencil
> Pencel holders are easy to make. First, cut the
>   at inch
> top and part of the sides off a small milk carton.
>   each side of
> Next trace the milk carton on a piece of paper.
> then, cut out what you have traced. Glue each
>   piece
> peece of paper to a side of the carton. Finally,
> decorate the carton with stickers glitter or
> cutouts that you glue to the carton.

Check Your Spelling

APPLY
STEP BY STEP

Use the proofreading marks to correct spelling mistakes. Add any misspelled words to your spelling log.

Write a Final Copy

Write a neat, final copy of your how-to paragraph. Proofread your work. Be sure all your changes are on your final copy. Save your work.

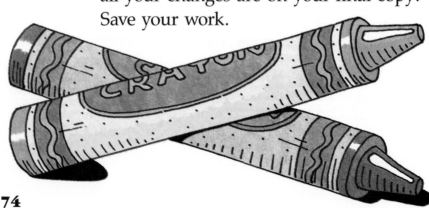

Sharing Your How-to Paragraph

Speaking/Listening Strategy

As you read aloud, try to avoid long pauses. Be familiar with the material. If you are in the audience, ask questions about information you missed or did not understand.

Choosing a Way to Share

Here are some ways to share your how-to paragraph.
Reading Aloud Prepare a few drawings or diagrams that show the steps of your how-to paragraph. Show them as you read your work.

Presenting a Demonstration As a friend reads each step of your paragraph, you can demonstrate the activity for your classmates.

Making a Book Put your paragraph together with your classmates' and make a collection. You might call it "Things to Do When There's Nothing to Do."

Share Your How-to Paragraph

Choose the way you want to share your paragraph. Present it and find out how many members of your audience think they might enjoy the activity.

Add to Your Learning Log
- What do I like best about my how-to paragraph?
- Which steps were hardest to explain?
- If I were assigned another how-to paragraph, what would I do differently?

The Literature Connection: Nouns

Are your dreams different from other people's dreams? Of course they are! To tell about any dream, however, you need nouns. **Nouns** are words that name persons, places, or things.

Did you ever dream about a turtle? If so, your turtle may have been like the one the poet describes in the poem below. What words for persons, places, or things can you find in the poem?

The Little Turtle
by
Vachel Lindsay

There was a little turtle.
He lived in a box.
He swam in a puddle.
He climbed on the rocks.

He snapped at a mosquito.
He snapped at a flea.
He snapped at a minnow.
And he snapped at me.

He caught the mosquito.
He caught the flea.
He caught the minnow.
But he didn't catch me.

Discussion

1. Which words in the poem name animals?
2. Which words in the poem name places or things?
3. Imagine you were a turtle. What people, places, and things would you see every day?

The Writing Connection: Nouns

Nouns are important words in all the sentences that you write. You can use nouns to tell about people or animals. Here are some examples of the way you could use nouns to tell about animals.

The horse stands by the fence.

The elephant picks up peanuts with his trunk.

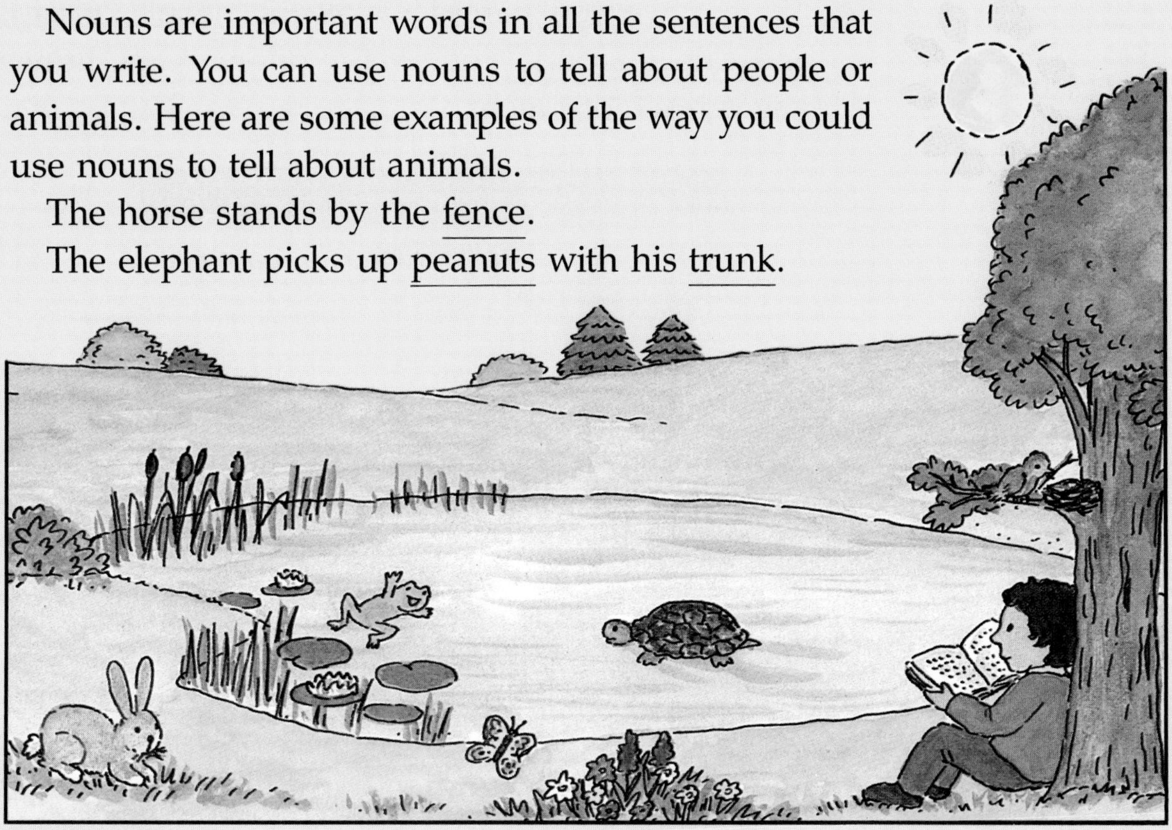

Activity

Look at the picture above. Then write about it. Try to paint a picture with words. You can write as many sentences as you wish.

- Read your sentences to a friend who did not see the picture. Have your friend draw a picture that shows everything you described in your word picture.
- Compare your friend's drawing with the picture on this page. Did it include all the details from the picture? Did it include all the details of your word picture? What nouns would make your word picture more precise?

Nouns

A **noun** is a word that names a person, place, or thing.

A. Nouns give you names for all the people, places, and things around you. Many nouns name things you can see or touch.

Person	Place	Thing
girl	playground	baseball
boy	school	pencil
carpenter	town	hammer

B. A sentence can have more than one noun.

The <u>girl</u> rides a <u>horse</u>.
A <u>carpenter</u> cuts a <u>board</u>.
A <u>boy</u> jumps in the <u>lake</u>.

Strategy

How can you be sure that a word is a noun? Ask yourself two questions: Can I see the thing it names? Can I touch the thing it names? If the answer is *yes*, the word is probably a noun.

Check Your Understanding

A. Write the letter of the noun in each sentence.
1. The house looks cozy.
    a. The   **b.** house   **c.** looks   **d.** cozy
2. A big tree grows nearby.
    a. A   **b.** big   **c.** tree   **d.** nearby

B. Write the letter of the nouns in each sentence.

3. The men carry a bucket.
   a. The, carry   **b.** men, a   **c.** men, bucket
4. A tall ladder touches the roof.
   a. ladder, roof   **b.** tall, the   **c.** A, touches

Practice

A. Write each sentence. Use the noun in parentheses.

5. A ____ begins with a plan. (house, the)
6. The plan shows each ____. (green, room)
7. Carpenters work with ____. (every, wood)
8. The ____ keeps out the rain. (roof, small)

B. Write each sentence. Underline all the nouns.

9. Early builders used logs.
10. Kings once built sturdy castles.
11. Other people lived in tents.
12. Steel makes modern buildings strong.

C. Mixed Practice   Write each sentence. Underline all the nouns.

13. Moles dig tunnels.
14. A large owl flew silently.
15. Baby owls lived in the old barn.
16. The young birds grew quickly.
17. The babies ate worms.
18. Farmers build pens for the pigs.
19. A mouse made a home in a cup.

Apply: Exploring Language

Write a sentence about where you live. Use one noun that names a person. Use one noun that names a place. Use one noun that names a thing. Be sure your sentence makes sense.

Singular and Plural Nouns

A **singular noun** is a word that names one person, place, or thing.

A **plural noun** is a word that names more than one person, place, or thing.

A. Nouns can be either singular or plural.

Singular	Plural
farmer	farmers
house	houses
flower	flowers

B. You can follow a rule to make most singular nouns plural. Add *s* to the singular.

tree ⟶ trees   ant ⟶ ants

Strategy

When you write, you use many nouns. Check the spelling of nouns that name more than one person, place, or thing. Be sure to end each noun correctly.

Check Your Understanding

A. Write the letter that tells whether the underlined word is singular or plural.

1. A bee has six legs.
   a. singular   **b.** plural
2. Many workers store honey in the hive.
   a. singular   **b.** plural

B. Write the letter of the correct plural form of the underlined nouns.

 3. friend **a.** friendse **b.** friends **c.** friend

 4. house **a.** houses **b.** house **c.** housess

Practice

A. Write whether each noun is *singular* or *plural*.

5. day	**9.** creek	**13.** inventions
6. hats	**10.** eagles	**14.** elbow
7. roses	**11.** parent	**15.** sunflower
8. planet	**12.** balloon	**16.** presidents

B. Write the plural form of each singular noun.

17. ball	**21.** paddle	**25.** pitcher
18. cart	**22.** spoon	**26.** farmhouse
19. team	**23.** visitor	**27.** dragon
20. dollar	**24.** tongue	**28.** monkey

C. Mixed Practice Write each sentence. Underline singular nouns once. Underline plural nouns twice.

 29. Many bees build a hive.

 30. Each bee does a special job.

 31. Guards protect the hive.

 32. The brave insects sting enemies.

 33. Many different animals build homes.

 34. Termites make nests in a log.

 35. A bear opens the nest with its claws.

Apply: Work with a Partner

 With a classmate, make a list of old toys you'd like to sell. Give the price for one toy. Then give the price for two or three toys. Spell each plural noun correctly. Example: one car, 10 cents, two cars, 20 cents.

More About Plural Nouns

There are several ways to form plural nouns.

A. You can follow rules to make most singular nouns plural.

Nouns ending with	Rule	Example
s, ss, ch, sh, x, z	add *es*	glass ⟶ glass<u>es</u> porch ⟶ porch<u>es</u> fox ⟶ fox<u>es</u>
consonant and *y*	change *y* to *i* and add *es*	penny ⟶ penn<u>ies</u> bunny ⟶ bunn<u>ies</u>

B. Some nouns do not follow rules. These nouns have special forms in the plural.

child ⟶ children	man ⟶ men
foot ⟶ feet	woman ⟶ women
goose ⟶ geese	mouse ⟶ mice
tooth ⟶ teeth	ox ⟶ oxen

Strategy

The nouns in Part B don't follow rules. You have to remember the plural form. Practice these words. Use the chart to help you.

Check Your Understanding

A. Write the letter of the correct plural of each under-lined noun.

    1. box
        a. boxs   **b.** box's   **c.** boxes

    2. city
        a. citys   **b.** cityes   **c.** cities

B. Write the letter of the correct plural of each under-lined noun.

3. <u>woman</u>   **a.** women   **b.** womans   **c.** wemen
4. <u>tooth</u>   **a.** tooths   **b.** toothes   **c.** teeth

Practice

A. Write the correct plural of each noun.

5. buzz   10. daddy   15. sky
6. dress   11. ash   16. box
7. lady   12. circus   17. princess
8. branch   13. class   18. eyelash
9. fox   14. bush   19. grocery

B. Follow the directions in Practice A.

20. goose   23. tooth   26. foot
21. ox   24. child   27. man
22. mouse   25. woman

C. Mixed Practice   Write each sentence. Use the plural form of the noun in parentheses.

28. A pioneer family had only a few _____. (dish)
29. Men cleared the land with _____. (ax)
30. Some families kept _____ in pens. (goose)
31. The horses wore leather _____. (harness)
32. Cattle roamed large _____. (ranch)
33. Boys and girls rode _____. (pony)
34. _____ picked wild _____. (Child, cherry)
35. _____ and _____ built log cabins. (Man, woman)

Apply: Exploring Language

Imagine that you and your family are moving. What types of things would you want to take? Write four labels to put on the boxes. Examples: toys, dolls, dishes.

Common and Proper Nouns

A **common noun** names any person, place, or thing.

A **proper noun** names a particular person, place, or thing.

A. A common noun begins with a small letter.

    <u>g</u>irl   <u>b</u>oy   <u>c</u>ity   <u>s</u>hip   <u>s</u>chool

B. A proper noun always begins with a capital letter. Some proper nouns are made up of more than one word. Capitalize the most important words. Do not capitalize short words such as *of*, *and*, or *a*.

Common Nouns	Proper Nouns
girl	Rosa
boy	John Wu
city	Atlanta
state	Georgia
country	Canada
statue	Statue of Liberty

Strategy

When you write sentences and paragraphs, be sure to start each proper noun with a capital letter. Check whether you have capitalized each important word.

Check Your Understanding

A. Write the letter of the common noun in each sentence.

    1. The boy jumps up and down.
        a. boy   **b.** jumps   **c.** up   **d.** and
    2. The girl always wins.
        a. The   **b.** girl   **c.** always   **d.** wins

B. Write the letter of the proper noun in each sentence.

3. Edwina plays three sports.
   a. Edwina   **b.** plays   **c.** sports
4. Jackie Robinson enjoyed baseball.
   a. Jackie Robinson   **b.** enjoyed   **c.** baseball

Practice

A. Write each sentence. Underline the common nouns.

5. Many people come to the field.
6. The women run quickly.
7. The boys watched eagerly.
8. The crowd cheers loudly.

B. Write each sentence. Capitalize the proper nouns.

9. chris evert lived in florida.
10. chris played tennis in france and england.
11. The star traveled around the united states.
12. chris saw the statue of liberty.

C. Mixed Practice Write each sentence. Underline the common nouns. Capitalize the proper nouns.

13. The team traveled in a bus.
14. The children beat the champions in chicago.
15. willie mays batted at yankee stadium.
16. The players visited china and japan.
17. Crowds cheered the boys and girls in ohio.
18. The coach took the team to new mexico.

Apply: Journal

What game do you like to play? In your journal, tell about the game, the friends you play with, and the items you use in the game. Capitalize all proper nouns.

Possessives

A **possessive** is a word that tells who or what owns or has something.

A. Many nouns can be changed into possessives. Look at the underlined nouns in the chart below. Notice the possessive form for each noun.

Owner	What Is Owned	Possessive	What Is Owned
A <u>boy</u> owns	a dog.	a <u>boy's</u>	dog
The <u>dog</u> has	paws.	the <u>dog's</u>	paws

B. Add 's to make most singular nouns possessive. The ' mark is an apostrophe.

Mike owns an airplane.   <u>Mike's</u> airplane
- owner
- name of one person
- singular noun
- possessive

The <u>airplane</u> has wings.   the <u>airplane's</u> wings

Strategy

When you talk, you don't need to think about how to form possessives. But when you write, you need to use an apostrophe with each possessive.

| one owner | + | 's | = | possessive |

Check Your Understanding

A. Write the letter of the correct possessive.
  1. The plane has seats.
    a. the seat's plane   **b.** the plane's seats
  2. The pilot has a hat.
    a. the pilot's hat   **b.** the hat's pilot

B. Write the letter of the possessive for the singular noun in parentheses.

    3. The (book) author is Jules Verne.

      a. book's   **b.** books   **c.** bookes'   **d.** bookse'

    4. The (author) books are exciting.

      a. author   **b.** authors   **c.** author's   **d.** authore's

Practice

A. Write who or what is the owner and what is owned.

    5. The ship has a sail.

    6. The submarine has engines.

    7. The captain owns maps.

    8. The navy has submarines.

B. Write each sentence. Write the noun in parentheses as a possessive.

    9. A Dutchman built the (world) first submarine.

    10. Robert (Fulton) ships ran on steam.

    11. One (inventor) submarine rolled on wheels.

    12. A (submarine) sailors live underwater.

C. Mixed Practice   Find the noun in each sentence that owns or has something. Then write that word as a possessive.

    13. The crew owns a pet seal. the _____ seal

    14. Jules Verne had a book. _____ book

    15. The captain has a ship. the _____ ship

    16. The storm has a roar. the _____ roar

    17. Subs of this navy dive deep. this _____ subs

    18. The sub that Nemo owns is fast. _____ sub

Apply: Test a Partner

Draw a robot. Have a partner write five possessives about it. Is each possessive correct?

More About Possessives

A **plural possessive** shows that more than one person, place, or thing has or owns something.

A. Study the chart below.

Owner	What Is Owned	Possessive	What Is Owned
The workers own The axes have	tools. blades.	the workers' the axes'	tools blades

If a plural noun ends in *s*, add an apostrophe (') after the *s* to form the plural possessive.

The cats have kittens.   the cats' kittens
owner   possessive
plural noun

If a plural noun does *not* end in *s*, add *'s* to form the plural possessive.

The children own a puppy.   the children's puppy

B. Add *'s* to form the possessive of singular nouns.

Hector owns a garden.   Hector's garden

Strategy

Watch out for plural nouns ending in *s*. They need only an apostrophe, not another *s*.

Check Your Understanding

A. Write the letter of the correct possessive.
  1. Francine paints the (swings) seats.
   a. swing's **b.** swings's **c.** swings'
  2. A worker builds the (oxen) pen.
   a. oxen's **b.** oxens' **c.** oxes's

B. Write the letter of the correct possessive.

   3. The (tree) leaves flutter.

      a. trees'   **b.** tree's

   4. Gina digs in the (garden) dirt.

      a. gardens'   **b.** garden   **c.** garden's

Practice

A. Write the correct possessive for each item.

   5. The children have a garden.

   6. The cities have parks.

   7. The parks have ponds.

   8. The carpenters own hammers.

B. Write the correct possessive for each item.

   9. The flower has blossoms.

   10. The blade has teeth.

   11. The hammer has a head.

   12. The child owns a sandbox.

C. Mixed Practice Write each sentence. Write the noun in parentheses as a possessive.

   13. The (workers) blade cuts a log in half.

   14. A gardener trims the (shrub) branches.

   15. Manuel visits the (children) zoo.

   16. A keeper gathers the (goose) eggs.

   17. The (geese) wings flap up and down.

   18. A (family) crumbs are the (mice) dinner.

   19. The (children) dog is in the (park) garden.

Apply: Learning Log

In your learning log, tell what is confusing about possessives. Make a plan for remembering how to form plural possessives.

Names and Titles

The first letter of a proper noun is capitalized.

A. The names of particular persons and places begin with a capital letter.

Jane Addams   Chicago, Illinois

The first letter of a name is called an **initial.** An initial that is used instead of a name is always capitalized and followed by a period.

Ralph Johnson Bunche   R. J. Bunche

B. Titles tell who a person is. A title comes before the person's name and begins with a capital letter. Most titles end with a period.

Ms.	a married or unmarried woman	Mr.	a married or unmarried man
Miss	an unmarried woman	Dr.	a doctor
Mrs.	a married woman		

Ms. Lidia Lopez   Dr. Paul J. Diamond

Strategy

When you write a title, be sure to start with a capital letter. Remember that most titles end with a period.

Check Your Understanding

A. Write the letter of the proper noun that is written correctly.

1. **a.** dorothy c hodgkin
   b. Dorothy C. Hodgkin
   c. Dorothy c. hodgkin

2. **a.** austin, texas
   b. Austin, texas
   c. Austin, Texas

B. Write the letter of the correct title.
   3. (doctor) Jonas Salk
       a. Doc   **b.** Dr   **c.** dr.   **d.** Dr.
   4. (a married woman) Annie Goodrich
       a. Mr.   **b.** Miss   **c.** Mrs.   **d.** ms.

Practice

A. Write each proper noun correctly.
   5. clara barton
   6. sally ride
   7. miami, florida
   8. newark, new jersey

B. Write each name with a correct title.
   9. (a married or unmarried man) Frederick Douglass
   10. (a married woman) Eleanor Roosevelt
   11. (doctor) Maria Mayer
   12. (a married or unmarried woman) Ella Fitzgerald

C. Mixed Practice Write each proper noun correctly.
   13. (doctor) david baltimore
   14. topeka, kansas
   15. (a married woman) emma miller
   16. (a married or unmarried man) Roland Hayes
   17. (an unmarried woman) maura riley
   18. chamber of commerce
   19. united states of america

Apply: Journal

Think of three different people you would like to be for one day. Write each person's name and title, if there is one. Write a sentence telling why you would like to be each person.

Names of Days and Months

◆

The names of days and months are proper nouns.

A. Names of days and months begin with a capital.

Tuesday, July 4   Saturday, August 3

B. Names of days and months can be shortened. The short form is called an **abbreviation**. Put a period after an abbreviation.

Sunday	Sun.	Wednesday	Wed.	Saturday	Sat.
Monday	Mon.	Thursday	Thurs.	Sunday	Sun.
Tuesday	Tues.	Friday	Fri.		

January	Jan.	May	none	September	Sept.
February	Feb.	June	none	October	Oct.
March	Mar.	July	none	November	Nov.
April	Apr.	August	Aug.	December	Dec.

May, June, and July already have short names. They do not need abbreviations.

Here's how to write days and months:

Oct. 26, 1990

Strategy

When writing paragraphs for school, do not use abbreviations. Spell out days and months.

Check Your Understanding

A. Write the letter of the correct form for each day and month.

    1. a. monday, march 15   **2. a.** Friday, June 8

      b. monday, March 15   **b.** friday, June 8

      c. Monday, March 15   **c.** friday, june 8

B. Write the letter of the correct abbreviation.

3. Thursday, April 2
   a. thurs., Ap. 2
   b. Thurs., Apr 2
   c. Thurs., Apr. 2

4. Sunday, January 1
   a. Sun., Jan. 1
   b. Sund., Ja. 1
   c. Sun, Jan 1

Practice

A. Write the sentences. Write correctly each day and month.

   5. Come on thursday, november 26.
   6. Ben has a birthday on saturday, may 12.
   7. Rosa got a new kitten in august.
   8. Astronauts landed on the moon on july 20, 1969.
   9. School begins on monday, september 5.

B. Write the abbreviation for each day and month.

   10. Thursday, March 29
   11. Sunday, April 17
   12. Tuesday, December 2
   13. Monday, October 31
   14. Friday, September 7
   15. Wednesday, August 9

C. Mixed Practice   Write each day and month correctly. Then write the abbreviation for each.

   16. Monday, August 6
   17. Friday, September 17
   18. Saturday, October 9
   19. Sunday, November 5
   20. Friday, April 16
   21. Thursday, December 2
   22. Tuesday, January 28
   23. Wednesday, March 14
   24. Wednesday, May 3
   25. Monday, June 19

Apply: Work with a Group

Work with several classmates to make a chart of birthdays for the students in your class. Use abbreviations for the names of days and months.

Compound Words

A **compound word** is a word made up of two shorter words.

A. Look at the sentences below. The compound words are underlined. Which words are they made from?

> Two brothers flew the first airplane.
> It took off from a hilltop.

B. You can figure out the meaning of a compound word if you know the two words from which it is formed.

> A spaceship is a ship that travels in space.
> A sailboat is a boat with a sail.

What do you think these words mean?

> playground   seaweed   footprint   doghouse

Strategy

It's easy to spell a compound word if you know how to spell the words it contains. If you're not sure, look up the word in a dictionary.

Check Your Understanding

A. Write the letter of the compound word.
  1. Our schoolwork was about inventors.
     a. Our   **b.** schoolwork   **c.** about   **d.** inventors
  2. Townspeople laughed at the Wright brothers.
     a. Townspeople   **b.** laughed   **c.** at   **d.** brothers

B. Write the letter of the missing word.

    3. A newspaper is a paper that brings you ____.

        a. movies **b.** paper **c.** news **d.** lunch

    4. Dinnertime is the time you eat ____.

        a. breakfast **b.** evening **c.** time **d.** dinner

Practice

A. Match each word with one from the box to make a compound word.

fire   tub   light   pin   flake   plane

    5. bath   **7.** camp   **9.** air

    6. clothes   **8.** moon   **10.** snow

B. Write each sentence, and supply the missing word.

    11. A motorbike is a bike that has a ____.

    12. A riverboat is a boat that sails on a ____.

    13. A flagpole is a pole that holds a ____.

    14. A bookstore is a store that sells ____.

C. Mixed Practice Write each sentence, and supply the missing word.

    15. A field where corn grows is a ____.

    16. A coat that you wear in the rain is a ____.

    17. The side of a mountain is called a ____.

    18. A house for birds is a ____.

    19. A room where you eat lunch is a ____.

    20. A pot for making tea is a ____.

    21. Land where people farm is called ____.

Apply: Work with a Partner

With a classmate, write six compound words. Each compound word should use one word from the box.

rain   snow   sun   house   food   shoe

LANGUAGE IN ACTION

Taking Messages

The phone rings, and you answer it. The call is for your mother and she's not home. What should you do?

- Listen carefully. If something is unclear, ask the caller to repeat the information.
- Be sure to write
    - the caller's name.
    - who the message is for.
    - the complete message.
    - the time of the call.
    - the caller's phone number.
    - who took the message.
- Read the message back to the caller to make sure you got it right.

Practice

Write two things that are wrong with each message below.

1. Abe —
   Larry called at 3:30. He said something about a baseball game. —Cindy
2. Dr. Johnson's office called. Call them back at 354-8628.
3. Theresa Lin called at 2:00. She will meet you at the mall tonight at 7. —Dave

Apply

Work with a partner. Pretend you are having a phone conversation. Take turns leaving and taking messages.

TEST TAKING

Studying for a Test

Do you know how to study for a test? Here are some ways to help you study better.

- First, know what the test will be about. Listen carefully when the teacher tells about the test. Ask questions if you don't understand.
- When it is time to study, make sure that you have the books and worksheets you need.
- Find a quiet place to study. Work at a desk or table. Make sure there is enough light.
- Set aside enough time to study. Don't wait until the last minute to study.
- Set up a study system that will work for you. Here are some ways to study.

Reread the things the test will be on.
Write down the main ideas as you study.
Think of questions that might be asked and answer them.

Practice

Answer the following questions.
1. When your teacher assigns a test, what do you need to know?
2. What things do you need to study for a test?
3. Where and when should you study?

Apply

Learning Log Decide what things from this lesson will help you. Write them in your learning log.

UNIT REVIEW

How-to Paragraph *(page 63)*

1. On your paper, list three features of a how-to paragraph.

Writing Steps in Correct Order *(pages 66-67)*

2. Put the steps below in correct order. Write them as a paragraph.

Next, spread jelly on bread.

Last, cut the sandwich into pieces for easier eating.

Making a peanut butter and jelly sandwich is easy.

Then, put the bread together to make a sandwich.

First, spread peanut butter on bread.

Giving Exact Information *(pages 70-71)*

3. Add exact details to the sentences you just wrote. Tell how many slices of bread you use and how many pieces you cut the sandwich into.

Using Commas *(pages 72-73)*

Write each sentence. Use commas where needed.

4. Jean do you know how to make a paper puppet?

5. Yes I just showed Tom Sue and George how to make one.

6. I will use this bag and you will use that one.

Singular and Plural Nouns *(pages 78-81)*

Write each sentence. Underline singular nouns once. Underline plural nouns twice.

7. The circus comes to town.

8. A clown chases the elephants.

9. All the clowns wear silly shoes.

10. The monkeys ride a bicycle in the tent.

More About Plural Nouns (pages 82-83)
Write the plural form of each singular noun.

11. tent   **13.** ash   **15.** box   **17.** woman

12. branch   **14.** child   **16.** city   **18.** foot

Common and Proper Nouns (pages 84-85)
Write each sentence. Underline the common nouns. Capitalize the proper nouns.

19. walt whitman wrote poems.

20. The poet lived in new york.

21. The statue of liberty is on an island.

22. The statue came from france.

Possessives (pages 86-89)
Write each sentence. Underline the word that owns or has something. Then write that word as a possessive.

23. P. T. Barnum owned an elephant. _____ elephant

24. The elephant had a trunk. the _____ trunk.

25. The clowns have hats. the _____ hats

26. The children have popcorn. the _____ popcorn

Names and Titles (pages 90-91)
Write each proper noun and title correctly.

27. (doctor) lydia suarez

28. (married or unmarried woman) judy burr

29. ames, iowa

Days and Months (pages 92-93)
Write the abbreviation for each day and month.

30. Sunday, October 1   **32.** Tuesday, February 5

31. Friday, April 10   **33.** Monday, November 22

Compound Words (pages 94-95)
Write each sentence and supply the missing compound word.

34. A book that tells how to cook is a _____.

35. A band that you wear on your head is a _____.

36. Work you do at school is _____.

MAKING ALL THE
CONNECTIONS

You and several classmates will now write as a group a news article. What you have learned about putting events in order will help you in your writing.

You will do the following in your news article:

♦ Describe an interesting or important event
♦ Tell about the event in time order
♦ Answer the questions *who*, *what*, *when*, *where*, *why*, and *how*

Reading a News Article

Read the following news article about a woman who built art. The side notes tell the main features of a news article.

The topic sentence tells the main idea of the paragraph. Details tell *who, what, when, how,* and *where.*

Details tell *why* the show was interesting and what its results were.

A show of Louise Nevelson's artwork opened at the museum last week. Nevelson made unusual statues from wood. She collected boxes and scraps of wood and painted them black. Then she placed the scraps inside the boxes. By stacking the boxes, she built sculptures. Some looked like cities. Others looked like strange creatures. Many people came to the show. They looked at the statues and talked about them. Louise Nevelson's artwork is very popular.

Speaking/Listening

Work in a group. Talk about these questions.

1. What important details about the art show did you learn from the news article on page 100? Include details that tell *who, what, when, where, how,* and *why* about the art show.

2. What details did you learn about the art show from the picture at the top of the page?

3. What materials would you use in a piece of art?

Thinking

Brainstorming

Choose a student from the group to take notes. Talk about these questions. Save your notes.

1. What interesting thing has your class made and put on display?

2. What details tell *who, what, when, where, why,* and *how* about the thing you showed?

3. What made your project interesting or unusual?

Organizing

To write a news article, you must first gather information. Then you must put the information into groups. The chart below shows the information that was used in the news article about Louise Nevelson.

Meet with your group. Look at the notes you made while brainstorming. Group them in a chart like the one below. Have one person write the ideas in the chart.

Who	What	When	Where	Why	How
Louise Nevelson	a show of her artwork	last week	the local art museum	Her work is interesting.	She used things she found.

Writing a News Article

Imagine that you and your group are newspaper reporters who have been asked to write an article about something special your class has shared. It might be a picture, a bulletin board display, or a science project. Together you will write a paragraph telling about the event. Use the chart of details you made.

Planning

Before writing your news article, you must plan it. Work with your group.

◆ Review your chart. Can you think of more details that tell *who, what, when, where, why,* and *how*? Add them to the chart.

- Organize your information in an outline. The first part will tell what happened. The middle part will give details. The last part will describe the results.
- Agree on the main idea and details for each part.

Composing

- Work with your group to write the news article. Have one student write down the first draft.
- Decide how to word the topic sentence. Then decide how to word each detail sentence.

Revising

- Read your news article with the members of your group.
- How can each sentence be improved?
- Make sure the main idea is clear.
- Check that all the details are correct.

Proofreading

As a group, proofread your news article. Choose one student to make the corrections.

- Does each sentence begin with a capital letter and end with the correct end mark?
- Does each sentence express a complete thought?
- Are names, titles, and proper nouns capitalized correctly?
- Are all words spelled correctly?

Presenting

- Choose one group member to write a final copy.
- Put your article on the bulletin board and share it with the rest of the class.

CUMULATIVE REVIEW

A. Write the letter of the group of words that is a sentence. (*pages 40-41*)

1. **a.** Every bike.
   b. Angus rode a bike.
   c. Rode quickly.

2. **a.** Fixed a flat tire.
   b. Leaked out slowly.
   c. Darleen stopped.

B. Write the letter of the word that names each kind of sentence. (*pages 42-45*)

3. The children are hungry.
   a. command   **b.** exclamation   **c.** question   **d.** statement

4. Fix lunch for the students.
   a. command   **b.** exclamation   **c.** question   **d.** statement

5. What did you eat for lunch?
   a. command   **b.** exclamation   **c.** question   **d.** statement

C. Write the letter of the sentence that has one line under the complete subject and two lines under the complete predicate. (*pages 46-51*)

6. **a.** Jill buys stamps.
   b. The stamp is red.
   c. Many stamps have pictures.

7. **a.** Jill sends a letter.
   b. A friend reads the letter.
   c. Jill tells much news.

D. Write the letter of the group of words that is in alphabetical order. (*pages 52-53*)

8. **a.** glad   more   teeth
   b. aunt   attic   baker
   c. line   baby   list

9. **a.** mile   mice   most
   b. purse   puppy   push
   c. walk   wall   warm

E. Write the letter of the word that would appear on a dictionary page with the guide words shown. (*pages 54-55*)

10. **scare/score**   **a.** school   **b.** skip   **c.** sand

11. **dime/doll**   **a.** dial   **b.** diet   **c.** dinner

F. Write the letter of the sentence that has the correct punctuation. (*pages 72-73*)

12. **a.** No Bob is not here
  b. Luz, come here.
  c. Next add flour.

13. **a.** Use pen ink and glue
  b. First cut the paper
  c. Well, that is all.

G. Write the letter of the words that are nouns. (*pages 78-79*)

14. The pilot talks on the radio.
  a. pilot, talks **b.** on, radio **c.** pilot, radio

15. The plane lands at an airport.
  a. plane, airport **b.** lands, at **c.** lands, airport

H. Write the letter of the correct plural noun. (*pages 80-83*)

16. Zelda puts both ___ on the diving board. (foot)
  a. foot **b.** foots **c.** feet

17. People sit around the pool on ___.
  a. bench **b.** benches **c.** benchs

I. Write the letter of the correct proper noun. (*pages 85-86*)

18. **a.** texas **b.** state **c.** United States

19. **a.** statue **b.** Statue Of Liberty **c.** Central Park

J. Write the letter of the correct possessive of each noun in parentheses. (*pages 86-89*)

20. Dad fed the ___ puppy. (children)
  a. childrens' **b.** children's **c.** childrens

21. Several ___ parents came to the pet show. (students)
  a. student's **b.** students's **c.** students'

K. Write the letter of the correct name or title. (*pages 90-91*)

22. **a.** Dr. Fran morris **b.** mr. Al Jones **c.** Ms. Loy Wu

23. **a.** parma, ohio **b.** j. b. Smith **c.** Mr. Juan Miro

L. Write the letter of the day and month that are correctly abbreviated. (*pages 92-93*)

24. **a.** Tues., March 7 **b.** Sund. Feb 2 **c.** Wed., Oct. 1

25. **a.** Fri, Ja. 23 **b.** Thurs., Aug. 9 **c.** Mndy May 3

PART TWO

Mysteries and Ventures

Something is there
there on the stair
coming down
coming down
stepping with care.
Coming down
coming down
slinkety-sly.
Something is coming and wants to get by.
"Something Is There"
by Lilian Moore

◆

The world is full of mysteries and adventures. We don't always understand how everything works or why it happens. Searching for answers can be an exciting adventure. In these units, think about mysteries that have puzzled you. What adventure might lead you to solve one of those mysteries?

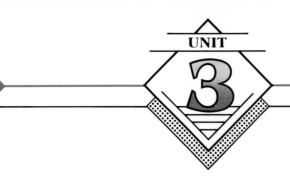
Book Report

◆

Verbs I

What Do You Know?

"What book should I read?"

From time to time, you may ask yourself this question. When you were younger, your teacher probably told you what books to read. Now, in the third grade, you will have a chance to choose books for yourself.

How do you know which books to choose? You may look through the library and see titles on book covers that look interesting. Friends may tell you about a book they enjoyed. You may also hear a classmate give a book report. A book report tells what a book is about. It also tells why the writer liked or didn't like the book.

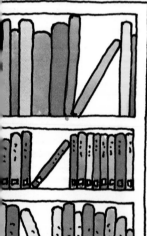

Thinking About Book Reports

What Is a Book Report?

A **book report** has these features:

- It lists the title and the author.
- It lists the main characters.
- It describes the time and place, or the setting, of the story.
- It tells the main events in the story, or the plot, without giving away the ending.
- It tells why the writer of the book report liked or disliked the book.

While you are in school, you will probably write many book reports. Each book report you write gives you a chance to share your opinion of a book. It also helps you think about what you liked or disliked. Thinking about what you like about books will help you make better book choices in the future.

Discussion

1. What was the last book you enjoyed?
2. How did you choose this book?
3. What would you say to get a friend interested in this book?

Reading a Book Report

Read the book report below. As you read, decide if you would like to read this book yourself.

The title and author are included.
The main character is named.

George Washington's Breakfast by Jean Fritz is about a young boy, George W. Allen, who wants to solve a very special mystery. George was born on George Washington's birthday and was named after him. George wants to find out everything he can about our first President. He already knows where President Washington lived and how tall he was. But after school one day he decides to find the answer to just one more question—what George Washington ate for breakfast. He looks for the answer in the school library and in his own house. His parents even take him on a weekend trip to Washington, D.C., and Mt. Vernon, where George Washington lived.

The main events are described.
The setting is described.

This is a well-written book that is informative and often very funny. Because the characters seem like real people, readers will be interested in finding out how George solved his mystery. The book also includes a lot of valuable information about the way President Washington lived.

The writer does not give away the ending.
The writer tells why he likes or dislikes the book.

Understanding What You've Read

Write the answer to each question below.

1. What is the title of the book?
2. Who is the main character in the book?
3. What do you think are the most important events in the book?
4. Do you think the person who wrote the report likes books about history? Explain.
5. How would you find information about a President?

Writing Assignment

Pretend that your school library is having a "Rate the Books" contest. There will be lists of the five best and five worst books of the year. You have to write a report that tells why you liked or disliked a book. In this unit, you will learn to write a book report. You will also see how another student, Maria, develops her book report.

Your **audience** for the report will be your classmates. Your **purpose** will be to include enough information so that the class can rate your book.

What book shall I write about?

Choose a Book

Make a list of the books that you've liked or disliked the most. Then, choose one book from the list that you'd like to write about. Save your work for the next lesson.

Using the Library

Maria decided to write a book report about *Something Queer on Vacation*, by Elizabeth Levy. She liked the book a lot the first time she read it. However, she couldn't remember all the details. Maria went to the library and asked the librarian to help her find the book.

The librarian told Maria about three types of books in the library. Each type of book is in a different part of the library.

- **Fiction** books are stories that writers make up from their imaginations.
- **Nonfiction** books tell facts about real people, animals, places, and events. Nonfiction books are grouped by subject. For example, books on science are separated from books on history.
- **Reference** books are special nonfiction books. These books give information about many different subjects. They include encyclopedias, dictionaries, and atlases.

Then the librarian took Maria around the library. Maria knew that *Something Queer on Vacation* was a made-up story. So, she went to the fiction section. The librarian had told her that fiction books were arranged alphabetically by the first letter of the author's last name. The book is by Elizabeth Levy. Maria looked for where the authors' last names begin with *L*.

When you do not know the author's last name, you can ask the librarian to check the library's listing of books for this information.

Practice

A. Tell where in the library you would find each topic. Write *fiction*, *nonfiction*, or *reference*. Some topics may be found in more than one place.

1. a mystery about ghosts
2. an atlas of the 50 states
3. Abraham Lincoln
4. a story about a talking horse
5. facts about elephants

B. Read each book title. Tell which type of book each is. Write fiction, nonfiction, or reference.

6. *Cinderella*
7. *The United States Atlas*
8. *Sewing Made Easy*
9. *Wishbone the Flying Cat*
10. *The Hopi Indians*
11. *The Adventures of Pinocchio*
12. *World Book Encyclopedia*
13. *The Inventions of Benjamin Franklin*
14. *All About Soccer*
15. *Dictionary of Rhyming Words*

Go to the Library

Decide whether the book you chose is fiction or nonfiction. Then, ask the librarian to show you where the fiction or nonfiction books are kept. Try to find your book. If you need help, ask the librarian.

Writing a Story Map

Maria reread *Something Queer on Vacation* very carefully. She decided to list important information about the book in a story map. The map would help her remember details to use later in her book report. Maria listed this information in her story map:

Setting—the time and place of the story

Characters—the people and animals in the story

Plot—the events that happen in the story

Maria divided the plot into three parts:

Problem—something that keeps a character from getting or doing what he or she wants

Solution Attempts—ways the character tries to solve the problem

Outcome—how the story ends

Here is the story map Maria made for her book.

Setting: The beach; the present		
Characters: Gwen, Jill		
Plot: Problem	Solution Attempts	Outcome
The girls are practicing for the July Fourth sandcastle contest, but someone keeps knocking over their sandcastles.	The girls find flipper prints near the sandcastles. They guard the castles and use the clues to solve the mystery.	The flipper prints belong to Gwen's younger sister. She was knocking down the sandcastles.

Maria knew that a book report should not give away the ending of the story. When she wrote her report, she left out the details in the chart under Outcome.

Practice

Read the story below. Then, on your paper, make a chart like the one on page 114. Fill in the chart with information from the story.

When Janet and Harold went out to play, they found their friends having a meeting. One of the kids had found dinosaur tracks! "There are no dinosaurs alive anymore," said Janet.

"Look for yourself," said Scott. "They're real. And they look like they were made last night."

Janet looked at the tracks. Then, she whispered to Harold, "Tonight we'll find out if there's a real dinosaur."

That night, Janet and Harold hid in the backyard with a flashlight. After a while there was a noise in the trees. They heard a thump, thump, thump and saw something appear in the yard. "Now!" shouted Janet. Harold turned on the flashlight and pointed it at the monster. It was Scott. In each hand he had a pole with a giant cardboard footprint attached to the bottom.

"So you're the dinosaur," laughed Janet.

"I guess I had you all fooled," said Scott as they all laughed together.

Make a Chart

Make a chart with the headings *Setting*, *Characters*, *Plot*, *Problem*, *Solution Attempts*, and *Outcome*. Fill in the chart with information from the book you've read. Save your chart. You will need it later.

Identifying Facts and Opinions

Maria will write her book report on a form. The top of the form tells facts about the book and what happens in it. A **fact** is a piece of information that can be proven or checked. Here are two facts about the book *Something Queer on Vacation*.

Jill and Gwen made sandcastles on the beach.
Jill and Gwen found flipper tracks in the sand.

Both of these statements are based on information in the book. Therefore, both statements can be checked and proven to be facts.

Maria's opinions about the book will be written in the bottom part of the book-report form. An **opinion** is how a person thinks or feels about something. It cannot be proved true or false. Maria wrote this opinion.

Something Queer on Vacation was good because Gwen and Jill were like detectives.

When you support an opinion with facts or reasons, your readers are more likely to agree with you. Which one of these facts do you think Maria should use to support her opinion?

The story took place in the summer.
Gwen and Jill used clues to solve the mystery.

Maria should use the second fact. The time of year that the story took place has nothing to do with her opinion.

116

Practice

A. Tell whether each sentence is a fact or an opinion.

    1. Sir Arthur Conan Doyle wrote 56 stories about Sherlock Holmes.

    2. These are the best detective stories ever written.

    3. In the stories, a friend named Dr. Watson helps Sherlock Holmes.

    4. Sherlock Holmes lives in London at 221B Baker Street.

    5. The mysteries he solves are quite interesting.

B. Write the fact from each group of sentences that supports the opinion.

    6. Opinion: Sherlock Holmes is very clever.
Sherlock Holmes often wears a hat.
In one story, Sherlock Holmes uses a part of a ticket to solve a mystery.
Sherlock Holmes lives in England.

    7. Opinion: Sherlock Holmes seems to be good at everything he does.
Sherlock Holmes plays the violin well and keeps bees.
Dr. Watson often helps Sherlock Holmes find clues.
Sir Arthur Conan Doyle also wrote *The Lost World*.

Support Your Opinion

Write a sentence that tells your opinion of the book that you have chosen. Make a list of facts that support your opinion.
Save your work for the next lesson.

Writing a First Draft

Read the first draft of Maria's book report. Because it's a first draft, she wasn't worried about making it perfect. It will be changed later.

Book Title   Something Queer on Vacation
Author   Elizabeth Levy
What Happens?   During their summer vacation, Jill and Gwen build sandcastles at the beech. They are practiceing for the July Fourth sandcastle contest Someone keeps knockking over their castles, But Gwen and Jill find flipper prints in the sand With this clue the girls try to solve the mystery.
My Opinion   I liked the book because Jill and Gwen were like reel detectives. They followed the clues. Anyone who likes to solve mysteries will like this book.

Write Your First Draft

APPLY STEP BY STEP

Use your chart and list of facts to help you in your writing. Write your report on the same kind of form that Maria used. Save your work for the next lesson.

Discussing a First Draft

Discussion Strategy

One way to improve your first draft is to discuss it with a classmate.

Take turns speaking during your discussion. If one partner talks all the time, the other classmate will probably stop listening.

Use this checklist to discuss Maria's book report with your class.

Content Checklist
- ✔ Does the book report name the title and the author?
- ✔ Does the book report tell about the main characters, setting, and plot of the story?
- ✔ Does the writer avoid giving away the story ending?
- ✔ Does the book report tell why the writer likes or dislikes the book?

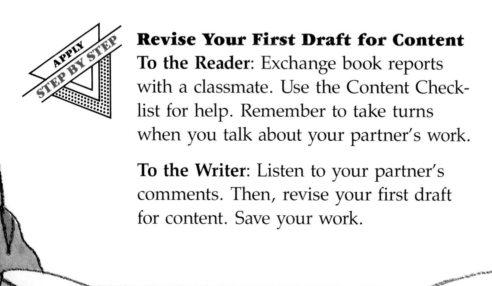

APPLY STEP BY STEP

Revise Your First Draft for Content

To the Reader: Exchange book reports with a classmate. Use the Content Checklist for help. Remember to take turns when you talk about your partner's work.

To the Writer: Listen to your partner's comments. Then, revise your first draft for content. Save your work.

Adding Descriptive Words

Jason enjoyed reading Maria's book report, but he had trouble imagining the clues that she described. Jason thought that Maria could tell more about the way the girls acted in the story.

You can use descriptive words to make your writing clearer. Some descriptive words tell more about a person, place, or thing.

> The garden was full of flowers.
> The garden was full of <u>bright</u>, <u>yellow</u> flowers.

Other descriptive words tell more about an action.

> Bill swims in the lake.
> Bill swims <u>slowly</u> in the lake.

Note the descriptive words Maria added to her report.

Maria added the descriptive words *small* and *shallow* to make her description of the prints clearer.
Maria added the word *eagerly* to tell more about how the girls search.
Maria added the word *always* to tell about the girls following the clues.

<u>What Happens?</u>   During their summer vacation, Jill and Gwen build sandcastles at the beech. They are practiceing for the July Fourth sandcastle contest Someone keeps knockking over their castles, But Gwen and Jill find flipper prints *small, shallow* in the sand With this clue the girls try to solve *eagerly* the mystery.
<u>My Opinion</u>   I liked the book because Jill and Gwen were like reel detectives. They followed the *always* clues. Anyone who likes to solve mysteries will like this book.

Practice

A. Add a descriptive word to tell more about the underlined person, place, or thing.

   1. I have some <u>books</u> about Einstein Anderson.
   2. He is a sixth <u>grader</u> who solves <u>mysteries</u>.
   3. Einstein Anderson figures out <u>puzzles</u>.
   4. He knows <u>facts</u> about science.

B. Add a descriptive word to tell more about the underlined action in each sentence.

   5. I <u>ran</u> to the store to get the new book.
   6. I <u>waited</u> for the store to open.
   7. When I got in, I <u>looked</u> through the shelves.
   8. At home, I <u>read</u> the book.

Revising Checklist

✔ Have I included all of the features of a book report?
✔ Can I combine subjects and predicates to make new sentences? (p. 32)
✔ Have I used exact information? (p. 70)
✔ Where can I add descriptive words?

APPLY STEP BY STEP

Revise Your First Draft For Style

Use the checklist above to help you revise your book report. Make changes on your draft, using proofreading marks. Save your work for later.

PROOFREADING
Writing Titles

Maria read her book report again to make sure it was written correctly. To help her check her work, she looked up the rules for writing titles. Here are the rules that Maria found.

Capitalize the first word and all important words in the title of a book, story, or poem.	"The Last of the Dragons"
Underline the titles of books	The <u>Big Orange Splotch</u> is by Daniel Pinkwater.
Use quotation marks for the titles of short stories and poems. When a story or poem title is at the end of a sentence that is a statement, the end mark is inside the quotation marks.	The short story I am now reading is called "The Two Detectives." "Helping" is one of my favorite poems.

Practice

Write the sentences below on another piece of paper. Make sure you write the titles correctly.

1. Another book by Elizabeth Levy is something queer at the ballpark.
2. I would like to read the poem the lost pony.
3. Maria wrote the story the wild fire.
4. Have you ever read the book the case of the elevator duck?
5. The last snowflake is a beautiful poem.
6. I wrote a report about the book charlotte's web.

Proofreading Checklist
- ✔ Did I begin each sentence with a capital letter? (p. 34)
- ✔ Did I use end marks correctly? (p. 34)
- ✔ Did I use commas correctly? (p. 72)
- ✔ Did I capitalize the first word and each important word in the title of the book?
- ✔ Did I underline the title of the book?
- ✔ Did I capitalize names and proper nouns correctly?

Proofreading Marks	
∧	add
⌇	take away
⁋	indent
≡	capitalize
/	small letter
◯	check spelling
∼	transpose

Proofread Your Book Report
Use the Proofreading Checklist to improve your work. Check for correct punctuation and capitalization. Make changes on your draft. Save your work.

Checking Spelling/Writing a Final Copy

Spelling Strategy

<u>Listen</u> carefully to the sounds in a word. Hearing the sounds helps you spell the word correctly. Say the word aloud. What letter or letters make each sound?

Here is part of Maria's book report.

> <u>Book Title</u> Something Queer on Vacation
> <u>Author</u> Elizabeth Levy
> <u>What Happens?</u> During their summer vacation,
> Jill and Gwen build sandcastles at the beech.
> They are practiceing for the July Fourth
> sandcastle contest Someone keeps knockking over
> their castles, But Gwen and Jill find flipper prints
> in the sand. With this clue the girls try to solve
> the mystery.
> <u>My Opinion</u> I liked the book because Jill and
> Gwen were like reel detectives. They followed the
> clues. Anyone who likes to solve mysteries will like
> this book.

 **Check Your Spelling**

Use the proofreading marks to correct spelling mistakes. Add any misspelled words to your spelling log.

Write a Final Copy

Write a neat, final copy of your book report. Proofread your work.

Sharing Your Book Report

Speaking/Listening Strategy

Speak clearly when you read aloud. Speak more slowly when you tell about important facts or strong opinions. If you are listening, pay careful attention to what the speaker is saying.

Choosing a Way to Share

Here are some ways to share your book report.

Reading Aloud Read your book report to your classmates. When you are finished, ask how many of them would like to read the book.

Make a Bulletin Board Put your book report on a class bulletin board. The bulletin board's title will be "Books We Have Read."

Share Your Book Report

Present your book report. Use one of the ways shown above, or use an idea of your own.

Add to Your Learning Log
- Am I proud of this book report? Explain.
- What part of doing the report was the most fun?
- If I could rewrite my book report, what things might I change?

The Literature Connection: Verbs

Think of some fun things you do every day. You go places and meet people. You play and read. To tell about these things, you need action words, or verbs.

Verbs help us picture actions in our minds. Verbs can tell about any action, no matter how fast or slow it might be.

Have you ever noticed that your feet go wherever you go? Read the poem below. It uses verbs to tell about some fun things that feet do.

Feet
by
Myra Cohn Livingston

Feet are very special things
For special kinds of fun.

On weekdays they walk off to school
Or skip — or hop — or run —

On Saturdays they roller-skate
Or bicycle — or hike —

On Sundays they just do the things
That other people like.

Discussion

1. What action words, or verbs, in the poem tell what feet do?
2. On Sundays feet do things "that other people like." What do you suppose those things are?
3. Do you think feet are special things? Name other actions they do that make them special.

The Writing Connection: Verbs

In your own writing, verbs help you tell about action. On the other page, you read about some things that feet do. What kinds of actions do the following sentences tell about?

Heather hopped over the sand castle.
Ralph raced down the beach.
Paula glides over the water on water skis.

Activity

What are the feet doing in this picture?

◆ Choose a pair of feet from the picture. Write at least one sentence that tells about the action of those feet.
◆ Use as many verbs as you want. Do not use the child's name in the sentence. Just tell what the feet are doing.
◆ Have a friend read what you wrote. See if your friend can look at the picture and tell which child you wrote about.

Action Verbs

An **action verb** is a word that tells what someone or something does.

A. Every sentence has a verb. Action verbs are easy to find. They tell what the subject part of the sentence does. Read the following sentences. Each underlined word is an action verb.

> People run.
> Everyone shouts loudly.
> A balloon rises.
> Boys and girls jump.

B. You have already learned that nouns are words that name people, places, and things. Verbs are words that tell what nouns do.

> A dog barks.   The balloons float.
> noun   action verb   noun   action verb

Strategy

Remember that an action verb tells what someone or something *does*. To find the verb in a sentence, look for the word that tells about *action*.

Check Your Understanding

A. Write the letter of the action verb in each sentence.
  1. The balloon sinks slowly to earth.
    a. balloon   **b.** sinks   **c.** slowly   **d.** earth
  2. The crowd cheers loudly.
    a. The   **b.** crowd   **c.** cheers   **d.** loudly

B. Write the letter that names the underlined word.

    3. The Montgolfier brothers <u>built</u> a balloon.

        a. noun   **b.** verb

    4. The <u>men</u> tied a basket under the balloon.

        a. noun   **b.** verb

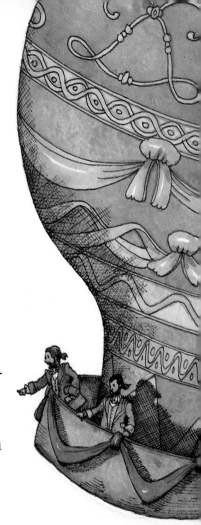

Practice

A. Write each sentence. Underline each action verb.

    5. The balloon carried some animals.

    6. Hot air filled the balloon.

    7. The balloon lifted the animals.

    8. The animals landed safely.

B. Write each sentence. Then write whether the underlined word is a *noun* or a *verb*.

    9. A Frenchman first <u>flew</u> in a balloon.

    10. Two <u>men</u> drifted from England to France in a balloon.

    11. The wind <u>blew</u> the balloon across the sea.

    12. The <u>balloon</u> landed in France.

C. Mixed Practice Write each sentence. Write whether each underlined word is a <u>noun</u> or a <u>verb</u>.

    13. People <u>sent</u> balloons <u>higher</u> and higher.

    14. Balloons <u>traveled</u> miles above the earth.

    15. Rockets <u>go</u> higher than balloons.

    16. Scientists <u>send</u> rockets to other planets.

    17. People still <u>like</u> balloons.

    18. A balloon <u>rises</u> and <u>floats</u> over a city.

Apply: Test a Friend

    On a piece of paper write all the action verbs you can think of in two minutes. Trade papers with a classmate. How many verbs did each of you write?

129

Present Tense

A verb in the **present tense** tells about an action that happens now.

A. Use the present tense of a verb to tell about actions that take place now.

> David reads about Japan today.
> Now Kenji writes a letter to David.
> This week David visits Kenji in Japan.

B. Verbs in the present tense have two forms. The correct form depends on the subject of the sentence. If the subject is a singular noun, the verb ends with *s*. If the subject is a plural noun, the verb does not end in *s*.

> David travels in a jet plane.
> The friends travel in a jet plane.
> Kenji climbs Mount Fuji.
> The boys climb Mount Fuji.

Strategy

In a sentence, the noun can end in *s* or the verb can end in *s*. Usually, the noun and the verb cannot both end in *s*.

Check Your Understanding

A. Write the letter of the present tense verb.
1. The plane lands in Tokyo this afternoon.
   a. plane   **b.** lands   **c.** this   **d.** afternoon
2. A subway takes the family to a hotel.
   a. subway   **b.** takes   **c.** family   **d.** hotel

B. Write the letter of the correct present tense verb.

    3. David ____ many new things in Japan.

        a. discover   **b.** discovers

    4. The boys ____ Japanese letters.

        a. write   **b.** writes

Practice

A. Write each sentence. Underline the verb.

    5. The family visits a Japanese restaurant.

    6. A waiter brings green tea.

    7. The boys eat with chopsticks.

    8. The cook makes bean cakes for the family.

B. Write each sentence with the correct present tense verb.

    9. David (visit, visits) Kenji's grandparents.

    10. The friends (travel, travels) on a train.

    11. Kenji (bow, bows) to his grandmother.

    12. The boys (sit, sits) on straw mats.

C. Mixed Practice Write each sentence with the correct present tense verb.

    13. Kenji (play, plays) a Japanese flute.

    14. David (speak, speaks) a few words of Japanese.

    15. The grandparents (give, gives) David a gift.

    16. An earthquake (shake, shakes) the house.

    17. David (watch, watches) a puppet show.

    18. Kenji (smile, smiles) and (wave, waves).

Apply: Work with a Group

Work with several classmates to write a story describing your city or town. What would a visitor see and do? Use verbs in the present tense.

Making Subjects and Verbs Agree

The subject and the verb in the present tense must work together in a sentence. When they work together, they agree.

A. If the main word in the subject part of a sentence is a singular noun, add *s* or *es* to the verb. Also add *s* or *es* if the subject is *he, she,* or *it.*

Type of Subject	Rule for Verb	Example
singular noun and he, she, it	add <u>s</u> or <u>es</u>	A diver swim<u>s</u>. She searche<u>s</u>.

B. If the subject part of a sentence is a plural noun, do not add *s* or *es* to the verb. Do not add *s* or *es* if the subject is *I, you, we,* or *they.* Study the chart below.

Type of Subject	Rule for Verb	Example
plural noun and <u>I</u>, <u>you</u>, <u>we</u>, <u>they</u>	do not add <u>s</u> or <u>es</u>	The divers swim. They search.

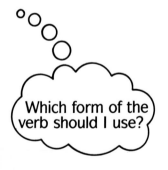

Which form of the verb should I use?

Strategy

To decide which form of the present tense verb to use, remember to look at the subject part of the sentence. Is it a singular noun? Add *s* or *es* to the verb. Is it a plural noun? You don't have to add any letters.

Check Your Understanding

A. Write the letter of the correct form of the verb.

    1. A diver ____ on a mask.

        a. put   **b.** puts

    2. He ____ into the water.

        a. splash   **b.** splashes

B. Write the letter of the correct form of the verb.

    3. Two sharks ___ nearby.

      a. circle   **b.** circles

    4. They ___ quietly.

      a. glide   **b.** glides

Practice

A. Write each sentence with the correct verb.

    5. Water (cover, covers) most of the earth.

    6. The ocean (hide, hides) mountains.

    7. Rain (wash, washes) salt into the oceans.

    8. The tide (rise, rises) twice each day.

B. Write each sentence with the correct verb.

    9. Scientists (search, searches) the ocean.

   10. They (catch, catches) strange sea creatures.

   11. We (watch, watches) a movie about sharks.

   12. Creatures (glow, glows) in the water.

C. Mixed Practice Write each sentence with the correct present tense of the verb in parentheses.

   13. A storm (form, forms) huge waves.

   14. Scientists (track, tracks) the storm.

   15. She (test, tests) the speed of the wind.

   16. Divers (explore, explores) the ocean depths.

   17. A submarine (dive, dives) very deep.

   18. Scientists (look, looks) and (listen, listens).

   19. I (swim, swims) and (watch, watches) you.

Apply: Exploring Language

Write each sentence using five different verbs.

Rita ___ all the way to school.

During recess, the students ___.

Spelling Present Tense Verbs

A. You must add *s* to many verbs in the present tense. If the verb ends in *ch*, *s*, *sh*, *ss*, or *x*, you must add *es*.

Type of Verb	Rule for Verb	Example
most present tense verbs	add <u>s</u>	swim ⟶ swim<u>s</u> race ⟶ race<u>s</u>
present tense verbs ending in <u>ch</u>, <u>sh</u>, <u>s</u>, <u>ss</u>, <u>x</u>, or <u>z</u>	add <u>es</u>	reach ⟶ reach<u>es</u> dash ⟶ dash<u>es</u> fix ⟶ fix<u>es</u>

B. If the present tense verb ends in a consonant and *y*, change the *y* to *i*. Then add *es*.

Type of Verb	Rule for Verb	Example
present tense verb ending in consonant and <u>y</u>	change the <u>y</u> to <u>i</u> and <u>es</u>	scurry ⟶ scurr<u>ies</u> copy ⟶ cop<u>ies</u> fry ⟶ fr<u>ies</u>

Strategy

To learn how to spell present tense verbs, remember the rules in this lesson. There are only a few rules, but there are hundreds of verbs.

Check Your Understanding

A. Write the letter of the correct present tense form of the verb in parentheses.
  1. A whale (leap) out of the water.
     a. leap   **b.** leaped   **c.** leaps
  2. The ship (approach) a group of whales.
     a. approaches   **b.** approach   **c.** approachs

B. Use the directions for Check Your Understanding A.

   3. A sailor (spy) a large whale.

      a. spies **b.** spy **c.** spys **d.** spyed

   4. A scientist (study) the whales.

      a. study **b.** studys **c.** studied **d.** studies

Practice

A. Write each sentence with the correct form of the verb in the present tense.

   5. Jacques Cousteau (search) for whales.

   6. A whale (pass) near his boat.

   7. The tail (brush) the little boat.

   8. The scientist (fall) into the sea.

B. Use the directions for Practice A.

   9. A baby whale (copy) its mother.

  10. The mother (carry) the baby on her back.

  11. Cousteau (study) sea animals.

  12. A whale (cry) to other whales.

C. Mixed Practice Write each sentence with the correct form of the verb in the present tense.

  13. A baby whale (wash) onto the shore.

  14. A scientist (carry) water to the whale.

  15. A helper (mix) food for the baby whale.

  16. A bird (snatch) some of the food.

  17. A blue whale (grow) and (reach) full size.

  18. A wave (approach) and (crash).

Apply: Test a Friend

Write five verbs ending in *ch, s, sh, ss, x, z,* or a consonant and *y*. Trade papers with a classmate. Write a singular noun to go with each verb. Add the correct ending to the verbs. Check your partner's work.

Past Tense

A verb in the **past tense** tells about an action that already happened. Most past tense verbs end in *ed*.

A. Verbs help you tell when an action takes place. Verbs can tell what happens in the present or what happened in the past.

Present Tense: The pilot <u>climbs</u> into the plane.
Past Tense: The pilot <u>climbed</u> into the plane.

Present Tense: The students <u>watch</u> a movie.
Past Tense: The students <u>watched</u> a movie.

B. Add *ed* to most verbs to form the past tense.

walk → <u>walked</u>   kick → <u>kicked</u>

twist → <u>twisted</u>   bounce → <u>bounced</u>

Strategy

How can you tell the difference between a verb in the present tense and a verb in the past tense? Look for *ed* at the end. A verb ending in *ed* tells about an action that happened in the past.

Check Your Understanding

A. Write the letter that tells the tense of the underlined verb.

  1. Michael <u>looked</u> for a book about Amelia Earhart.

    a. present tense   **b.** past tense

  2. Aretha <u>opens</u> the book.

    a. present tense   **b.** past tense

B. Write the letter of the correct past tense form of the verb in parentheses.

    3. Young Amelia Earhart (play) a banjo for fun.
        a. play   **b.** played   **c.** plays

    4. The girl also (hike) in the mountains.
        a. hiked   **b.** hike   **c.** hikes

Practice

A. Write whether the underlined verb is in the *present tense* or the *past tense*.

    5. Wilma tells the class about Amelia Earhart.
    6. Amelia earned money for an airplane.
    7. The young pilot raced from California to Ohio.
    8. The teacher asks Michael about Amelia's plane.

B. Write each sentence with the verb in the past tense.

    9. The little plane (bump) down the runway.
  10. The brave pilot (cross) the Atlantic Ocean alone.
  11. Amelia Earhart (land) in Ireland.
  12. The young woman (return) to the United States.

C. Mixed Practice Write each sentence. Change the underlined present tense verb into the past tense.

  13. Earhart starts on a trip around the world.
  14. The plane disappears in the Pacific Ocean.
  15. Many people search for the plane.
  16. Lina wonders about Amelia Earhart.
  17. A ship carries the search team.
  18. People finally stop the search for Earhart.

Apply: Journal

Write a journal entry describing three things you did yesterday. Use action verbs in the past tense.

Spelling Past Tense Verbs

A. You have already learned how to form most past tense verbs by adding *ed*. Study the chart below.

Type of Verb	Rule for Verb	Example
most verbs	add <u>ed</u>	march ⟶ march<u>ed</u>
verbs ending in <u>e</u>	drop the <u>e</u>, add <u>ed</u>	race ⟶ rac<u>ed</u>

B. Some verbs change in a different way. Look at the chart below and learn the rules.

Type of Verb	Rule for Verb	Example
verbs ending in a consonant and <u>y</u>	change <u>y</u> to <u>i</u> and add <u>ed</u>	try ⟶ tr<u>ied</u> hurry ⟶ hurr<u>ied</u>
verbs ending in one vowel and a consonant	double the last consonant and add <u>ed</u>	drop ⟶ drop<u>ped</u> hum ⟶ hum<u>med</u>

Strategy

Remember the rules for spelling past tense verbs. They will help you form hundreds of verbs correctly.

Check Your Understanding

A. Write the letter of the correct past tense form of the verb in parentheses.

1. Hiram Bingham (discover) a lost city in Peru.
   a. discoverd   **b.** discovers   **c.** discovered
2. Hiram (save) money for the trip.
   a. saved   **b.** saves   **c.** saveed

138

B. Use the directions for Check Your Understanding A.

    3. Hiram Bingham (study) at Yale University.

      a. studyed   **b.** studied   **c.** studed

    4. The young man (plan) a trip to Peru.

      a. planned   **b.** planed   **c.** pland

Practice

A. Write each sentence. Use the verb in the past tense.

    5. Hiram Bingham (sail) to South America.

    6. A farmer (describe) the lost city.

    7. Hiram (climb) high into the mountains.

    8. A guide (point) to a hillside.

B. Use the directions for Practice A.

    9. Hiram (spy) the lost city.

   10. A jungle (bury) the old buildings.

   11. The workers (carry) tools.

   12. The men (clip) away the brush.

C. Mixed Practice Write each sentence. Use the correct form of the verb in the past tense.

   13. Hiram (touch) the walls of the stone buildings.

   14. Incas (carve) giant blocks of stone.

   15. The explorers (map) the ancient city.

   16. Clouds (cover) the mountain peaks.

   17. Hiram (name) the city Machu Picchu.

   18. Incas (marry) in the temples at Machu Picchu.

   19. People (visit) the city and (snap) pictures.

   20. Hiram (dream) about the city and (smile).

Apply: Learning Log

In your learning log, tell what was difficult in this lesson. Then tell what you can do to improve your skill in spelling past tense verbs.

Synonyms and Antonyms

◆

A. Read the sentences below.

The garden is <u>pretty</u>. The garden is <u>beautiful</u>.

Both sentences mean almost the same thing. The words *pretty* and *beautiful* are synonyms.

Synonyms are words with the same or similar meanings.

Look at these pairs of synonyms.

big, large   gift, present   smile, grin

B. Read the sentences below.

Maria is <u>tall</u>. Tanika is <u>short</u>.

The words *tall* and *short* are antonyms.

Antonyms are words with opposite meanings.

Look at these pairs of antonyms.

open, shut   always, never   hot, cold

Strategy

When you write, try not to use the same word over and over. Synonyms help make your sentences more interesting. Pick the synonym that means exactly what you want to say.

Check Your Understanding

A. Write the letter of the synonym for the underlined word.

1. Pirates sailed the <u>ocean</u>.
   a. lake   **b.** sea   **c.** land   **d.** river
2. They <u>looked</u> for treasure.
   a. asked   **b.** found   **c.** dug   **d.** searched

B. Write the letter of the antonym for the underlined word.

    3. The large chest held jewels.

        a. big   **b.** small   **c.** square   **d.** open

    4. Pirates flew a black flag.

        a. white   **b.** dark   **c.** gray   **d.** cloth

Practice

A. Write each sentence. Replace the underlined word with its synonym in parentheses.

    5. Captain Kidd sailed a pirate ship. (boat, hat)

    6. The captain was very clever. (wicked, smart)

    7. His ship traveled quickly. (once, fast)

B. Write each sentence. Replace the underlined word with its antonym in parentheses.

    8. Blackbeard shouted. (whispered, yelled)

    9. People hated the wicked pirate. (liked, fought)

   10. Blackbeard wore a long beard. (black, short)

   11. Some women were pirates, too. (men, robbers)

C. Mixed Practice Write each sentence. Write *synonym* or *antonym* to name the underlined words.

   12. Kidd took a long trip on a short boat.

   13. The big ship crossed a huge ocean.

   14. The ship sailed both night and day.

   15. Pirates stole from the rich and the poor.

   16. Blackbeard robbed on land and sea.

   17. A small pirate opened a little, tiny box.

   18. A stout sailor captured the slender pirate.

Apply: Exploring Language

Write a synonym and an antonym for *happy, small,* or *quiet*. Write a sentence using each.

LANGUAGE IN ACTION

Making Introductions

You are walking down the street with your cousin. You see a friend and stop to talk. Your cousin and your friend look at each other. What should you do?

It is polite to introduce people to one another. Here's what you should do.

- ◆ Say each person's name, and introduce the other person.
  "Esteban, this is Lisa." "Lisa, this is Esteban."
- ◆ Don't just say the person's name. If possible, say something about each person. You can also tell why you know each of them.
  "Tracy, this is Ho-il. He lives next door to me."
  "Ho-il, this is Tracy. She's visiting from Montana."
- ◆ If you are being introduced to someone, say the person's name. This will help you remember it.
  Right: "It's nice to meet you, Wilson."

Practice

On a separate piece of paper, answer these questions.
   1. When should you introduce people?
   2. What do you say besides their names?
   3. What should you do when you are introduced to someone?

Apply

Work in groups of three. Each person in the group should introduce the other two.

HISTORY OF LANGUAGE

Days of the Week

Judy looked at her plans for next week. On Monday, she had soccer practice. On Wednesday, she had a piano lesson. On Saturday, she planned to help Mr. Wilson weed his garden. Monday, Wednesday, Saturday . . . Judy wondered how the days got their names.

She found that the names of all the days of the week come from myths. Myths are stories that people told a long time ago to explain things they didn't understand, such as lightning.

Some names come from Norse myths. Tyr was a brave, strong Norse god. To honor Tyr, a day of the week was named for him. In England, Tyr was called Tiw (pronounced *too*), and his day was called *Tiw's day*.

Names for other days come from Roman myths. For the Romans, planets and stars were very important. The sun and the moon had days named for them. They were called Sun's day and Moon's day.

People shortened the names for days of the week. *Tiw's day* became *Tuesday*. *Sun's day* became *Sunday*, and *Moon's day* became *Monday*.

Activity

Rewrite this list of days of the week. After each day, write the god or goddess for whom the day is named.

1. Wednesday   **a.** Frigga, Norse goddess of the home
2. Thursday   **b.** Saturn, a Roman god of farming
3. Friday   **c.** Thor, Norse god of thunder
4. Saturday   **d.** Woden, the main German god

UNIT REVIEW

Book Report *(page 109)*
1. On your paper, list three features of a book report.

Identifying Facts and Opinions *(pages 116-117)*
Write whether each sentence below is a *fact* or an *opinion*.
   2. *Hans Brinker* was written by Mary Mapes Dodge.
   3. It is a wonderful story that everyone should read.
   4. It tells about Dutch children who lived in the 1800s.
   5. The story has a very exciting ending.

Adding Descriptive Words/Writing Titles
(pages 120-123)
Add a descriptive word to tell more about each underlined word.
   6. The class read the book by Mary Mapes Dodge.
   7. Students talked about the skating race in the book.
   8. The teacher showed a picture of a real skating race.
   9. Classmates looked at the picture.
Write each sentence. Write all titles correctly.
   10. Have you read the book ramona the brave?
   11. Meg called her poem the tree and the bush.
   12. My favorite story is the lion and the mouse.

Action Verbs *(pages 128-129)*
Write each sentence. Then write whether each underlined word is a *noun* or a *verb*.
   13. The skaters glide on the ice.
   14. The children race swiftly.
   15. Melba crosses the finish line.
   16. The wind blows the snow.

Present Tense   *(pages 130-133)*
Write each sentence with the correct present tense of the verb in parentheses.
17. Bears (roam, roams) the forest.
18. A mother bear (catch, catches) some food.
19. The bear (share, shares) the food with her cubs.
20. The bears (walk, walks) into a cave.

Spelling Present Tense Verbs   *(pages 134-135)*
Write each sentence with the correct form of the verb in the present tense.
21. Moy (mix) seed for the birds.
22. The girl (carry) the seeds outside.
23. Snow (crunch) under each boot.
24. Moy (brush) snow from the bird feeder.
25. The girl (hurry) back to the warm house.

Spelling Past Tense Verbs   *(pages 136-139)*
Write each sentence with the correct form of the verb in the past tense.
26. Pilgrims (sail) from England.
27. The settlers (carry) only a little food.
28. The ship (land) at Plymouth.
29. An Indian tribe (live) nearby.
30. The Pilgrims (try) Indian foods.
31. The settlers (plan) a big feast.

Synonyms and Antonyms   *(pages 140-141)*
Write each sentence. Then write whether the underlined words are *synonyms* or *antonyms*.
32. A cool breeze blows over the warm desert.
33. A level road crosses the flat land.
34. A fast car passes a slow truck.
35. The noisy bird makes a loud sound.
36. The sun shines from dawn until dusk.

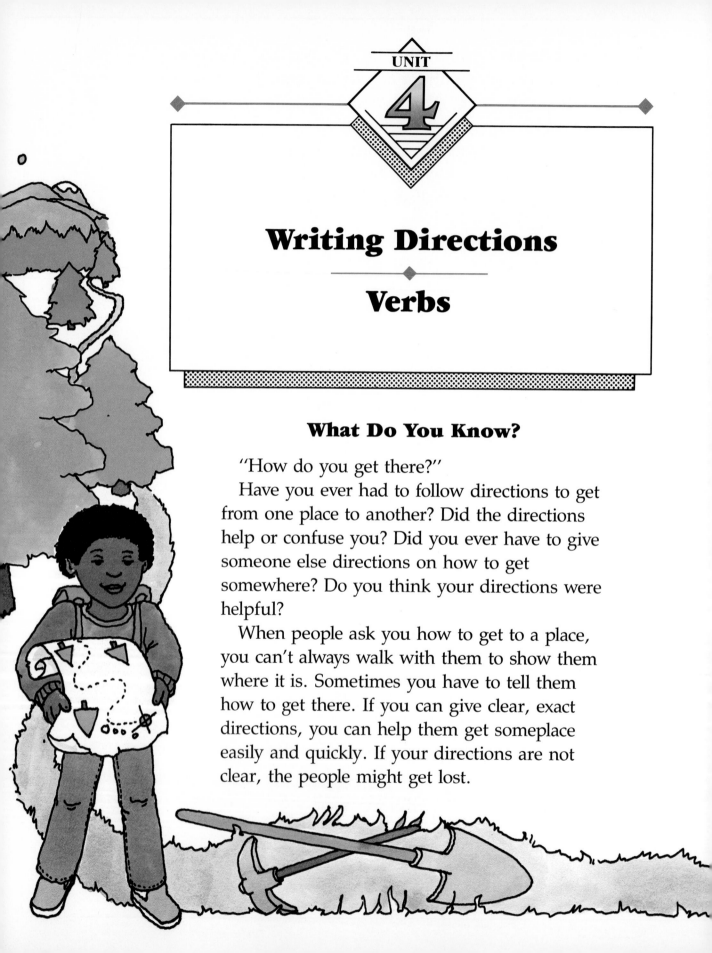

Writing Directions

Verbs

What Do You Know?

"How do you get there?"

Have you ever had to follow directions to get from one place to another? Did the directions help or confuse you? Did you ever have to give someone else directions on how to get somewhere? Do you think your directions were helpful?

When people ask you how to get to a place, you can't always walk with them to show them where it is. Sometimes you have to tell them how to get there. If you can give clear, exact directions, you can help them get someplace easily and quickly. If your directions are not clear, the people might get lost.

Thinking About Directions

What Are Directions?

Directions have these features:

- They name the place where you are and the place where you are going.
- They are divided into simple steps.
- The steps are given in order.
- They include landmarks that make them easy to follow. A landmark is something easy to spot, such as a firehouse or a radio tower.
- The directions are clear and exact.

You are often asked to give directions to get from place to place. If a friend is visiting you for the first time, you may need to tell him or her how to get to your home. You may have to tell a new classmate how to get from your classroom to the auditorium or the lunchroom. Directions can be for fun, too. You could direct people to a prize in a treasure hunt.

Exact directions can make the difference between getting there and getting lost. In this unit, you will learn how to give clear directions.

Discussion

1. Have you ever given someone directions? If so, what did you say?
2. What things do you think are important to say when you are giving directions?
3. What things should you think about before giving someone directions?

147

Reading Directions

Read the following selection. It tells about the famous reporter Nellie Bly, and the route of her trip around the world. The directions that she followed are also shown on the map.

Although Nellie wrote many stories that helped people, she became best known for her trip around the world. She had read Jules Verne's *Around the World in Eighty Days*, a make-believe story about a man who went around the world in eighty days. Although going around the world in only eighty days

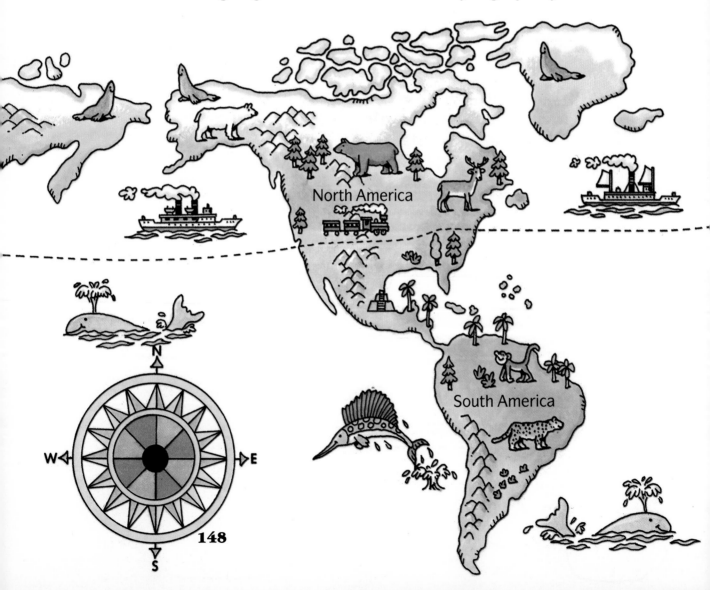

North America

South America

N

W E

S

sounded impossible, Nellie thought that it could be done. Joseph Pulitzer agreed with her. He gave her money for the trip.

On November 14, 1889, at 9:40 a.m., Nellie left New Jersey on a steamship headed for England. The steamship crossed the Atlantic Ocean and landed on a southern shore of England.

From England, Nellie sailed to France. Jules Verne came to greet her and wish her luck. Then she rode a train to Italy.

Nellie boarded another steamship to travel across the Mediterranean Sea, the Suez Canal, and the Red Sea. Then she went across the Indian Ocean and on to China and Japan.

All along the way, she sent back stories about her trip. These stories were used in the *World*. Soon many people had learned of Nellie's race against time. Each day they looked in the *World* for a story by Nellie. Would Nellie make it?

In Japan, Nellie boarded a steamship to cross the Pacific Ocean. When the ship landed in San Francisco, thousands of people were there to greet Nellie. She was filled with joy.

Then Nellie crossed the United States by train. Each time the train stopped, hundreds of people were there to meet Nellie. They had to see Nellie to believe the exciting stories they had read.

On January 26, 1890, at 3:15 P.M., Nellie was back in New Jersey. She had gone around the world faster than any other person. It took her seventy-two days, six hours, and eleven minutes.

First sailed from New Jersey to England.
Then sailed from England to France.
Next rode from France to Italy by train.
Then sailed from Italy across the Mediterranean, the Suez Canal, and Red Sea.
Then sailed from the Red Sea across the Indian Ocean to China and Japan.
Next sailed from Japan to San Francisco.
Finally rode from San Francisco to New Jersey by train.

Understanding What You've Read

Write the answers to these questions.

1. Where did Nellie Bly go after she left England?
2. How did Nellie travel to get to Italy?
3. How did Nellie get from Japan to San Francisco?
4. At the beginning of the selection, how do you know that Nellie will end up at the same place that she started?
5. How is Nellie Bly's trip different from a trip around the world that someone would take today?

Writing Assignment

Imagine your school is having an Open School Day. You must help prepare by writing directions on how to get between any two points in or around your school.

Your **audience** will be your teacher and classmates. Your **purpose** will be to work up a set of clear, exact directions that someone could use even if you were not there to explain them.

Choose a Route

- Make a list of five routes that you could give directions for. Make sure the places are not next to each other. For example, you might tell how to get from the library to the lunchroom.
- Decide which of the five routes you would most like to give directions for. Save your choice for the next lesson.

How would I direct someone?

151

Observing and Taking Notes

Laura needs to tell her uncle how to get from the Third Street bus stop to the gym. To make sure she will give exact directions, Laura walks the route herself. She takes notes on where she walks and what landmarks she sees. Landmarks are special points along a route. They help people remember the route. Here are Laura's notes.

```
Key
⊢⊣ = door
c = classroom
h = hallway
```

--entered by Third Street door, walked down hall
--turned left at the library and kept walking
--walked straight past the auditorium
--turned left at the nurse's office
--the gym is at the end of the hall

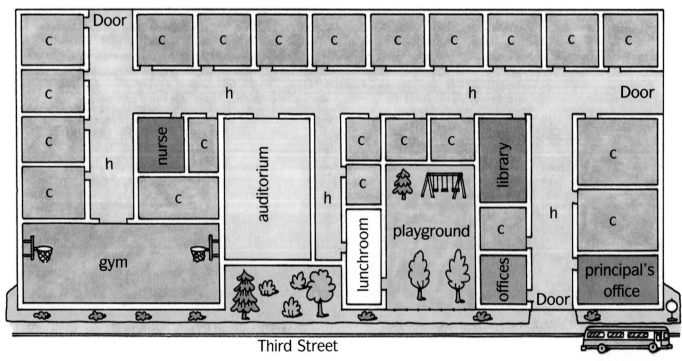

Third Street

bus stop

When taking notes as you walk a route, think about the points where you must make a decision. Exactly where do you make a turn? What landmarks help you? Write these details down. The decision points will become the steps in your directions.

Practice

A. The notes below tell how to get from the playground to the principal's office in Laura's school. Rewrite the notes so they are correct. Fill in any decision points that are missing. Change any incorrect details. Use the map on page 152 to help you.

—walked through the lunchroom to the lunchroom's other door

—turned right into the hallway

—turned right at the library

—walked straight down that hall to principal's office, which was to my left

B. Use the map on page 152 to make notes on how to get from the gym to the playground.

Take Notes on Your Route
- Walk the route you plan to give directions for.
- Take notes on your decision points and landmarks. You do not have to use complete sentences.
- Put your notes in order. Add sequence words such as *first*, *next*, and *last*.
- Save your notes.

Did I take the easiest route?

Writing a First Draft

Read the first draft of Laura's set of directions. She wasn't worried about making it perfect. It will be changed later.

> This is how to get from the Third Street bus stop to the gym in my school.
> First, enter by the Third Street door and walk downe the hall.
> Next, turn at the library.
> Then, turn left at the nurse's office.
> finally, walk straight down the end of the hall to the gym

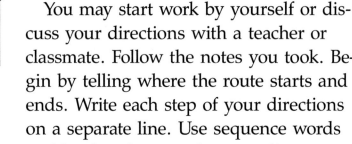

Write Your First Draft

You may start work by yourself or discuss your directions with a teacher or classmate. Follow the notes you took. Begin by telling where the route starts and ends. Write each step of your directions on a separate line. Use sequence words and landmarks to make your directions easy to follow. Save your work.

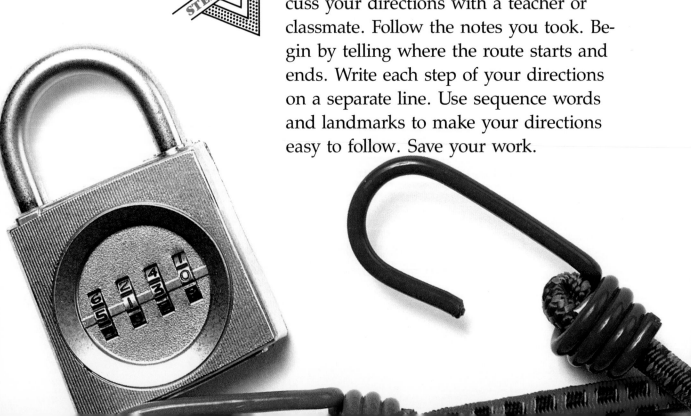

Discussing a First Draft

After you finish your first draft, discuss your work with a partner.

Discussion Strategy

Let your partner finish what he or she is saying. You will have a chance to give your own ideas *after* your partner has finished.

Use this Content Checklist to discuss Laura's directions with your class.

Content Checklist
- ✔ Do the directions tell where the route starts and ends?
- ✔ Are the directions divided into easy steps?
- ✔ Are the steps given in order?
- ✔ Are the directions clear and exact?
- ✔ Do the directions include landmarks that will make them easy to follow?

Revise Your First Draft for Content

To the Reader: Trade papers with a classmate. Try to see your partner's route in your mind. Use the Content Checklist and Discussion Strategy.

To the Writer: Listen to what your partner says. Then revise your draft for content. Save your work.

155

Revise for Complete Information

When you prepare directions, you must make sure no detail is left out. A good set of directions includes every step that is needed to get from one place to another. Here is a list to help you check the information in your directions.

1. Mention all turns. Say whether they are right or left turns.

   Turn <u>left</u> when you get to the office.

2. Tell how far to go. Be as exact as possible.

   Stay on Vine Street <u>for three miles.</u>

3. If you can, give a landmark that will help explain the directions.

   Walk straight and <u>pass the library.</u>

4. If there is anything difficult about a direction, give a special tip about it.

   Walk to the back door, <u>which is under the stairs.</u>

Here is how Laura added details to her directions.

First, enter by the Third Street door and walk downe the hall.
Next, turn ^left at the library.
^Then, walk straight and pass the auditorium⊙
Then, turn left at the nurse's office.
finally, walk straight down the end of the hall to the gym

Practice

A. These are the treasure rooms below the Ice King's castle. Here are his directions for getting from the elevator in the Gold Room to the Robot Lab.

Rewrite the directions. Put in any missing details. Here is how to get from the elevator to the Robot Lab.

1. First, walk from the Gold Room through the Silver Room.

2. Then, go to the hallway and turn.

3. Next, turn right and walk down the hallway past the Room of Maps.

4. Finally, keep walking straight ahead until you reach the Robot Lab.

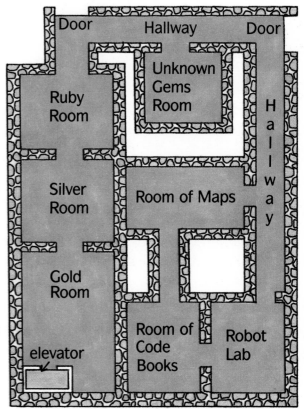

Revising Checklist

✔ Have I included all the features of a set of directions?
✔ Can I combine subjects and predicates to make new sentences? (p. 32)
✔ Have I included exact information? (p. 70)
✔ Where can I add information to make my work complete?

Revise Your First Draft for Style

Check for the items on the Revising Checklist. If you need to, add information to make your directions clearer. Mark your changes on the draft.

Abbreviations of Place and Time

Laura used a street name in her directions. She decided to use an abbreviation for the ordinal number *third* and for the word *street*. An abbreviation is a shortened form of a word. Laura checked the following rules for writing abbreviations.

Rule	Examples		
An abbreviation of a word like <u>street</u> begins with a capital letter and ends with a period when it is part of a proper noun.	Street St. Road Rd. Avenue Ave. Boulevard Blvd.		
Capitalize the abbreviations of days of the week. Place a period after each abbreviation.	Sun.	Mon.	Tues.
	Wed.	Thurs.	
	Fri.	Sat.	
Use a capital letter to begin the abbreviation for each month. Place a period after it. May, June, and July are not abbreviated.	Jan.	Feb.	Mar.
	Apr.	Aug.	Sept.
	Oct.	Nov.	Dec.
Abbreviate ordinal numbers like first and second by using the numeral and an ending. Do not use a period.	1st	2nd	3rd
	4th	5th	6th
	10th	12th	13th
	21st	22nd	23rd

Reminder: In most writing you do in school, such as reports and stories, you do *not* use abbreviations. You may use abbreviations in writing notes, lists, and addresses.

Practice

Here are some notes a reporter took for a story about a treasure hunt. Write each numbered item. Use abbreviations for the underlined words.

1. hunt began on Friday, October 19
2. treasure hidden near one of the streets that crosses Mackie Boulevard
3. hunt supposed to end Wednesday, October 7
4. crowds hunted along Second Avenue and Sixth Road
5. Oak Street and Bay Road full of treasure hunters
6. on Monday, September 7, Karen Hong of Tenth Road found a rare coin at First Street
7. no one found treasure, which was at Sixth Avenue
8. on Thursday, October 8, Karen Hong declared the winner of the hunt

Proofreading Marks	
^	add
℘	take away
¶	indent
≡	capitalize
/	small letter
⬭	check spelling
∾	transpose

Proofreading Checklist

- ✓ Did I begin each sentence with a capital letter? (p. 34)
- ✓ Did I use the correct end marks for sentences? (p. 34)
- ✓ Did I use commas correctly? (p. 72)
- ✓ Did I use the correct capitalization and punctuation for all my abbreviations?
- ✓ Do my subjects and verbs agree?

APPLY STEP BY STEP

Proofread Your Directions

Check for correct capitalization and punctuation. Use the Proofreading Checklist. Make the changes on your draft. Save your work for the next lesson.

Checking Spelling/Writing a Final Copy

Spelling Strategy

To learn the spelling of a word, write it often. Trace the letters with your fingertip. What is the shape of each letter?

Read Laura's revised and proofread directions.

> This is how to get from the Third Street bus stop to the gym in my school.
> First, enter by the Third Street door and walk ~~downe~~ down the hall.
> Next, turn left at the library.
> Then, walk straight and pass the auditorium.
> Then, turn left at the nurse's office.
> finally, walk straight down the end of the hall to the gym.

Check Your Spelling

Use the proofreading marks to correct any mistakes in spelling. Apply the Spelling Strategy. Add any misspelled words to your spelling log.

Write a Final Copy

Write a neat, final copy of your directions. Be sure to proofread your work. Keep your final copy.

Sharing Your Directions

Speaking/Listening Strategy

When giving directions aloud, make each step perfectly clear. Pause briefly between steps in your description of the route. As a listener, note decision points.

Choosing a Way to Share

Here are some ways to share your directions.
Reading Aloud Imagine you are giving someone directions over the telephone. Since you can't use hand gestures to make your directions clear, your directions must be exact.

Demonstrating Your Directions Pretend you are running an information booth at Open School Day. Explain your directions to a classmate.

Making a Map Draw a map to use with your directions. Have your classmates try to follow your directions on the map.

Share Your Directions

Choose the way you want to share your paragraph. After you present it, answer any questions your audience may have.

Add to Your Learning Log

How do I feel about my directions?
What did I like most about writing them?
If I could rewrite my directions, what would I change?

The Literature Connection: Verbs

Think about the way different animals move. Some walk, some fly, some crawl or sneak. Action words that tell about how things move are called **verbs**.

Good writing always contains many colorful verbs. Each verb you read should form an action picture in your mind.

In the poem below, verbs are used to tell about the mysterious way that snakes move. As you are reading, try to picture an actual snake crawling along the ground.

The Snake
by
Karla Kuskin

A snake slipped through
the thin green grass
A silver snake
I watched it pass
It moved like a ribbon
Silent as snow.
I think it smiled
As it passed my toe.

Discussion

1. Which words in the poem are verbs? Explain what actions they tell about.
2. What do you think the snake was smiling about as it passed the poet's toe?
3. Suppose this poem were about a bear instead of a snake. Which verbs would need to be changed?

The Writing Connection: Verbs

Some verbs tell about actions done only by certain animals or things. Here are some examples.

The angry snake <u>hissed</u> at the dog.

The frog <u>croaked</u> all night long.

Can you imagine a snake that *croaked*, or a frog that *hissed*? You can't, because these verbs are usually special for the animals they tell about. In your writing, choose verbs that match the thing you are telling about.

Activity

Think of an animal you would like to write about. If you want to, you can use one from the picture.

◆ Write about the animal you chose. Use as many action verbs as you need. Try to make such a clear picture of the animal that your reader can see what it is doing.

◆ Look at the poem "The Snake" to get good ideas.

The Verb *Be*

The verb *be* is a **linking verb**. A linking verb joins the subject of a sentence with words that name or describe it.

A. The verb *be* has several different forms.

Subject	Form of *be*	Example
I	*am* and *was*	I <u>am</u> a student. I <u>was</u> brave.
singular nouns and *he, she, it*	*is* and *was*	The puzzle <u>is</u> fun. It <u>was</u> easy.
plural nouns and *we, you, they*	*are* and *were*	Stones <u>are</u> heavy. We <u>were</u> friends.

B. You know that an action verb tells what the subject *does*. A linking verb tells what the subject *is* or *is like*. It does not tell about action.

Action verb: Ancient people <u>built</u> Stonehenge.
Linking verb: Stonehenge <u>is</u> a ring of stones.

Strategy

It's easy to find action verbs and linking verbs. An action verb tells what the subject *does*. A linking verb tells what the subject *is* or *is like*.

Check Your Understanding

A. Write the letter of the form of the verb *be*.
  1. The stones are very heavy.
    a. stones **b.** are **c.** very **d.** heavy
  2. Chris is a student.
    a. Chris **b.** is **c.** a **d.** student

B. Write the letter that names the underlined verb.

    3. Builders <u>carried</u> stones to a field.

        a. action verb   **b.** linking verb

    4. The workers <u>were</u> strong.

        a. action verb   **b.** linking verb

Practice

A. Write each sentence. Then underline the form of the verb *be*.

    5. Stonehenge is an ancient monument.

    6. It was a special place.

    7. Some stones are as large as trucks.

    8. I am curious about Stonehenge.

B. Write each sentence. Write if the underlined verb is an *action verb* or a *linking verb*.

    9. Workers <u>carved</u> the pieces of stone.

   10. They <u>were</u> skillful stoneworkers.

   11. We <u>are</u> visitors at Stonehenge.

   12. Many people <u>travel</u> to Stonehenge.

C. Mixed Practice Write each sentence. Underline the verb. Write if it is an *action verb* or a *linking verb*.

   13. Rosa drew a picture of Stonehenge.

   14. The picture is very beautiful.

   15. Juanita tells the class about Indian mounds.

   16. The mounds are in Mississippi.

   17. What was their purpose?

   18. Mark is happy and walks to school.

   19. There will be a movie at school today.

Apply: Test a Partner

Write nouns for five persons, places, or things in a column. Ask a classmate to write a sentence using each noun with a linking verb. Check your partner's work.

Main Verbs and Helping Verbs

The verb part of a sentence can have one or more verbs. A **main verb** is the most important verb in a sentence. A **helping verb** helps the main verb tell about an action.

A. The helping verbs *have*, *has*, and *had* often help the main verb tell about an action in the past.

The hikers have arrived.
helping verb   main verb

Todd has greeted them.
helping verb   main verb

Gabriella had visited the park last year.
helping verb   main verb

B. Add *ed* to most main verbs that follow the helping verbs *have*, *has*, or *had*. Look at the chart below.

Helping verb	Main verb	Example
have	camped	The children have camped.
has	cooked	John has cooked hamburgers.
had	sliced	She had sliced the potatoes.

Strategy

To find the helping verb in a sentence, look for the main verb with an *ed* ending. The helping verbs *have*, *has*, and *had* come before the main verb.

Check Your Understanding

A. Write the letter of the helping verb.
   1. The leader has pointed the way.
      a. leader   **b.** has   **c.** pointed   **d.** way
   2. The children have started the trip.
      a. children   **b.** have   **c.** started   **d.** trip

B. Write the letter of the main verb in each sentence.

   3. The climbers have prepared for the trip.
      a. climbers   **b.** have   **c.** prepared   **d.** trip
   4. Cindy has jumped over a log.
      a. has   **b.** jumped   **c.** over   **d.** log

Practice

A. Write each sentence. Underline the helping verb once. Underline the main verb twice.

   5. The children have filled their bags.
   6. The climbers have packed food and water.
   7. Mother had camped here before.
   8. Todd has lifted his pack.

B. Write each sentence with the correct form of the main verb.

   9. The leader has _____ the children. (call)
   10. The climbers have _____ all morning. (walk)
   11. They had _____ several miles. (hike)
   12. Gabriella has _____ a stream. (cross)

C. Mixed Practice Write each sentence. Form the main verb correctly. Underline the helping verb.

   13. The children have _____ very high. (climb)
   14. A cloud has _____ the sun. (cover)
   15. The climbers have _____ the top. (reach)
   16. Todd has _____ at another mountain. (look)
   17. That rock had _____ down earlier. (tumble)
   18. The children have _____ for lunch. (stop)
   19. The climbers have _____ down. (sit)

Apply: Work with a Group

   Take turns writing sentences with the verbs below. Use the helping verbs *have*, *has*, or *had*. Verbs: chase, fix, help, hurry, laugh, play, rise.

Irregular Verbs

Some verbs do not form the past tense by adding *ed*.

A. You have already learned to add *ed* to change most present tense verbs to the past tense. **Irregular verbs** change in a different way.

Present	Past		Present	Past
come	came		go	went
do	did		run	ran
eat	ate		see	saw

B. The main verb changes when it is used with the helping verbs *have*, *has*, and *had*.

Present	Past with *have*, *has*, or *had*
come	(have, has, had) come
do	(have, has, had) done
eat	(have, has, had) eaten
go	(have, has, had) gone
run	(have, has, had) run
see	(have, has, had) seen

These verbs don't follow the regular rules. I need to remember them.

Strategy

Irregular verbs are hard to learn. Use the chart to remember the past tense of the verbs in this lesson.

Check Your Understanding

A. Write the letter of the correct past tense verb.

1. Phileas Fogg ____ around the world.

    a. go   **b.** went   **c.** goes

2. Fogg ____ to the train station.

    a. run   **b.** runs   **c.** ran

B. Write the letter of the correct form of the main verb.

    3. Phileas has ___ something exciting.

        a. done   **b.** does   **c.** do

    4. The man has ___ many interesting places.

        a. see   **b.** sees   **c.** seen

Practice

A. Write each sentence with the correct past tense form of the verb in parentheses.

    5. Phileas Fogg ___ to Egypt. (come)

    6. He ___ to India on a boat. (go)

    7. Fogg ___ a princess in trouble. (see)

    8. The man ___ something clever. (do)

B. Follow the directions for Practice A.

    9. The princess has ___ with Fogg. (come)

   10. The train had ___ across India. (go)

   11. Fogg and the princess have ___. (eat)

   12. The travelers have ___ to the boat. (run)

C. Mixed Practice Write each sentence with the correct form of the main verb in parentheses.

   13. Fogg has ___ many unusual foods. (eat)

   14. The man ___ to the United States. (come)

   15. He and the princess ___ to New York. (go)

   16. They had ___ many different sights. (see)

   17. Fogg has ___ around the world. (go)

   18. He had ___ and ___ to the train. (eat, run)

   19. We have ___ a book about Fogg. (read)

Apply: Learning Log

Describe the most difficult part of this lesson. Tell what you can do to learn the irregular verbs.

Contractions with *Not*

A **contraction** is a shortened form of two words. An apostrophe (') takes the place of the missing letter or letters in a contraction.

A. Some verbs can be combined with the word *not* to form contractions. Look at the chart below.

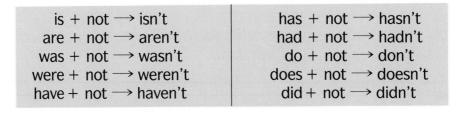

is + not ⟶ isn't	has + not ⟶ hasn't
are + not ⟶ aren't	had + not ⟶ hadn't
was + not ⟶ wasn't	do + not ⟶ don't
were + not ⟶ weren't	does + not ⟶ doesn't
have + not ⟶ haven't	did + not ⟶ didn't

B. To write a contraction, join the verb with the word *not*. Replace the letter *o* in *not* with an apostrophe.

is not ⟶ isnot ⟶ isn't

Strategy

When you speak, you use many contractions. You don't have to think about adding an apostrophe. When you write, remember to add an apostrophe where a letter or letters are missing.

Check Your Understanding

A. Write the letter of the two words that make up each contraction.

1. Camels aren't like most animals.
  a. is not   **b.** are not   **c.** were not
  d. had not

2. They don't need water for many days.
  a. did not   **b.** does not   **c.** done not
  d. do not

B. Write the letter of the contraction for each pair of underlined words.

    3. A camel is not very friendly.

        a. isn't   **b.** is'nt   **c.** isno't   **d.** is't

    4. Chan had not seen a camel before.

        a. ha'dnt   **b.** hadn't   **c.** hadnt'   **d.** had'nt

Practice

A. Write the two words from which each contraction is made.

    5. don't   **8.** weren't   **11.** hasn't

    6. aren't   **9.** isn't   **12.** doesn't

    7. didn't   **10.** hadn't   **13.** wasn't

B. Write the contraction for each pair of words.

    14. have not   **17.** did not   **20.** is not

    15. does not   **18.** was not   **21.** has not

    16. are not   **19.** do not   **22.** were not

C. Mixed Practice Write each sentence. Form a contraction for the underlined words.

    23. Long ago camels were not tame.

    24. Today most camels do not live in the wild.

    25. The children have not taken a camel ride.

    26. Food does not grow in the desert.

    27. Camels are not part of the horse family.

    28. The camel was not used in Europe.

    29. A camel's fur is thick, but it is not long.

    30. A camel's foot cannot sink into soft sand.

Apply: Journal

Write a journal entry telling about five things you have not done but would like to do. Use the contractions you studied in this lesson.

Homobphones

◆

Homophones are words that sound the same but have different spellings and different meanings.

A. Read the pairs of sentences. The underlined words in each pair are homophones. How are they the same? How are they different?

My <u>aunt</u> had a picnic. Some <u>ants</u> came to it.
The cupboard was <u>bare</u>. A <u>bear</u> ate all the food.

B. The correct homophone to use depends on the meaning of the sentence.

Which word belongs in each sentence below: *here* or *hear*?

The race starts ____. I ____ the whistle.

Which word belongs in each sentence below: *won* or *one*?

This boat ____. It is the ____ I sailed.

Strategy

Homophones can be confusing when you write. Which spelling should you use? Think about the meaning of the word. Check the spelling in a dictionary.

Check Your Understanding

A. Write the letter of the homophone for the underlined word.
  1. Four ships set <u>sail</u>.
    a. fear **b.** for **c.** far **d.** five
  2. Our ship sailed fast.
    a. or **b.** air **c.** their **d.** hour

B. Write the letter of the homophone that correctly completes each sentence.

    3. One ____ has seven days.
        a. weak **b.** week
    4. Yolanda ate the ____ sandwich.
        a. whole **b.** hole

Practice

A. Write each sentence. Underline the homophones.

    5. Two boats sailed to Nantucket.
    6. The wind blew over the blue water.
    7. People see the boats at sea.

B. Write each sentence using the correct homophone.

    8. ____ family played on the beach. (Hour, Our)
    9. Helen filled a ____ with water. (pail, pale)
  10. The ____ felt very hot. (son, sun)

C. Mixed Practice Write the sentences. Use each homophone in the correct place.

  11. I ____ along the ____ to the lake. (road, rode)
  12. Lions ____ here. They eat ____. (meet, meat)
  13. The hunters ____. The lion licks its ____. (paws, pause)
  14. ____ got some dust in my ____. (I, eye)
  15. We ____ there are ____ lions here. (no, know)
  16. The baby lion looked for ____ mother. ____ time for lunch. (it's, its)
  17. ____ jeep is over ____. (there, their)

Apply: Work with a Partner

Think of two pairs of homophones. Write one word from each pair. Trade papers with your partner. Complete the pairs.

LANGUAGE IN ACTION

Using the Phone Book

You want to call your friend Raoul. You know his last name, but you don't know his phone number. What should you do?

Here are some tips for using a phone book:

- People are listed alphabetically by last name. After each name, the address and phone number are given.
- At the top of each page you will see two key names. These are the first and last names on the page. Every name on the page comes between the key names. For example, Gollin appears on a page with the key names of *Gerber* and *Green* because *Go* is between *Ge* and *Gr* alphabetically.

Practice

Look at this page from a telephone book. On a separate piece of paper, answer the following questions.

Cogswell-Danly

Cogswell, C   86 Star Dr 493-4288
Cohen, Beth   21 Surrey Rd 723-3372
Cole, Daniel   326 Bay Rd   493-7623

Connaly, Brian   8 Webster Ave 723-6468
Connaly, Colleen   24 Surrey Rd 517-6984
Contabos, Arsenio   5 Rose Lane . . . 493-8266

1. What is Daniel Cole's phone number?
2. Where does Arsenio Contabos live?
3. Your friend Ann Connaly lives on Surrey Road. What is her phone number?

Apply

At home, look up the phone numbers of three classmates. In class tomorrow see if you got them right.

TEST TAKING

Following Directions

When you take a test, read the directions carefully. If there is a sample, study it before going on. Make sure you know what to do.

Study the test directions and samples below.

Directions: Underline the word in each group that does not belong.
Sample: fish cat dog box

Directions: Circle the letter of the correct answer.
Sample: $12 - 5 =$ _____ a. 17 b. 12 (c.)7

Directions: Write the word that makes sense in the sentence.
Sample: The rain came falling ^down^ .
         above through down

Practice

Answer the questions about the sample test.

Directions: Fill the circle of the correct answer.
Sample: $3 + 2 =$ ___ ○ 3 ○ 2 ● 5
        1. $4 + 2 =$ __6__ ○ 5 ○ 6 ○ 7
        2. $5 - 1 =$ ___ ○ 6 ○ 4 ○ 1

---

1. How does the sample follow the directions?
2. What is wrong with the answer for question 1?
3. What is wrong with the answer for question 2?

Apply

Learning Log Decide what things from this lesson will help you. Write them in your learning log.

175

UNIT REVIEW

Writing Directions   *(page 147)*

1. On your paper, list three features of a set of directions.

Observing and Taking Notes   *(pages 152-153)*

2. The notes below tell how to get from the bears to the food stand. Write them in correct order.
Then, turn at the lions and go to the goats.
Last, turn at the birds and go to the food stand.
First, walk from the bears to the lions.
Next, turn left at the goats and go to the bird building.

Revise for Complete Information   *(pages 156-157)*

3. Rewrite the second and third sentences above to make them more complete. Add any missing information.

Abbreviations of Place and Time   *(pages 158-159)*

Write the abbreviation for each word.

4. Street   Road   Avenue   Boulevard
5. Sunday   April   Friday   October
6. first   fifth   twelfth   tenth

The Verb *Be*   *(pages 164-165)*

Write each sentence. Underline the verb. Write whether it is an *action verb* or a *linking verb*.

7. The ocean is deep.

8. Waves crash on the shore.

9. Fish swim in the water.

10. The fish are hungry.

11. Sharks chase the fish.

12. The sea is home to many fish.

13. A crab hurries past.

14. The crab is quick.

Main Verbs and Helping Verbs   *(pages 166-167)*
Write each sentence with the correct past tense form of the main verb in parentheses. Then underline the helping verb.
15. The plane has _____ in San Francisco. (land)
16. Many people have _____ the city. (visit)
17. Joanne has _____ the Golden Gate Bridge. (cross)
18. Raul has _____ Telegraph Hill. (climb)
19. The Barnes family had _____ there last year. (walk)
20. A cable car has _____ down the hill. (roll)

Irregular Verbs   *(pages 168-169)*
Write each sentence with the correct past tense form of the main verb in parentheses.
21. A grasshopper _____ a blade of grass. (eat)
22. A frog has _____ the grasshopper. (eat)
23. The children _____ the frog. (see)
24. The frog had _____ from the pond. (come)
25. Now the frog has _____. (go)
26. The children _____ after the frog. (run)

Contractions with *Not*   *(pages 170-171)*
Write the contraction for each pair of words.
27. did not   **30.** was not   **33.** has not
28. is not   **31.** does not   **34.** are not
29. had not   **32.** were not   **35.** have not

Homophones   *(pages 172-173)*
Write the sentences. Use each homophone in the correct place.
36. The squirrel had brown _____. It climbed a tall _____ tree. (fir, fur)
37. The baby _____ was very _____ to its mother. (dear, deer)
38. Mindy had a _____ in the school play. In one scene, she ate a _____. (role, roll)
39. Dwayne _____ a postcard from Spain. The stamp cost one _____. (cent, sent)

MAKING ALL THE
CONNECTIONS

You and several classmates will now write as a group a character sketch. What you have learned about story characters will help you in your writing.

You will do the following in your character sketch:

+ Clearly describe a character from a story
+ Tell what the character does
+ Tell what the character is like
+ Tell what the character likes or dislikes
+ Tell what is special about the character

Reading a Character Sketch

Read the following character sketch about a scientist who solves mysteries. The side notes tell the main features of a character sketch.

The writer tells:
+ who the character is
+ what the character does
+ what the character likes
+ what makes the character special
+ how the character acts
+ what the character dislikes

Dr. Anne Huttle is a famous scientist. In the day, she works in a lab. There, she makes and tests perfume. Outside of work, Dr. Huttle likes to solve mysteries. She has invented a "smell machine" that can be used to find robbers. Dr. Huttle has shown that smells are as good as fingerprints in solving crimes. Her friends say that she's very funny and knows just about everything. Dr. Huttle laughs at this. She says she has no interest in baseball and cooking. Therefore, they are real mysteries to her.

178

Speaking and Listening

HUTTLE 'S MOVEABLE LAB

Work in a group. Talk about these questions.

1. What important details did you learn about
   Dr. Anne Huttle from the reading on page 178?
2. What details about characters and setting did you
   learn from the picture above?
3. What makes Dr. Huttle such a special character?
4. Would Dr. Huttle make a good friend?

Thinking

Brainstorming

Choose one person from your group to be a note
taker. Have the person take notes as you discuss these
questions. Save your notes.

1. Which characters from stories do you think are most
   interesting?
2. What do the characters do?
3. How do the characters act? Tell about the things they
   like or do not like.
4. What makes the characters special?

Organizing

When you are writing a character sketch, it is helpful to make a list of notes describing the person. The chart below shows details that were used to write the character sketch on Dr. Huttle.

With the rest of your group, look back at your brainstorming notes. Decide how to use them to fill in a chart like the one below. Have one group member write down your ideas in the chart.

What she/he does	What she/ he is like	Likes	Dislikes	What makes her/ him special
scientist, works in a lab	funny, smart	solving mysteries;	cooking, baseball	tracks down robbers with "smell machine"

Writing a Character Sketch

Imagine that your group has to choose a "Character of the Year" and write a paragraph that describes this character. Use the chart of details you made as a group to help you write the paragraph.

Planning

- Review the chart you made as a group. Add new details you think of now.
- Decide which details from the chart you will include in your paragraph.
- Organize your information in a list. First, write the character's name. Then, write your details in the

order you wish to present them. For example, start with what the character does or what is special about the character.

Composing

- Work with your group to write your character sketch. Choose someone to write down the first draft as all group members suggest ideas.
- Decide exactly how to word the topic sentence. Then decide how to word each detail sentence.

Revising

- As a group, read over your character sketch. Think of ways to improve each sentence.
- Check that the first sentence names the character.
- Check that you have included all the details that tell what the character is like.

Proofreading

Now as a group, proofread your character sketch. Choose one group member to make the proofreading changes on your draft. Answer these questions:

- Do your subjects and verbs agree?
- Are you using the right verb tenses?
- Are you using the right form of the verb **be**?
- Are all words spelled correctly?
- Are all contractions written correctly?

Presenting

- Choose one group member to write a final copy.
- Display your group's character sketch on the bulletin board.

CUMULATIVE REVIEW

A. Write the letter of the group of words that is a sentence. (*pages 40-41*)

    1. a. Dad washed the car.   **2. a.** Turned on the water.
       b. Filled a bucket.   **b.** Kyle rinsed the hood.
       c. Soapy water.   **c.** The shiny metal.

B. Write the letter of the word that names each kind of sentence. (*pages 42-45*)

    3. Please bring the rake.

       a. command   **b.** exclamation   **c.** question   **d.** statement

    4. How tall the weeds are!

       a. command   **b.** exclamation   **c.** question   **d.** statement

C. Write the letter of the sentence that has one line under the complete subject and two lines under the complete predicate. (*pages 46-51*)

    5. a. The children gather leaves.
       b. Mom rakes the leaves.
       c. Dad puts the leaves in a basket.
    6. a. The playful dog jumps into the basket.
       b. Bright leaves scatter everywhere.
       c. The family laughs.

D. Write the letter of the group of words that is in alphabetical order. (*pages 52-53*)

    7. a. aboard toast flower   **8. a.** shine ship shirt
       b. carve busy cave   **b.** jelly jeans jewel
       c. gang garden gasp   **c.** lamp letter lane

E. Write the letter of the word that would appear on a dictionary page with the guide words shown. (*pages 54-55*)

    9. offer/olive   **a.** open   **b.** old   **c.** once
   10. walrus/wash   **a.** voice   **b.** wish   **c.** warn

F. Write the letter of the sentence that has commas in the correct place. (*pages 72-73*)

11. a. Mix oats, milk, and salt
    b. Yes the oven is hot.
    c. Rosa try a cookie.

12. a. Next wash the dishes.
    b. I eat, and you play.
    c. No I have enough.

G. Write the letter of the words that are nouns. (*pages 78-79*)

13. Oats grow on the farm.
    a. Oats grow   **b.** grow, the   **c.** Oats, farm

14. The farmer sells many vegetables.
    a. sells, many   **b.** farmer, vegetables   **c.** The, many

H. Write the letter of the correct plural noun. (*pages 80-83*)

15. Many ____ live in the barn. (mouse)
    a. mouse   **b.** mice   **c.** mouses

16. The children saw two ____ in the woods. (fox)
    a. foxes   **b.** foxs   **c.** foxse

I. Write the letter of the correct proper noun. (*pages 84-85*)

17. a. Jane Austen   **b.** phillis wheatley   **c.** author
18. a. lake   **b.** Lake Michigan   **c.** Missouri river
19. a. doctor   **b.** Doctor Rivera   **c.** montana

J. Write the letter of the correct possessive. (*pages 86-87*)

20. Jake paddled ____ canoe. (Mindy)
    a. Mindys   **b.** Mindy's   **c.** Mindie's

21. The ____ team won the canoe race. (women)
    a. women's   **b.** womens   **c.** womens'

K. Write the letter of the correct name or title. (*pages 90-91*)

22. a. MR Tim Korf   **b.** Mr. Sam Lee   **c.** Mr. don jones
23. a. Miss Loy Ku   **b.** Ms. Ina Lopez   **c.** MRs. Joy king

L. Write the letter of the day and month that are correctly abbreviated. (*pages 92-93*)

24. a. Sat., Nov. 2   **b.** Thur., Aug 10   **c.** Tusd., Feb. 1
25. a. Wdnesday, Ju. 7   **b.** Fri, Jan 5   **c.** Sun., Mar. 23

M. Write the letter that tells whether the title is written correctly in each sentence. (*pages 122-123*)

26. Roxanne read the poem "Mending Wall."
    a. correct   **b.** incorrect

27. The short story "Call of the Loon is about a bird.
    a. correct   **b.** incorrect

28. I liked the book "Jerry And The Jumping Beans".
    a. correct   **b.** incorrect

N. Write the letter of the verb in each sentence. (*pages 128-129*)

29. Animals make many different sounds.
    a. Animals   **b.** make   **c.** many   **d.** different

30. A cricket rubs its legs together.
    a. cricket   **b.** rubs   **c.** legs   **d.** together

O. Write the letter of the correct present tense verb. (*pages 130-135*)

31. A frog ____ its throat with air.
    a. fill   **b.** fills

32. Dolphins ____ objects with sound.
    a. find   **b.** finds

33. A bat ____ for a cave.
    a. search   **b.** searches   **c.** searchs

34. The fly ____ around an apple.
    a. buzz   **b.** buzzs   **c.** buzzes

P. Write the letter of the correct past tense verb. (*pages 136-139*)

35. Tina ____ water to the paint.
    a. adds   **b.** added   **c.** add

36. The children ____ many pictures.
    a. paint   **b.** paints   **c.** painted

37. All the students ____ art last year.
    a. studied   **b.** studyed   **c.** studyd

38. Hector ____ the paint brush.
    a. dropped   **b.** droped   **c.** drops

Q. Write the letter that names the verb in each sentence. (*pages 164-165*)

39. A brass band marches down the street.
   a. action verb   **b.** linking verb
40. The music is very loud.
   a. action verb   **b.** linking verb
41. The musicians are students.
   a. action verb   **b.** linking verb

R. Write the letter of the correct form of the main verb. (*pages 166-167*)

42. The members of the band have ____ the music.
   a. practice   **b.** practiced
43. The students had ____ together before.
   a. played   **b.** play
44. The drummer has ____ the drum.
   a. pounded   **b.** pound
45. The leader has ____ the marchers.
   a. guide   **b.** guided

S. Write the letter of the correct form of the past tense verb. (*pages 168-169*)

46. The children ____ to the zoo.
   a. go   **b.** gone   **c.** went
47. The children ____ to the otter cage.
   a. ran   **b.** run   **c.** runned
48. The otters had ____ already.
   a. eat   **b.** ate   **c.** eaten
49. The funny animals ____ many tricks.
   a. did   **b.** do   **c.** done

T. Write the letter of the correct contraction. (*pages 170-171*)

50. are not   **a.** arent   **b.** arn't   **c.** aren't
51. does not   **a.** does'nt   **b.** doesnot   **c.** doesn't
52. was not   **a.** wasn't   **b.** was'nt   **c.** wasnt'

PART THREE

Discoveries and Changes

So many little flowers
Drop their tiny heads
But newer buds come to bloom
In their place instead.

"Cycle"
by Langston Hughes

---◆---

Everywhere you look, there are discoveries and changes happening. Every day we learn a little more about the world around us. In the coming units, think about discoveries you have made and changes that have taken place in your life.

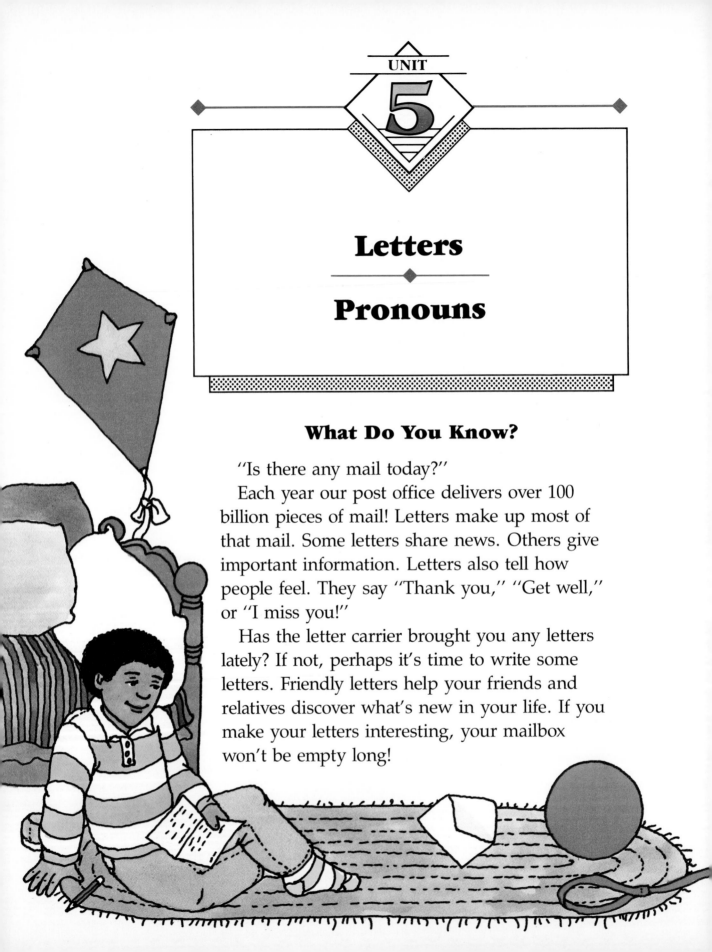

UNIT 5

Letters

Pronouns

What Do You Know?

"Is there any mail today?"

Each year our post office delivers over 100 billion pieces of mail! Letters make up most of that mail. Some letters share news. Others give important information. Letters also tell how people feel. They say "Thank you," "Get well," or "I miss you!"

Has the letter carrier brought you any letters lately? If not, perhaps it's time to write some letters. Friendly letters help your friends and relatives discover what's new in your life. If you make your letters interesting, your mailbox won't be empty long!

Thinking About Letters

What Is a Friendly Letter?

A **friendly letter** has these features:

- It shares news with a friend or family member.
- It is written in a friendly way.
- It has a heading, a greeting, a body, a closing, and a signature.

Are friendly letters necessary in the age of telephones? Of course they are! The letters we receive are lasting. We can read them over and over—when and where we want. Letters are a lasting record. They show how people grow and change. A handwritten letter is as welcome as the sound of a friend's voice. Like a present, it shows someone cares about us. Writing letters is also fun. It is a chance to say something well. Unlike talking on the phone, you can change and improve what you say. You can send your message anywhere in the world and not worry about a high phone bill. And a quick reply is always a nice surprise!

Discusssion

1. What friendly letters have you gotten in the mail lately?
2. What are some reasons for which you write letters?
3. Why are some letters more interesting than others?

Reading a Friendly Letter

The following friendly letter is taken from "Where the Bear Went Over the Mountain," by Blaine Goodman. In this story, Judy and her brother Stan have moved to a small log cabin in the mountains. Above the fireplace, they find this old letter:

This heading gives only the date.

July 26, 1974

Dear Jim,

When I first came to Germany, I did not intend to stay, but I've changed my mind. I concealed all the Indian artifacts in the cave where I found them, and I put the artifacts from the gold-rush days with them. Thought they'd be safe there until you moved into the cabin.

The body is written in everyday language.

Now, if you intend to open a store, the artifacts are all yours, or if not, just leave them. If someone can locate the cave "where the bear went over the mountain," well, finders keepers.

Yours,
Bill

There are many different closings.

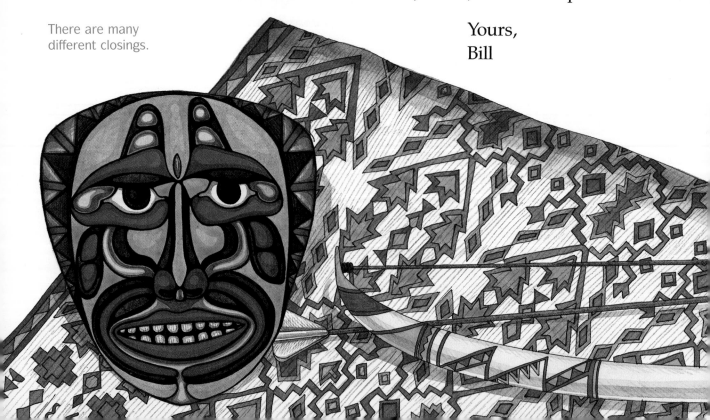

Understanding What You've Read

Answer these questions about the letter.

1. When did Bill write the letter?
2. Where did Bill put the Indian artifacts?
3. Do you think Bill thought his artifacts were valuable? Why?
4. What might Jim have done with the artifacts?
5. An artifact is anything made by human work or skill. What might some Indian artifacts be?
6. Judy and Stan found Bill's letter at the beginning of the story. What do you think the rest of the story tells about?

Writing Assignment

Have you wondered what's new in the life of a friend or relative lately? Is there some author, TV star, or other famous person you've always wanted to exchange letters with? Try writing a letter to someone you've wanted to share news with or hear from. You may just get a letter back!

In this unit, you will learn to write and send a letter, step by step. You will also see how another student, Matt, writes and sends his letter. The **audience** for your letter is whoever you are writing to. Your **purpose** is to share news or tell how you feel about something.

APPLY STEP BY STEP

Decide Who You're Writing To

Get the person's name and address. Then, write a few notes about things that you might want to tell this person. Save this information. You will use it later.

Parts of a Letter

Matt got this friendly letter in the mail. Notice each part of the letter and where it is placed on the page. Can you find its five parts?

---

heading —
11 Rose Lane
Rockport, Massachusetts 01966
July 25, 1987

Dear Matt, — greeting
Remember how worried I was about my cat, Norman? He was missing for over a week. Now I know why.
Today I found Norman in the garage. He was sitting in a box of old rags. Only he wasn't alone. Norman now has six kittens!
Do you want a kitten? Should I change Norman's name? Write and let me know.

body

Your cousin, — closing
Carla — signature

- The **heading** gives the reader your address. It also tells when you wrote the letter.
- The **greeting** opens the letter. It is a way to say "hello" to the person you are writing to.
- The **body** is the main part of the letter. In it, you share news and tell how you feel.
- The **closing** ends the letter. It says "good-bye."
- The **signature** is your name. When writing to friends or relatives, you only need to use your first name.

Practice

Read Matt's answer to Carla's letter. Then, answer the questions.

> 11 Honeycutt Street
> Hampton, New Hampshire 03842
> August 1, 1987
>
> Dear Carla,
>   I'm glad you found Norman. Or should I say Norma? I'd like to come see the kittens. But Mom says I can't have one. She thinks it wouldn't get along with my dogs, birds, goldfish, and white mice. Maybe we should open a pet shop?
>
>   Yours truly,
>   Matt

1. What name is in the greeting?
2. Who wrote the letter?
3. What part of the letter tells when it was written?
4. What does the closing say?
5. What is the name of the letter part that tells about Matt's pets?

Plan Your Letter

   Think about what you will say in your letter. Look in your journal for ideas. Then, list the events or feelings you will include in the body of your letter. Save your work.

Addressing an Envelope

The envelope is an important part of sending a letter. An envelope must be addressed correctly. Otherwise, the post office will not be able to figure out who to deliver the letter to.

Here is the envelope for Carla's letter to Matt.

Matt is the receiver. The **receiver's address** is in the middle of the envelope. The receiver's full name is on one line. On the second line is the street address. The third line contains the city, the state, and the ZIP code. The ZIP code is a number that helps the post office sort and deliver mail more quickly.

Carla is the sender. The sender's address is in the upper left-hand corner. The sender's address is called the **return address**. It tells where to return the letter if the letter cannot be delivered.

The stamp is in the upper right-hand corner of the envelope. The post office will not deliver a letter without a stamp.

Practice

A. Eddie Cunningham is sending a letter to his friend Lisa Wells. Eddie lives at 311 Jefferson Street, Charlotte, North Carolina 28222. Lisa's address is 126 Valley Road, Amarillo, Texas 79106. Draw an envelope. Then, address it correctly so that Lisa will receive the letter from Eddie.

B. Karen McCarthy is sending a letter to her friend Iris Gomez. Karen McCarthy just moved to 32 Oakdale Court in Mobile, Alabama. Her ZIP code is 36609. Iris lives at 3120 Spring Road, Laguna Hills, California. Iris's ZIP code is 92653. On your paper, draw an envelope. Then, show how Karen should address it so that Iris will receive the letter from Karen.

STEP BY STEP

APPLY

Address Your Envelope

You already know who will receive the letter you write. Get an envelope, and write that person's name and address at the center of the envelope. Then, write your name and address in the top left-hand corner. Put a stamp on your envelope in the top right corner. Save the envelope for later.

Writing a First Draft

Read the first draft of Matt's next letter to Carla. He wasn't worried about making it perfect. It will be changed later.

---

11 Honeycutt street
Hampton New Hampshire
August, 11 1987

Dear Carla

I heard the actor Rex Wright was making a movie in town. Dad and I rode down to watch I saw the movie director waving to us. I went over to him with my heart beating fast. he said he needed a young boy for a small part. I will have to lines to say.

I alwaes wanted to be an actor. Mabe I have been discovered. The movie's name is Only Yesterday.

Your star cousin
Matt

Write Your First Draft

If you wish, discuss ideas for the body of the letter with your teacher or a classmate. Remember to include:

• a heading
• a greeting
• a closing and signature

Save your work for the next lesson.

Discussing a First Draft

A letter isn't like a telephone call. You can improve a letter by revising it. One way to revise a draft is to discuss it with a classmate.

Discussion Strategy

If a classmate asks you to discuss a draft, try not to hurt his or her feelings. For example, don't say, "Huh? This part is awful." Instead, you might say, "I don't understand what you mean here."

Use this checklist to discuss Matt's draft.

Content Checklist

✔ Does the letter have a heading, a greeting, a body, a closing, and a signature?
✔ Does the letter share news with a friend or with a family member?
✔ Is it written in a friendly way?

Revise Your First Draft for Content

To the Reader: Read your partner's draft. Tell what you think the purpose of the letter is. Then, imagine how you would feel if you received the letter in the mail. Point out parts of the letter that could be clearer or more complete.

To the Writer: Listen to your partner's ideas. Then, revise your draft. Save your work.

Varying Your Sentences

Matt sent his letter to a classmate named Wilma. "You have an exciting topic," said Wilma, "but your letter doesn't show much excitement. Maybe it's because so many of your sentences begin with I."

You can vary your sentences by changing the word order. Notice how the comma is used.

I rushed to the theatre to get a good seat.
<u>To get a good seat,</u> I rushed to the theatre.

Another way to vary your sentences is to add time or order words at the beginning. Put a comma after the words you use.

<u>Yesterday afternoon,</u> I saw a poster for the movie.
<u>Later,</u> I called the theater.

Here is how Matt varied his sentence beginnings.

The writer has added a word or words to the sentence beginning.
The writer has changed the word order.

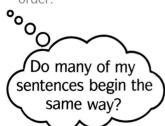

Do many of my sentences begin the same way?

Last week, I heard the actor Rex Wright was making a movie in town. Dad and I rode down to watch suddenly, I saw the movie director waving to us. I went over to him with my heart beating fast. He said he needed a young boy for a small part. I will have to lines to say.

198

Practice

A. Vary the word order in each sentence.

1. I went to see *Only Yesterday* the other night.

2. I waited for your part for over an hour.

3. I got thirsty and got a drink, unfortunately.

4. I missed your two lines as a result.

B. Vary each sentence beginning by adding a word or words from the box or words of your own.

5. I waited for the star to come to the theater.

6. I saw a big, black car pull up.

7. I tried to look in the car window.

8. I saw the star step out of the car.

Finally
After a while
Yesterday
Eagerly

◆─────────────────────────────◆

Revising Checklist

✔ Have I included all the features of a friendly letter?
✔ Can I combine subjects and predicates to make new sentences? (p. 32)
✔ Have I included exact information? (p. 70)
✔ Can I add descriptive language? (p. 120)
✔ Can I add information to make my work complete? (p. 156)
✔ Where can I vary the beginnings of sentences?

◆─────────────────────────────◆

APPLY STEP BY STEP

Revise Your First Draft for Style

Use the Revising Checklist. Make the changes on your draft. Save your work.

Punctuating Letters

After revising his draft, Matt checked the rules for punctuating friendly letters. He used these rules and proofreading marks to correct his letter.

◆ Place a comma between the city and the state in the heading of a letter.

    San Francisco, California   Chicago, Illinois

◆ Use a capital letter to begin each proper noun. The names of streets, cities, states, and months are proper nouns.

Maple Avenue	Kent Place	Orchard Street
Dallas	New York	Iowa
June	August	January

◆ Place a comma between the day and year of the date in the heading of a letter.

    July 24, 1988   August 17, 1990

◆ Place a comma after the greeting of a letter.

    Dear Uncle Frank,   Dear Joan,

◆ Place a comma after the closing of a letter. Only the first word in the closing begins with a capital letter.

    Your cousin,   Yours truly,   Love,

Practice

Write the letter below correctly. Add capital letters and punctuation marks where necessary.

Dear Matt Phillips   11 Ridge road
                              springfield Illinois 62705
                              may 11 1988

Was that you I saw for a second or two at the theatre. If so, please send me your autograph. Do you remember me. i was in first grade with you until I moved to Illinois.

                      Your old friend Allan Graye

Proofreading Checklist

✔ Did I indent the first sentence of each paragraph? (p. 34)
✔ Did I begin each sentence with a capital letter? (p. 34)
✔ Did I use the correct end marks? (p. 34)
✔ Did I use commas correctly? (p. 72)
✔ Did I use the correct capitalization and punctuation for all my abbreviations? (p. 158)
✔ Did I capitalize and punctuate all of the letter parts correctly?

Proofreading Marks	
∧	add
⌀	take away
¶	indent
≡	capitalize
/	small letter
◯	check spelling
∿	transpose

Proofread Your Letter

Reread your letter to check for correct punctuation and capitalization. Use the Proofreading Checklist for help. Make corrections on your draft. Save your work.

Checking Spelling/Writing a Final Copy

You can learn to spell a word in three ways. Which way works best for you?

◆ Look at the word. See the letters in it.
◆ Listen to the word. Hear its sounds.
◆ Write the word. Trace the letters.

Here is part of Matt's corrected letter.

---

11 Honeycutt Street
Hampton, New Hampshire
August 11, 1987

Dear Carla,
Last week
I heard the actor Rex Wright was making a movie in town.
Suddenly
Dad and I rode down to watch. I saw the movie director waving
to us. I went over to him with my heart beating fast, he said
two
he needed a young boy for a small part. I will have to lines
to say.
always   *Maybe*
I alwaes wanted to be an actor. Mabe I have been discovered.
The movie's name is Only Yesterday.

Your star cousin,
Matt

Check Your Spelling

Use the spelling strategy and proofreading marks to correct errors in spelling. Then, write a neat, final copy of your letter. Be sure to include all your corrections on your final copy. Proofread your work.

Sharing Your Letter

◆

After making a neat, final copy of your letter, share it with others. There are many ways to share a letter.

Speaking/Listening Strategy

Speak loudly and clearly. Try to become familiar with what you are reading. That way you won't have to read it word for word. If you are listening to someone, guess what the writer's main purpose is.

Choosing a Way to Share

Here are some ways to share your letter.

Reading Aloud Before you mail your letter, read it aloud to the class. When all the letters have been read, vote for the letter that is the funniest, the most interesting, or the most unusual.

Making a Letter Collection Make copies of each letter you write. Place the copies and any replies you get into a scrapbook. Call it "The Collected Letters of (your name)."

Share Your Letter

Mail your letter, but first make a copy of it to share with your classmates. Use one of the ways explained on this page. It's your choice!

Add to Your Learning Log

- Am I happy with my letter?
- What part of writing the letter was the most fun?
- If I could rewrite my letter, what changes would I make?

The Literature Connection: Pronouns

Words such as *you, she,* and *him* are called **pronouns**. Pronouns take the place of nouns in sentences.

Pronouns can be used in place of the word that names any person or thing. Writers use pronouns when they don't want to repeat names over and over again. Pronouns help make sentences easy to read and understand.

Read the poem to see how pronouns are used in place of the words that name people.

Little
by
Dorothy Aldis

I am the sister of him
And he is my brother.
He is too little for us
To talk to each other.

So every morning I show him
My doll and my book;
But every morning he still is
Too little to look.

Discussion

1. In this poem, who is named by the pronouns *he* and *him*?
2. What two people does the word *us* replace in the poem?
3. Can you think of names for the two people in the poem? Read the poem using the names you chose instead of pronouns.

The Writing Connection: Pronouns

Pronouns can make your own writing easy to read and understand. Each pronoun you use takes the place of a noun. The following sentences show how you might use pronouns in your writing.

Margie and Amos rode in a bike race.
They rode in a bike race.

Harry poured water into a cup.
Harry poured it into a cup.

Activity

Look at the picture above. Think about what is taking place.

♦ Write about the picture. Don't use any of these words: *he, she, it, they, him, her, them.*
♦ Read your story. How does it sound? Is it boring or difficult to understand?
♦ Write the story again. This time, use pronouns from the list where you need to. What difference do the pronouns make?

Subject Pronouns

A **pronoun** is a word that takes the place of a noun.

A. One kind of pronoun is a subject pronoun.

A **subject pronoun** takes the place of one or more nouns in the subject part of the sentence. The subject pronouns are *I, you, he, she, it, we,* and *they*.

> Eric walks to the park. He walks to the park.
> People look at the sky. They look at the sky.

B. Use the subject pronoun that tells about the same number and kind as the noun it replaces.

Subject Pronoun	Whom or What It Tells About
I	myself (the person speaking)
you	person or persons I am talking to
he	one boy or man
she	one girl or woman
it	one thing
we	myself and one or more persons
they	two or more persons or things

Strategy

Pronouns are useful words. Study the chart above so that you can remember all the subject pronouns.

Check Your Understanding

A. Write the letter of the subject pronoun.
1. They saw Halley's Comet.
   a. They   **b.** saw   **c.** Halley's   **d.** comet
2. It looks like a star with a tail.
   a. It   **b.** like   **c.** star   **d.** with

B. Write the letter of the pronoun that takes the place of the underlined noun.

    3. Eric sees many stars in the sky.
        a. She **b.** You **c.** He **d.** We

    4. The stars shine brightly.
        a. It **b.** They **c.** I **d.** She

Practice

A. Write each sentence. Underline the subject pronoun.

    5. I watch the sky.   **7.** You see a comet.
    6. We use a telescope.   **8.** It has a long tail.

B. Write each sentence. Replace the underlined subject noun with the correct subject pronoun.

    9. William points to the comet. (He, They)
  10. Comets flash in the sky. (We, They)
  11. Ann read about comets. (She, We)
  12. The sky blazes with light. (It, He)

C. Mixed Practice   Write each sentence. Replace each subject noun with a pronoun.

  13. Edmund Halley discovered a comet.
  14. The comet is called Halley's comet.
  15. Scientists study the comet.
  16. People watch for the comet.
  17. Mother saw the comet through a telescope.
  18. The man and woman studied the comet.
  19. My parents and I saw the pictures.

Apply: Work with a Group

With several classmates, write newspaper headlines telling what has happened at your school. Then replace the noun in the subject part with a subject pronoun.

Object Pronouns

A. Another kind of pronoun is an object pronoun.

An **object pronoun** takes the place of a noun after an action verb. It is found in the predicate part of a sentence. The object pronouns are *me, you, him, her, it, us,* and *them.*

Ben Franklin flew a <u>kite</u>. Ben Franklin flew <u>it</u>.

B. Use the correct object pronoun to replace a noun in the predicate part of a sentence.

Object Pronoun	Whom or What It Stands For
me	myself (the person speaking)
you	person or persons I am talking to
him	one boy or man
her	one girl or woman
it	one thing
us	myself and one or more other persons
them	two or more persons or things

Strategy

You use many object pronouns when you speak or write. Use the chart above to help you remember them.

Check Your Understanding

A. Write the letter of the object pronoun.
   1. The teacher taught us about electricity.
      a. teacher **b.** us **c.** about **d.** electricity
   2. An Englishman named it.
      a. An **b.** Englishman **c.** named **d.** it

B. Write the letter of the object pronoun that takes the place of the underlined word or words.

    3. Electricity interests <u>the students</u>.

        a. me   **b.** you   **c.** him   **d.** them

    4. Franklin studied <u>electricity</u>.

        a. us   **b.** it   **c.** them   **d.** you

Practice

A. Write each sentence. Underline the object pronoun.

    5. The teacher told me about his work.

    6. Franklin's son helped him.

    7. A kite and a key taught them about electricity.

    8. A movie showed us about Franklin's work.

B. Write each sentence. Replace the underlined noun with the correct object pronoun in parentheses.

    9. I told <u>Lori</u> about the movie. (her, us)

   10. Many scientists visited <u>Franklin</u>. (them, him)

   11. Franklin greeted <u>the scientists</u>. (them, him)

   12. The scientists discussed <u>electricity</u>. (it, him)

C. Mixed Practice   Write each sentence. Replace the underlined words with the correct object pronoun.

   13. The experiment worried <u>Mrs. Franklin</u>.

   14. An electrical storm approached <u>Franklin</u>.

   15. Rain soaked <u>Franklin and his son</u>.

   16. Electricity struck <u>the kite</u>.

   17. Ben Franklin told <u>Mrs. Franklin</u> the results.

   18. The teacher tested <u>the other students and me</u>.

Apply: Work with a Partner

Work with a friend. See if you can write sentences using all seven object pronouns correctly. Use the chart in this lesson to check your work.

I and *Me*

Use the pronouns *I* and *me* to talk about yourself.

A. *I* is a subject pronoun. Use it in the subject part of a sentence. Always capitalize the pronoun *I*.

> I visited the natural history museum.

Me is an object pronoun. Use it in the predicate part of a sentence.

> The teacher told me about dinosaurs.

B. *I* or *me* may be used with the name of another person. When you write or speak, use *I* or *me* last to be polite.

> Tom and I went to the museum.
> The guide took Tom and me to the gems.

Strategy

Should I use *I* or *me* in this sentence?

It's hard to know when to use *I* and when to use *me*. Say the sentence aloud without the other name. Which sounds right, *I* or *me*? That's the one to use.

> Sentence: Tom and (I, me) collect rocks.
> Try: *Me* collect rocks. Wrong!
> *I* collect rocks. Right! Use the pronoun *I*.

Check Your Understanding

A. Write the letter that names the underlined word.
  1. I enjoyed the museum.
   a. subject pronoun   **b.** object pronoun
  2. Gems and minerals interest me.
   a. subject pronoun   **b.** object pronoun

210

B. Write the letter that uses *I* or *me* correctly.

    3. A movie showed ____ about volcanoes.
        a. Tom and me   **b.** Tom and I
    4. ____ looked at the dinosaur skeletons.
        a. I and Tom   **b.** Tom and I

Practice

A. Write each sentence using the correct pronoun.

    5. ____ saw many strange dinosaurs. (I, me)
    6. The guide told ____ about them. (I, me)
    7. A huge dinosaur frightened ____. (I, me)
    8. ____ drew a picture of it later. (I, me)

B. Write each sentence and supply the correct word.

    9. Tom and ____ ate in the cafeteria. (I, me)
    10. Tom and ____ saw a movie later. (I, me)
    11. It showed Tom and ____ about snakes. (I, me)
    12. Tom and ____ wrote a report. (I, me)

C. Mixed Practice   Write each sentence using the correct word to fill each blank.

    13. Snakes interest my brother and ____. (I, me)
    14. ____ bought a book about dinosaurs. (I, me)
    15. Tom and ____ went home. (I, me)
    16. Mom measured ____ that evening. (I, me)
    17. ____ am smaller than a dinosaur. (I, me)
    18. Tell Tom and ____ about dinosaurs. (I, me)
    19. ____ asked Dad to give Tom and ____ a dinosaur model. (I, me) (I, me)
    20. ____ asked Tom to help ____. (I, me) (I, me)

Apply: Journal

In your journal, describe what makes you different from anyone else. Use the pronouns *I* and *me*.

Possessive Forms of Pronouns

Possessive forms of pronouns tell who or what owns or has something. They take the place of possessives.

A. The possessive forms of pronouns are *my, your, his, her, its, our,* and *their.*

> The class read about *Marie Curie's* work.
> The class read about *her* work.

B. Use the possessive form of the pronoun that tells about the same kind and number as the possessive it replaces.

Possessive Pronoun	Whom or What It Tells About
my	belonging to myself
your	belonging to you
his	belonging to one boy or man
her	belonging to one girl or woman
its	belonging to one thing
our	belonging to myself and one or more other persons
their	belonging to more than one person or thing

Strategy

Study the chart above to learn the possessive forms of pronouns. Remember that forms of possessive pronouns usually come before a noun in a sentence.

Check Your Understanding

A. Write the letter of each possessive form of the pronoun.

1. Their family had many scientists.
   a. Their   **b.** had   **c.** many   **d.** scientists

2. How many scientists are in your family?
   a. many   **b.** in   **c.** your   **d.** family

212

B. Write the letter of the possessive form of the pronoun that takes the place of the underlined word.

   3. Marie's family came from Poland.
      a. His **b.** Their **c.** Her **d.** Our
   4. Marie worked in Pierre's laboratory.
      a. our **b.** my **c.** his **d.** their

Practice

A. Write each sentence. Underline the possessive form of the pronoun.

   5. My class learned about famous scientists.
   6. May found a book in our school library.
   7. Its title is *Madame Curie*.

B. Read each sentence. Write the second sentence with the correct possessive form of the pronoun.

   8. Marie's husband was Pierre. _____ husband was Pierre.
   9. Pierre's work was hard. _____ work was hard.
  10. The Curies discovered the atom's secret. The Curies discovered _____ secret.

C. Mixed Practice   Write each sentence. Replace the underlined possessives with pronouns.

  11. The Curies' work was very important.
  12. Pierre's brother helped the Curies.
  13. Marie's discovery surprised other scientists.
  14. The metal's name was polonium.
  15. The Curies' discovery was named for Marie's country.
  16. Ted's class read about other scientists' work.

Apply: Learning Log

Describe the hardest part of this lesson. What can you do to learn about possessive forms of pronouns?

Contractions

A **contraction** is a shortened form of two words that are joined together. An apostrophe (') takes the place of the missing letter or letters in a contraction.

A. Pronouns can be joined with the verbs *am, is,* or *are* to form contractions. Look at the chart below.

Contraction	Means	Contraction	Means
I'm	I am	he's	he is
you're	you are	she's	she is
we're	we are	it's	it is
they're	they are		

B. Pronouns can also be joined with the verbs *will* or *have* to form contractions. Look at the chart below.

Contraction	Means	Contraction	Means
I'll	I will	we'll	we will
you'll	you will	they'll	they will
she'll	she will	I've	I have
he'll	he will	you've	you have

Strategy

Sometimes it is hard to know whether to use *it's* or *its.* Just remember:

it's = it is   its = belonging to it

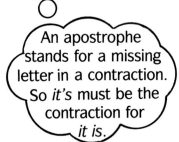

An apostrophe stands for a missing letter in a contraction. So *it's* must be the contraction for *it is.*

Check Your Understanding

A. Write the letter of the correct contraction for the underlined words.

1. <u>We are</u> reading about Sequoia National Park.
a. Wer'e   **b.** We're   **c.** We'are   **d.** Were

2. <u>It is</u> named for a famous Cherokee Indian chief.
a. Its   **b.** Its'   **c.** It's   **d.** I'ts

214

B. Use the directions for Check Your Understanding A.

   3. I will tell you about Chief Sequoya.
      a. Iw'll **b.** Ill **c.** I'wl **d.** I'll

   4. She will draw Sequoya's famous alphabet.
      a. She'll **b.** She'wl **c.** Shell **d.** Shew'l

Practice

A. Write each sentence. Use the correct contraction for the underlined words.

   5. It is used for Cherokee words.
   6. I am interested in Sequoya's alphabet.
   7. He is the inventor of the alphabet.
   8. They are unusual letters.

B. Use the directions for Practice A.

   9. You will find the alphabet difficult.
 10. I have tried it several times.
 11. She will tell about the Greek alphabet.
 12. You have learned the Roman alphabet.

C. Mixed Practice   Write each sentence. Use the correct contraction for the underlined words.

 13. He is the person who invented the alphabet.
 14. You have seen a Cherokee newspaper.
 15. We will remember Sequoya's work.
 16. She is a Cherokee Indian.
 17. You will visit Sequoia National Park.
 18. It is a very beautiful place.
 19. We will see if you are ready for the trip.
 20. They have learned a new alphabet.

Apply: Test a Friend

Write four contractions from this lesson. Ask a partner to use each one in a sentence and tell what it means. Check your classmate's work.

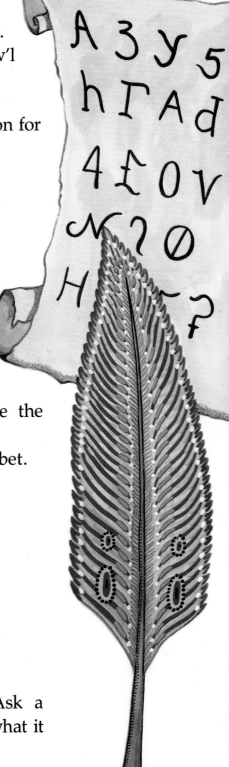

Context Clues

A. You can often figure out the meaning of a word from its context, or the words around it. Synonyms and antonyms are good context clues.

> We stood at the <u>bow</u>, or front, of the ship.

The synonym *front* tells you what *bow* means.

> A storm came <u>gradually</u>, not suddenly.

The antonym *suddenly* tells you what *gradually* means.

B. Other sentences may also give clues to the meaning of an unfamiliar word.

> The captain stood on the <u>bridge</u>. He steered the ship from this platform above the deck.

What special meaning does *bridge* have in the sentence above? What clues tell you the meaning?

Strategy

If you find an unfamiliar word while you're reading, be a detective. Look for clues around or near the word. If you're still not sure, use a dictionary.

Check Your Understanding

A. Write the letter that tells the meaning of the underlined word.
  1. A ship's sails hang from a tall pole, or <u>mast</u>.
     a. ship   **b.** sails   **c.** pole
  2. The captain was <u>alert</u>, not sleepy.
     a. awake   **b.** half asleep   **c.** angry

B. Use the directions for Check Your Understanding A.

   3. Workers cut long, flat pieces of wood. They built the ship from these <u>planks</u>.

   a. Workers   **b.** pieces of wood   **c.** ship

   4. We walked to the end of the ship. From the <u>stern</u> we watched the waves.

   a. front of a ship   **b.** bow   **c.** end of a ship

Practice

A. Write each sentence. Write the meaning of the underlined word.

   5. Sea trips are filled with <u>peril</u>, or danger.

   6. Sailors must be <u>cautious</u>, but not careless.

   7. A wave can smash a ship and <u>destroy</u> it.

B. Use the directions for Practice A.

   8. <u>Galleons</u> were fast. These ships had many sails.

   9. Ships carry <u>cargo</u>. Goods such as oil and coal are often sent by ship.

   10. Many ships travel in a group. They form a <u>fleet</u>.

C. **Mixed Practice** Write each sentence. Write the meaning of the underlined word.

   11. Modern ships are <u>spacious</u>, or roomy.

   12. A <u>ferocious</u> storm arose. Fierce winds blew.

   13. A crew <u>cooperates</u>. Everyone works together.

   14. A <u>cruise</u> is fun if you like sea travel.

   15. It was a <u>distinctive</u> ship, not an ordinary ship.

Apply: Work with a Partner

   With a classmate, write sentences using three underlined words on this page. Include clues to help.

Invitations and Thank-You Notes

Have you ever been to a birthday party? Have you had one? How did you invite people? How did you thank them?

Here are some tips on invitations.
- Tell what the invitation is for.
- Include your last name as well as your first name.
- Give the time and date of the party.
- Give the full address of the party.
- Include your phone number so your friends can tell you whether they can come to the party or not.

Here are some tips on writing thank-you notes.
- Use the right form for a friendly letter.
- Tell why you're writing. Write, "Thank you for inviting me," or, "Thank you for the teddy bear."
- Tell something else. Describe your favorite part of the party or how you will use the gift.

Practice

On a separate piece of paper, answer these questions.
1. On an invitation, how should you give the name of the person for whom the party is for.
2. What should you say about the party?
3. Is a thank-you note a letter?

Apply

Write an invitation to your party. Then write a thank-you note for a gift.

HISTORY OF LANGUAGE

Native American Words

Sally went to a special zoo yesterday. There she saw a moose, a chipmunk, a skunk, an opossum, a racoon, and a coyote. Do you know what is special about those animals?

When settlers came from England, they saw many things they had never seen. Because they hadn't seen them before, they didn't have names for them. They asked the Native Americans what these things were called. The settlers used the names that the Native Americans taught them, and these names entered the English language.

Animal names are not the only Native American words we use in English. There are also plant names and other words, too. *Potato*, *squash*, and *hurricane* are Native American words. So are *chili* and *teepee*. You probably know more Native American words than you think you do.

Activity

Rewrite the following sentences. Complete each sentence with a Native American word from the box.

pecans   canoe   moccasins   hammock   tomatoes

1. We like to paddle our _____ on the lake.
2. Rosa's favorite crunchy snack is _____.
3. I bought some ripe, red _____.
4. My feet feel good in _____.
5. Darryl took a nap in a _____.

UNIT REVIEW

Letters *(page 189)*
1. On your paper, write three features of a letter.

Parts of a Letter *(pages 192-193)*
Write the name of each part of the letter below. Then write the letter correctly.

2. 11 Rose Road
Spur,TX79370
June 9, 1987

3. Gary
4. Dear Sam,
5. Your friend,

6. Thank you for visiting. Come back soon!

Varying Your Sentences/Punctuating Letters
(pages 198-201)
Vary the word order in each sentence below.

7. I started dance lessons last month.
8. I will be in my first dance show someday.
9. I must practice every day in order to prepare.

Write each item below. Add correct capital letters and punctuation.

10. 18 alton street
atlanta georgia 30355
february 10 1990

11. your friend
jane

12. dear sue

Subject Pronouns and Object Pronouns
(pages 206-209)
Write each sentence. Replace the underlined words with a pronoun. Write if it is a *subject pronoun* or an *object pronoun*.

13. Carrie Bond wrote many songs.
14. Theodore Roosevelt invited Carrie to the White House.
15. Carrie and Enrico Caruso met the President.
16. Jill and I wrote a song.

I and Me *(pages 210-211)*
Write each sentence. Use the correct word to fill each blank.
17. Mitos and ____ baked muffins. (I, me)
18. First, ____ went to the store. (I, me)
19. Then mom helped ____ in the kitchen. (I, me)
20. Mitos and ____ gave everyone a muffin later. (I, me)
21. The whole family thanked Mitos and ____. (I, me)

Possessive Forms of Pronouns *(pages 212-213)*
Write each sentence. Replace each underlined possessive with a possessive form of the pronoun.
22. Tim's family lives in London.
23. London's harbor is filled with ships.
24. The children's class visits the harbor.
25. Mrs. Bunting's husband is a sea captain.
26. The children look at the captain's ship.

Contractions *(pages 214-215)*
Write a contraction for each pair of words.

27. it is	**30.** I have	**33.** she is
28. we will	**31.** he will	**34.** you have
29. they are	**32.** you will	**35.** we are

Context Clues *(pages 216-217)*
Write each sentence. Write the meaning of the underlined word. Use context clues to help you.
36. A young monkey feels secure, or safe, with its mother.
37. Monkeys mature slowly. They grow up after a long time.
38. A mother monkey grooms her baby. She keeps it neat.
39. A young monkey's play is vigorous, not weak.
40. Male baboons show affection, or love, to the babies.

UNIT
6

Research Report

◆

Adjectives

What Do You Know?

"What is that place like?"

Imagine you are going to visit or move to another state or country. What might you want to find out about that place? How would you find it out? One way to answer your questions is to read about the place and then write a report on the information you have gathered.

A research report tells only facts, not how you feel about something. It gives information in a clear way. When you work on a research report, it helps answer questions you had about your topic. A research report tells the facts you have learned. When you share your report, it will also help your friends learn things they wanted to find out about the same topic.

Thinking About Research Reports

What Is a Research Report?

A **research report** has these features:

- It gives information on a topic you have looked up and researched. It is not based only on information you already know.
- The topic may be divided into two or more main ideas.
- Each main idea is supported with facts.
- All information in the report is true. It does not contain opinions.

Until now, you have been able to find the facts you needed for your school work in textbooks. Now, you will be asked to write research reports using information that you will find in other books. These reports may be on topics in science, social studies, or some other area. For a social studies report, you may be asked to find out what a state or country was like in the past and how it has changed. A science report might be about a discovery, such as electricity. It could also be about inventions such as the telephone or the jet plane.

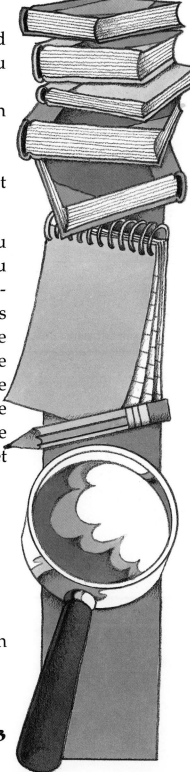

Discussion

1. What places are you interested in visiting?
2. What questions do you have about these places?
3. Where do you think you might find the information to answer these questions?

Reading a Research Report

Read the following research report about Japan. Notice how the main idea in each paragraph is supported with facts.

The first sentence of this paragraph states the paragraph's main idea. It answers the question, What is unusual about Japan?

The main idea is supported by facts about Japan's islands.

Japan is a country of islands. It is made up of four large islands and thousands of smaller ones. The largest island is Honshu. Most of Japan's people live on Honshu. This is where Japan's largest cities are found. Mount Fuji, Japan's tallest mountain, is also on Honshu. The next-largest island is Hokkaido. Hokkaido lies to the north of Japan's other islands. It has long, snowy winters. Many people travel to Hokkaido to play winter sports. In 1972, the Winter Olympic Games were held on the island of Hokkaido.

The first sentence of this paragraph states the main idea. It answers the question, What is Japan's capital city like?
The main idea is supported by facts about Tokyo.

Tokyo is the capital of Japan. It is one of the world's largest cities. More than eight million people live in Tokyo. Tokyo was first built before the year 1300. It was not Japan's first capital. It became the capital in 1868. Some of Tokyo's oldest buildings are still around today. They stand next to tall office buildings that have been built all over the city.

Understanding What You've Read

Write the answers to these questions.

1. What is Japan's largest island?

2. What is the capital of Japan?

3. Where in Japan were the 1972 Olympic Games held?

4. On what island would you probably find Tokyo?

5. How can you tell from the report that Japan is a very old country?

6. What other questions would you like a report on Japan to answer?

Writing Assignment

Imagine your class is having a Social Studies Information Exchange Day. Each student will share information on a social studies subject. To prepare, you will write a research report on a topic you choose.

Your **audience** for the report will be your teacher and classmates. Your **purpose** will be to study a subject you are curious about and to share what you learned.

What do I want to find out more about?

Choose a Topic

Make a list of five social studies topics that interest you. Examples are Texas, farming, Boston, Canada, or the Great Lakes.

Making a Topic Wheel

Luis decided to do a two-paragraph research report about Alaska. But he knew he could not tell all about Alaska in a short report. He had to narrow his topic to more specific ideas.

Luis made a topic wheel. A **topic wheel** lists questions about a large topic. The questions are placed in a circle around the topic. After you make your topic wheel, choose two of the questions to discuss in your report.

Luis's topic wheel is below. He has listed the questions that interest him most about Alaska. Under each question, he has put facts he found out from his teacher. He will look in books and magazines for more facts.

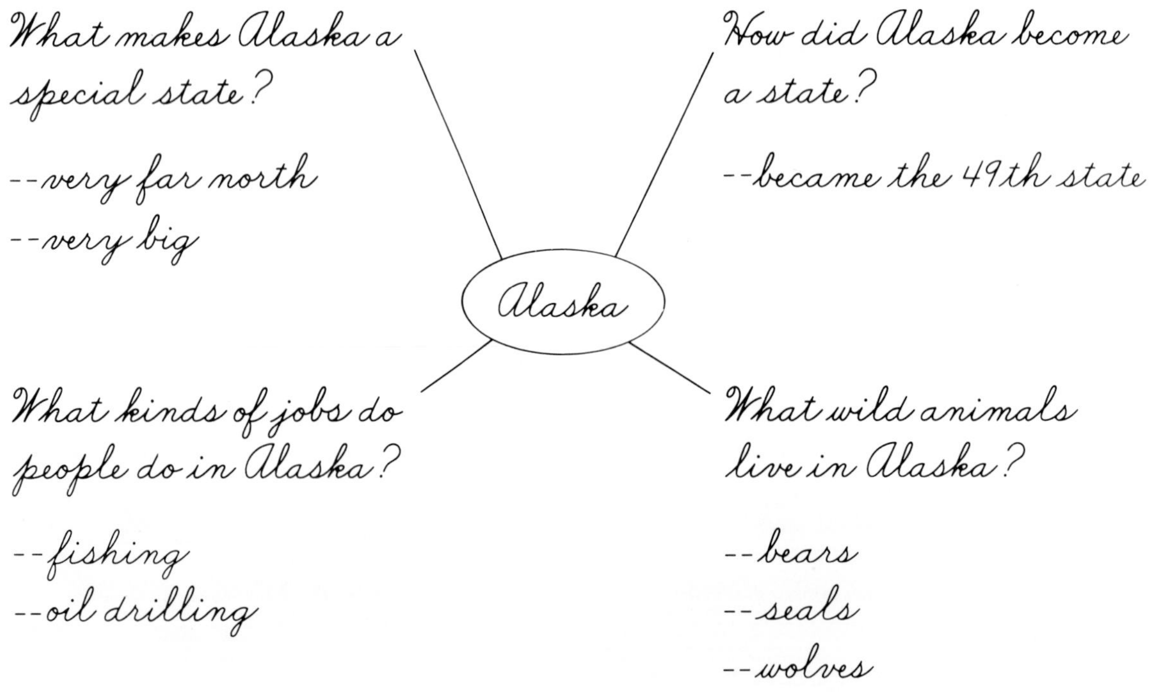

What makes Alaska a special state?

--very far north
--very big

How did Alaska become a state?

--became the 49th state

Alaska

What kinds of jobs do people do in Alaska?

--fishing
--oil drilling

What wild animals live in Alaska?

--bears
--seals
--wolves

Practice

Make a topic wheel for each topic below. Write at least four questions about each topic.

1. maps
2. California
3. Spain
4. the city of Philadelphia
5. the first American cities
6. the United States Southwest
7. Benjamin Franklin
8. the first railroads

Make a Topic Wheel

Get out the list of five topics you wrote for your report. Choose the topic you would like to write about. Make a topic wheel. On the wheel, write at least four questions you have about your topic. Under each question, write any facts you already know that could answer the question.

Using an Enyclopedia

Luis chose Alaska as the subject of his report. He wanted to use the encyclopedia to find out about Alaska. An encyclopedia has many volumes that are numbered and are in alphabetical order. On the side of each volume are the number and the letter. Inside each volume are articles on many topics. These articles are also arranged alphabetically.

To find the article you want, look in the volume with the same first letter as your topic. Luis found the article on *Alaska* in Volume 1, the *A* volume. An article on the *Rocky Mountains* would be in the *R* volume, Volume 16.

To find an article on a person, look in the volume with the same first letter as the person's *last* name. Use Volume 8, the *H* volume, to read about *Sam Houston*, an early hero of Texas.

Your topic might be a group of words. In that case, choose the *key* word, the most important word. If your topic is *the world's longest rivers*, the key word is *rivers*. You would look in the *R* volume.

Practice

Use the encyclopedia described on the previous page. Write the key word you would look up and the number of the volume in which you would find information on each topic below.

1. the discovery of Canada
2. Daniel Boone
3. Sweden
4. Captain John Smith
5. the Mississippi River
6. the capital city of India
7. where gold is found
8. countries that grow rice
9. where sheep are raised
10. what life is like in Kansas

Find Your Topic in the Encyclopedia

Look up information for your topic in an encyclopedia. Look in any volume that might hold information. For example, Luis looked in the *A* volume for *Alaska*. Write down the page numbers where any information you plan to use can be found. Save your work.

Using the Parts of a Book

Luis wanted to answer these two questions in his research report:

What makes Alaska a special state?
How did Alaska become a state?

Luis found many books about Alaska. The main parts of each book helped him learn more about the information inside.

Our Alaska
  by Linda Cernak

Worldwide Publishing Company
Boston, Massachusetts

The title page appears at the front of a book. It gives the title and author. It gives the name and location of the publishing company. The back of that page tells the year the book was printed.

Table of Contents

The table of contents comes next. It lists the chapter titles in the order in which they appear. It shows the page on which each one begins.

Index

The index is at the back of the book. It lists the book's main topics in alphabetical order. Some topics also have more specific details listed under them. The index shows the page or pages on which each item can be found.

Practice

Use the title page, table of contents, and index on the previous page to answer these questions.

1. Who is the author of *Our Alaska*?
2. Which company published the book?
3. What is the first chapter of the book about?
4. On which page does Chapter 3 begin?
5. Which chapter tells about wild animals in Alaska?
6. In 1899, gold was found in Alaska. Which chapter would give information on that part of Alaska's history?
7. On what page in the book could you find out how tall Mount McKinley is?
8. What page tells who William H. Seward was?
9. What page gives information on the city of Nome?
10. Why might someone doing a research report be interested in the year a book was published?

Find Books on Your Topic
- Find books on the topic you chose for your research report. Use library books or your textbooks. (p. 112)
- Learn more about what is in the book by checking the title page, table of contents, and index.
- List the title of books you can use.
- Under each title, list the page numbers that show where you will find useful information.
- Save your work.

Taking Notes in Your Own Words

Luis chose some books and encyclopedia articles for his report. Next, he took notes on what he read.

To take notes, write down only the most important information you find. Your notes do not have to be in complete sentences. Do not copy from the book. Use your own words instead.

Here is one article Luis read and the notes he took.

Alaska, which became a state in 1959, is west of Canada. It is farther north than any other state. Temperatures in parts of Alaska can drop to 60° below zero. It is the only state where wild polar bears can still be found. Alaska is also the largest state. North America's tallest mountain, Mount McKinley, is in Alaska.

People in Alaska do many kinds of jobs. Many Alaskans drill for oil in Alaska's large oil fields. Other people mine for coal, gold, silver, or copper. Many people work on fishing boats. Others work in fish canning plants. A great number of Alaskans work in factories that turn wood into pulp for making paper.

What makes Alaska a special state?
--farthest north of any state
--can reach 60° below zero in places
--only wild polar bears in U.S.
--largest state
--Mount McKinley, tallest North American mountain

How did Alaska become a state?

--became a state in 1959

Notice that Luis wrote down both questions he wanted to answer. This helped him decide what notes to take. He didn't need to take notes on the second paragraph. There was nothing in it about his questions.

Luis still had very little information that answered his question about how Alaska became a state. He needed to find another book or article.

Practice

A. Read the following article on Alaska. Take notes that Luis could use to answer the question of how Alaska became a state.

The 49th and 50th states, Alaska and Hawaii, have unusual histories. In 1867, the United States bought land that later became Alaska. Hawaii became United States land in 1898. People did not think about making these lands states right away. In 1912, some other areas, including Arizona, became new states. But Alaska and Hawaii did not. Finally, in the middle of the 1900s, Congress decided it was time for Alaska and Hawaii to become states. On January 3, 1959, President Dwight D. Eisenhower signed a bill that made Alaska a state. Hawaii was voted on by Congress later that year. It became a state on August 21, 1959. Each time a new state was added, a new star was put on the American flag.

B. Imagine you are doing a report on what jobs people in Alaska do. Take notes on the second paragraph of the article on page 232. Put the notes in your own words.

Take Notes for Your Report

Look back at the two questions you asked about your topic. Write each question at the top of a notecard or a piece of paper. Take notes about each question from the books and encyclopedia articles you chose. Save your work.

Writing a First Draft

Read the first draft of Luis's research report. He wasn't worried about making it perfect. It will be changed later.

Alaska is a special state in many ways. It is the largest state in the United States. Alaska is also the state that is farthest north. Sometimes it can get as cold as 60° below zero in parts of the state. Alaska is the only state with wild polar bears. It is also the state with North America's tallest mountain, Mount McKinley. The story of how alaska became a state is an unusual one. In 1867, the united states bought the land that bekame alaska. but alaska did not become a state until almost a hundred years later On January 3, 1959, president dwight d eisenhower made alaska a state. A 49th star was added to the American flag. This star honored the country's newest state. This star honored the country's largest state. This star honored the country's coldest state.

Write Your First Draft

You may discuss your report with your teacher or classmates or start work by yourself. Answer your two questions in separate paragraphs. Use the notes you took. Begin the first paragraph with your first main idea. Then write the details that tell more about it. Do the same for the second paragraph. Save your work.

Discussing a First Draft

Luis finished his first draft. He wanted to improve it. He talked about the report with his classmate Alison.

Discussion Strategy

Before your discussion, think carefully about what you are going to say. This will make it easier for you to say what you really mean.

Use this Content Checklist to discuss with your class the research report that Luis wrote.

Content Checklist
- ✔ Does the report give information on one topic?
- ✔ Does each paragraph discuss a separate main idea?
- ✔ Do details in each paragraph explain the main idea?
- ✔ Are all details in the report facts?

Revise Your First Draft for Content

To the Reader: Trade papers with a classmate. Read your partner's report. Try to identify the main idea in each paragraph. If anything is unclear, discuss ways to improve it. Use the Content Checklist and Discussion Strategy for help.

To the Writer: Listen to the things your partner says. Take notes if you need to. If your partner could not guess your main idea or any of your details, revise your draft to make it clearer.

Combining Sentences for Style

◆

You can combine short sentences that describe the same person, place, or thing.

Use *and* when you have only two describing words.

Alaska's south is warm. Alaska's south is damp.
Alaska's south is warm and damp.

Use commas and *and* for three or more describing words.

Polar bears are huge. Polar bears are fierce.
Polar bears are strong.
Polar bears are huge, fierce, and strong.

You can also combine sentences that describe the same action.

The sun shines warmly on the ice.
The sun shines brightly on the ice.
The sun shines warmly and brightly on the ice.
Climb the hill carefully. Climb the hill slowly. Climb the hill safely.
Climb the hill carefully, slowly, and safely.

Here is how Luis combined sentences in his draft.

> On January 3. 1959. president dwight d eisenhower made alaska a state. A 49th star was added to the American flag. This star honored the country's newest state. ~~This star honored the country's largest state. This star honored the country's coldest state.~~
>
> *largest, and coldest*

Practice

Read each group of sentences. Combine them into one sentence by joining the describing words. Write your new sentence.

1. a. Watching sled dog races in Alaska is popular.
   b. Watching sled dog races in Alaska is fun.
2. a. Sled dogs are strong.
   b. Sled dogs are fast.
   c. Sled dogs are clever.
3. a. One race, the Iditarod, is long.
   b. One race, the Iditarod, is difficult.
4. a. The crowds cheer the winning sled loudly.
   b. The crowds cheer the winning sled wildly.
   c. The crowds cheer the winning sled happily.

Revising Checklist

✔ Have I included all the features of a research report?
✔ Can I combine subjects and predicates to make new sentences? (p. 32)
✔ Have I included exact information? (p. 70)
✔ Can I add descriptive language? (p. 120)
✔ Can I add information to make my work complete? (p. 156)
✔ Where can I vary the beginnings of sentences? (p. 198)
✔ Where can I combine sentences by joining describing words?

Revise Your First Draft for Style

Check for the items on the Revising Checklist. Where possible, combine sentences by joining adjectives or adverbs with *and* or with *and* and commas. Mark your changes on the draft. Hold onto your work.

Writing Names and Titles

Luis used several proper nouns in his report. He checked the following rules for writing proper nouns, titles, and initials.

Rule	Examples
Begin every important word in a proper noun with a capital letter. Proper nouns include names of people, countries, states, cities, and mountains.	Dwight Eisenhower United States of America Alaska Boston Canadian Rocky Mountains
Capitalize the initials in a person's name. Place a period after each initial.	Dwight D. Eisenhower D. David Eisenhower D. D. Eisenhower
Begin the title of a person with a capital letter. If the title is an abbreviation, place a period after it.	President Eisenhower Mr. Eisenhower Mrs. Mamie Eisenhower

Practice

Write each sentence correctly. Use capital letters and periods when necessary.

1. Instead of states, canada has provinces.
2. manitoba, quebec, and ontario are all places in Canada.
3. canada's largest cities are montreal and toronto.
4. In 1791, john g simcoe started building toronto.
5. At the time, mr simcoe named the city york.
6. Other important cities are ottawa and vancouver.
7. The capital of alberta is calgary.

Proofreading Checklist

✔ Did I indent the first sentence of each paragraph? (p. 34)
✔ Did I begin each sentence with a capital letter? (p. 34)
✔ Did I use the correct end marks for sentences? (p. 34)
✔ Did I use commas correctly (p. 72)
✔ Did I use the correct capitalization and punctuation for all my abbreviations? (p. 158)
✔ Did I write all proper nouns, titles, and initials correctly?
✔ Do my pronouns refer to the correct noun?

Proofreading Marks	
∧	add
⅃	take away
¶	indent
≡	capitalize
/	small letter
◯	check spelling
∿	transpose

Proofread Your Research Report

Check for correct capitalization and punctuation. Use the Proofreading Checklist. Make the changes on your draft. Save your work for the next lesson.

Checking Spelling/Writing a Final Copy

Spelling Strategy

Always check your spelling when you proofread. Follow these steps:
- Circle each word you think is misspelled.
- Write the word again.
- See if it looks right to you.
- Check in a dictionary if needed.

Here is part of Luis's revised and proofread report:

> ¶The story of how alaska became a state is an unusual one. In 1867, the united states bought the land that ~~bekame~~ *became* alaska. but alaska did not become a state until almost a hundred years later. On January 3, 1959, president dwight d. eisenhower made alaska a state. A 49th star was added to the American flag. This star honored the country's newest state. *largest, and coldest* This star honored the country's largest state. This star honored the country's coldest state.

Check Your Spelling

Use the proofreading marks to correct any mistakes in spelling. Add any misspelled words to your spelling log.

Write a Final Copy

Write a neat, final copy of your research report. Proofread your work. Keep your final copy.

Sharing Your Research Report

Speaking/Listening Strategy

Before you speak, look up any unusual words or names in a dictionary to see how they are pronounced. When someone else is speaking, listen carefully for the main points of what that person is saying.

Choosing a Way to Share   Here are some ways to share your report.

Presenting a TV Show   Set up a TV interview show to explain your report. Luis played a movie star who had just finished making a film in Alaska. A classmate played a TV talk show interviewer who asked him questions about Alaska.

Making a Book   Put all the class reports into a *Guidebook to Our Planet*. Make a title page, table of contents, and index for the book. Display the book in your school.

Share Your Research Report
Choose the way you prefer to share your report. After you present it, answer questions from your audience.

Add to Your Learning Log
- What makes me happiest about my research report?
- What is the best part of my report?
- What would I like to change about my research report?

The Literature Connection: Adjectives

A discovery is something new to you. A discovery can be any color or size. You make a discovery when you see new people, places, or things, or when you read about them.

Words that describe people, places, or things are called **adjectives**. When adjectives are used, they can make what is being described seem real. The poem below uses adjectives to tell about a place the poet discovered and has remembered.

A Memory
by
William Allingham

Four ducks on a pond,
A grass-bank beyond,
A blue sky of spring,
White clouds on the wing;
What a little thing
To remember for years—
To remember with tears!

Discussion

1. How many ducks are on the pond? Name the word that tells you.
2. What colors are the sky and clouds? Name the words that tell you.
3. Imagine that you have visited the place described in the poem. What other things might you see? Use adjectives to tell about them.

The Writing Connection:
Adjectives

You can use adjectives to make your writing more colorful. Picture this sentence in your mind.

Ducks played in a pond.

How many ducks were there? What kind of pond was it? Adjectives can help give a clearer picture. Now read this sentence.

Three ducks played in a shallow pond.

The picture is clearer now. Use adjectives to tell more about the people, places, and things you see.

Activity

Imagine you are at the bottom of the sea. You are watching the fish swim.

- Start with this sentence: The fish are swimming.
- Make a picture with words. Try to make your word picture so clear that readers will be able to see the fish in their minds.
- Add any words that will help you make a clear word picture of the fish. The sentence can be as long as you wish. You can write more than one sentence.

Adjectives

An **adjective** is a word that tells about a noun.

A. Adjectives give details that make a clear picture for the reader. Many adjectives tell what kind, size, shape, or age a noun is.

> A <u>tiny</u> bird sang. (*Tiny* tells what size.)
> The <u>old</u> dog yawned. (*Old* tells what age.)

B. Adjectives also form a clear picture by telling how a noun looks, sounds, smells, tastes, or feels.

> I petted the <u>soft</u> bunny. (*Soft* tells how the bunny feels.)
> It nibbled <u>sweet</u> clover. (*Sweet* tells how the clover tastes.)

Strategy

To find the adjective in a sentence, look for the noun. Then, ask which word tells about the noun. An adjective usually comes before the noun it describes.

Check Your Understanding

A. Look at the underlined noun. Write the letter of the adjective that tells about the noun.

   1. A fat <u>puppy</u> drank a bowl of milk.
      a. fat **b.** drank **c.** bowl **d.** of

   2. It liked the warm <u>milk</u> very much.
      a. It **b.** liked **c.** warm **d.** very

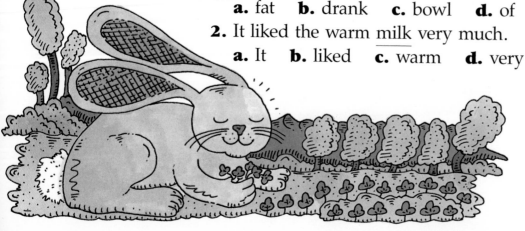

B. Use the directions for Check Your Understanding A.

   3. My rabbit eats crunchy <u>lettuce</u>.

      a. My   **b.** rabbit   **c.** eats   **d.** crunchy

   4. Your kitten has silky <u>fur</u>.

      a. Your   **b.** kitten   **c.** has   **d.** silky

Practice

A. Write each sentence. The noun is underlined. Put two lines under the adjective that tells about it.

   5. A little <u>kitten</u> sleeps in a box.

   6. The young <u>cats</u> chase each other.

   7. The mother flicks her long <u>tail</u>.

   8. An angry <u>cat</u> hisses.

B. Use the directions for Practice A.

   9. Frogs breathe through slippery <u>skin</u>.

 10. They catch insects with sticky <u>tongues</u>.

 11. The frog croaks with a gruff <u>voice</u>.

 12. It hops into a damp <u>puddle</u>.

C. Mixed Practice Write each sentence. Put two lines under each adjective. Put one line under the noun it tells about.

 13. A robin lays a blue egg.

 14. It hatches in a snug nest.

 15. The hungry babies cry.

 16. The parents bring juicy worms.

 17. Robins also eat sweet berries.

 18. An adult robin has a red breast.

 19. Many animals grow and change.

Apply: Work with a Group

Take turns choosing something in the classroom. Use adjectives to describe the object. See if the others can guess the mystery item.

More About Adjectives

Some adjectives answer the question "How many?" to tell about a noun.

A. Numbers are special kinds of adjectives. They give the reader a clear picture by telling how many nouns there are. Look at the following examples.

> Nine planets circle the sun. (*Nine* tells how many planets.)
> Two astronauts landed on the moon. (*Two* tells how many astronauts.)

B. Some adjectives tell how many without giving the exact number. Words such as *few*, *many*, *several*, and *some* all answer the question "How many?"

> Some scientists study the planets. (*Some* gives an idea of how many scientists.)

Strategy

To find certain adjectives in a sentence, look for the noun. Then, find the word that answers the question "How many?"

Check Your Understanding

A. Write the letter of the adjective in each sentence.
   1. The earth has one moon.
      a. earth **b.** has **c.** one **d.** moon
   2. Seven spacecraft have flown to Mars.
      a. Seven **b.** spacecraft **c.** have **d.** Mars

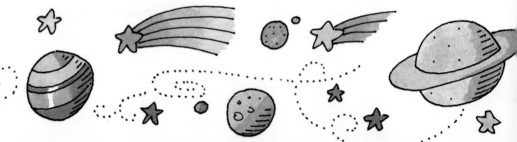

B. Write the letter of the adjective in each sentence.

3. Mars has many mountains.
   a. Mars   **b.** has   **c.** many   **d.** mountains
4. There are also several canyons.
   a. There   **b.** are   **c.** also   **d.** several

Practice

A. Write each sentence. Underline the adjective.
   5. The Romans counted only five planets.
   6. Galileo saw four moons through his telescope.
   7. Scientists found three planets beyond Saturn.
   8. Two spacecraft flew past Jupiter.

B. Use the directions for Practice A.
   9. A few astronauts walked on the moon.
   10. They brought back many rocks.
   11. Several rings are around Saturn.
   12. We saw some pictures of the rings.

C. Mixed Practice Write each sentence. Underline each adjective that tells how many.
   13. Many clouds cover Venus.
   14. One planet circles near the sun.
   15. A few moons have volcanoes.
   16. Earth has one moon.
   17. Some scientists plan trips to Mars.
   18. They study several moons of Saturn.
   19. Mercury has no moons.
   20. Saturn has many small moons.

Apply: Journal

In your journal, write several sentences about things you have discovered in your neighborhood. In each sentence, use an adjective that tells how many.

247

A, An, and *The*

The words *a*, *an*, and *the* are special adjectives. They are called **articles**.

A. An article points to the noun that follows it. *A* and *an* are used only before singular nouns.

> Louisa May Alcott was an author.
> She wrote a book.

The can be used before singular or plural nouns.

> The book is very popular.
> All the children like the story.

B. *A* and *an* are used before different words. Use *a* before nouns that begin with a consonant sound.

> a poem   a story   a writer   a girl

Use *an* before nouns that begin with a vowel sound.

> an author   an editor   an adjective

A apple? No.
An apple? Yes!
That's right.

Strategy

If you don't know whether to use *a* or *an* with a noun, say the article and the noun out loud. Usually, only the correct article sounds right.

Check Your Understanding

A. Write the letter of the article in each sentence.
   1. Louisa lived on a farm.
      a. lived   **b.** on   **c.** a   **d.** farm
   2. The children played outdoors.
      a. The   **b.** children   **c.** played   **d.** outdoors

B. Write the letter of the correct article.

    3. They picked fruit in ____ orchard.

        a. a   **b.** an

    4. Vegetables grew in ____ garden.

        a. a   **b.** an

Practice

A. Write each sentence. Underline each article.

    5. Louisa's father ran a school.

    6. He called the school Pine Place.

    7. The family was very poor.

    8. Louisa kept a journal.

B. Write each sentence using the correct article.

    9. The children slept in ____attic. (a, an)

   10. Rain made ____noise on the roof. (a, an)

   11. Young Louisa wrote ____poem. (a, an)

   12. ____editor printed it. (A, An)

C. Mixed Practice Write each sentence, using the correct article.

   13. Louisa became ____ author. (a, an)

   14. She was ____ nurse during wartime. (a, an)

   15. Louisa helped ____ soldiers. (the, a)

   16. Someone gave Louisa ____ idea. (a, an)

   17. Many people read ____ stories. (a, the)

   18. She wrote ____ book about her family. (a, an)

   19. ____ American writer wrote ____ book. (A, An) (a, an)

   20. We read her story ____ year ago. (a, an)

Apply: Test a Partner

Have a classmate write two sentences. Each sentence should use two of the three articles. Check to make sure they are used correctly.

Adjectives That Compare

Adjectives can be used to compare two or more nouns.

A. Add *er* to an adjective to compare two persons, places, or things. Look at the following sentences.

> Malcolm is tall.
> Angela is taller than Malcolm.

The word *than* follows an adjective ending in *er*.

B. Add *est* to an adjective to compare three or more persons, places, or things.

> Our school building is tall.
> An apartment building is taller than the school.
> A skyscraper is the tallest building of the three.

You also add *est* when the words *of all* are part of the sentence.

> A skyscraper is the tallest building of all.

Strategy

When comparing two nouns, add the ending with *two* letters (*er*). When comparing three or more nouns, add the ending with *three* letters (*est*).

Check Your Understanding

A. Write the letter of the correct adjective.
    1. A hill is ____ than a mountain.
        a. low **b.** lower **c.** lowest
    2. Winter is ____ than summer.
        a. colder **b.** cold **c.** coldest

B. Write the letter of the correct adjective.

    3. A redwood is the ____ tree of all.

        a. great   **b.** greatest   **c.** greater

    4. The Columbia is the ____ river of the three.

        a. long   **b.** longer   **c.** longest

Practice

A. Write each sentence, using the correct form of the adjective in parentheses.

    5. The Pacific Ocean is (deep) than the Atlantic.

    6. Lake Superior is (broad) than Lake Erie.

    7. A pond is (small) than a lake.

    8. A hurricane is (strong) than a breeze.

B. Follow the directions for Practice A.

    9. A horse is the (fast) animal of the three.

    10. A cheetah is the (fast) animal of all.

    11. A snail is the (slow) creature of the three.

    12. A parrot is the (bright) bird of all.

C. Mixed Practice Write each sentence, using the correct form of the adjective in parentheses.

    13. Mount Logan is (high) than Mount Rainier.

    14. Mount McKinley is (low) than Mount Everest.

    15. Everest is the (high) mountain of all.

    16. It is (steep) than Mount Shasta.

    17. The Amazon River is (long) than the Potomac.

    18. The Nile is the (long) river of all.

    19. The (big) mountains of all are in Asia.

    20. A desert is the (dry) place on earth.

Apply: Learning Log

What part of this lesson was hardest for you? Make a plan for learning adjectives that compare.

Prefixes

A **base word** is a word to which other word parts can be added. A **prefix** is a word part that is added to the beginning of a base word.

A. Study the prefixes in the chart below.

Prefix	Meaning	Example
pre	before	preview
re	again	refill
un	the opposite of; not	unfold

B. A prefix changes the meaning of a base word. The new word has the meaning of its two parts.

re + do⟶*re*do Redo means *do again*.
un + wise⟶*un*wise Unwise means *not wise*.

You can make new words by adding prefixes to many words you already know.

re + play⟶*re*play pre + heat⟶*pre*heat

Strategy

When you read, it helps to know the meaning of prefixes. Prefixes can help you figure out the meanings of words you don't already know.

Check Your Understanding

A. Write the letter of the prefix in the underlined word.
   1. He unwrapped a gift. **a.** re **b.** un **c.** pre
   2. She remailed the box. **a.** re **b.** un **c.** pre

B. Look at the underlined word in each sentence. Write the letter that tells what it means.

3. Liz <u>rewrote</u> her story.
    a. wrote before   **b.** told   **c.** wrote again

4. Bob's new shoes felt <u>uncomfortable</u>.
    a. ugly   **b.** not comfortable   **c.** soft

Practice

A. Write each sentence. Put a line under each word that has a prefix. Put two lines under each prefix.

5. People rediscovered an old city in Greece.
6. The city was unknown for hundreds of years.
7. Workers uncovered old buildings.

B. Write a new word by adding each prefix to the base word. Then, write the meaning of the new word.

8. re + tell: ____
9. pre + pay: ____
10. un + certain: ____
11. pre + cook: ____
12. un + like: ____
13. re + count: ____

C. Mixed Practice Write each sentence. Underline each word with a prefix. Write the meaning of the word.

14. Mayan builders used precut blocks of stone.
15. Traders unpacked shells and feathers.
16. Unfriendly tribes attacked the Mayas.
17. The people did not reunite.
18. Workers found unbroken statues.
19. We revisited the city they uncovered.
20. Our precooked food was uninteresting.

Apply: Exploring Language

Make up some words of your own using the prefixes *pre*, *re*, and *un*. Use each word in a sentence.

LANGUAGE IN ACTION

Giving an Oral Report

What is an oral report? An oral report is like a research report. The difference is that you present it aloud, instead of writing it down. You tell the class what you learned. Here's what you do.

- Start off as if you were writing a report. Find out all you can about the subject.
- Make notes. You can write them on a piece of paper, or you can use index cards. Write down what you want to talk about. These notes are only for you. They don't have to be complete sentences.
- Read your report. Speak loudly and clearly. Make sure everyone can hear you. Remember, you're talking to your friends and classmates. There's no need to be nervous.

Practice

On a separate sheet of paper, answer these questions.
1. What is the first thing you do to prepare an oral report?
2. When you are giving the report, how do you know what to say?
3. When you are giving the report, how should you speak?

Apply

Give an oral report to your class. Pick any topic you like. You may ask your teacher to suggest one.

TEST TAKING

Using Time Well

When you are taking a test, you need to use your time well. Then, you can finish the test and get full credit for what you know.

Here are some ways to use your time better when you take a test:

- Read every question on the test. Answer the questions you know. Skip any questions you can't answer.
- After reading the test once, go back and work on any unanswered questions. If you still have trouble with a question, skip it and go on.
- After you've gone through the test a second time, go back and work on any questions that are left.
- If there is still time after you finish the test, check your answers.

Practice

Answer the following questions.
1. What should you do if you get stuck on a problem the first time through a test?
2. What should you do after you read through the test once?
3. What should you do if you've finished the test and there is still some time left?

Apply

Learning Log   Decide what things from this lesson will help you. Write them in your learning log.

UNIT REVIEW

Research Report   *(page 223)*

1. On your paper, list three features of a research report.

Using an Encyclopedia   *(pages 228-229)*

Read each topic. Write the key word you would look up in an encyclopedia to find more information on that topic.

  2. the first bicycles   **4.** the life of a cowboy

  3. cities in Illinois   **5.** the Atlantic Ocean

Combining Sentences/Capitalization and Punctuation   *(pages 236-239)*

Write each pair of sentences as one sentence by combining the describing words.

  6. a. Model ships are   **7. a.** Build the ship carefully.
      unusual.   **b.** Build the ship slowly.
     b. Model ships are fun.   **c.** Build the ship well.

Write each sentence with correct capitalization and punctuation.

  8. The city of denver is the capital of colorado.

  9. This city is in the rocky mountains.

10. It was named for james w denver.

11. mr denver was an important person in the state.

Adjectives   *(pages 244-245)*

Write each sentence. Put two lines under each adjective. Put one line under the noun it tells about.

12. A tree grows from a tiny seed.

13. The young tree has smooth bark.

14. Red apples grow on the long branches.

15. We pick the sweet fruit.

More About Adjectives *(pages 246-247)*
Write each sentence. Underline each adjective that tells how many.
16. Insects have six legs.
17. Some insects live in groups.
18. Several butterflies have four wings.
19. A mayfly dies after a few hours.
20. Many insects have two feelers.

A, An, and The *(pages 248-249)*
Write each sentence, using the correct article.
21. _____ insect's eyes never close. (A, An)
22. _____ eyes have hundreds of lenses. (A, The)
23. _____ flea has no eyes. (A, An)
24. A bee hears through _____ hairs on its body. (a, the)
25. All insects hatch from _____ egg. (a, an)

Adjectives That Compare *(pages 250-251)*
Write each sentence, using the correct form of the adjective in parentheses.
26. A bee flies (fast) than a grasshopper.
27. A dragonfly is the (fast) insect of all.
28. A cricket is (loud) than a grasshopper.
29. The cicada is the (loud) of the three insects.
30. A honey bee is (small) than a bumblebee.

Prefixes *(pages 252-253)*
Write each sentence. Underline the word with a prefix. Then write the meaning of the word.
31. All the students took a pretest.
32. The teacher read a story with an unexpected ending.
33. Tricia retold the story to her brother.
34. She was unsure of the ending.
35. She relearned the story the next day.
36. The teacher gave the students a pretest.

MAKING ALL THE
CONNECTIONS

You and several classmates will now write as a group a business letter about a problem. What you have learned about letter writing will help you.

You will do the following in your letter:
♦ Describe a problem and suggest a solution
♦ Give facts and reasons to support your solution
♦ Include all the parts of a letter

Reading A Business Letter

Read the following business letter and side notes.

Heading

6453 Summit Road
Provo, Utah 84602
September 23, 1988

Inside
Address

Mr. Tom Wu
Provo Elementary School
616 Oakdale Street
Provo, Utah 84602

Greeting

Dear Principal Wu:

Body

The problem is
described here.

A solution is
suggested.

Facts support the
solution.

There is a problem at our school. During lunch a few students stay on the swings. They won't let other students take a turn. I think everyone who wants to swing should get a five-minute turn. In a forty-minute break, many more students will be able to use the swings.

Closing

Sincerely,

Signature

Jonathan Snyder

Speaking and Listening

Work in a group. Talk about these questions.

1. What was the problem stated in the letter?

2. What details about Jonathan's problem did you learn from the picture at the top of the page?

3. What facts did he use to support his solution?

Thinking

Brainstorming

Choose one person to be a note taker. Have the person take notes as you discuss these questions.

1. What problems does your school or town have? Explain why the problems need to be solved.

2. What are some facts and opinions that could support your solution?

Organizing

When you plan a business letter, it is helpful to organize what you want to write. Study the chart below. It shows how Jonathan organized his letter.

With the rest of your group, look back at your brainstorming notes. Decide how to use them to fill in a chart like the one below. Have one group member write down your ideas in the chart.

Problem	Solution	Facts	Opinions
Students weren't sharing the swings.	Everyone take a 5-minute turn.	More people would be able to swing.	There will be less fighting and more fun.

Writing a Business Letter

Imagine that you and other group members are part of a student council. The student council's president has asked you to write a letter to the principal about a problem. Use the chart you made to help you plan and write a letter.

Planning

+ Review the chart that your group made. Add any new details you think of.
+ Discuss the problem and possible solutions.
+ Think of facts and details that support your solution.
+ Organize your information in a list. State the problem. Then write your solution.

Composing

- Work with your group to write your letter. Choose someone to write down the first draft as all group members suggest ideas.
- Write the correct heading and greeting.
- Decide how to word the problem, solution, and supporting facts.
- End the letter with a closing and signature.

Revising

- As a group, read over your letter.
- Check that the information in the heading is correct.
- Check that you have stated the problem and your solution.

Proofreading

As a group, proofread your letter. Have one member make the proofreading changes on your draft.

- Are all pronouns used correctly?
- Are all contractions correctly formed?
- Are all words spelled correctly?
- Is correct punctuation used in the heading, greeting, and closing?

Presenting

- Choose one group member to write a final copy.
- Send the letter.

CUMULATIVE REVIEW

A. Write the letter of the correct punctuation to end each sentence. (*pages 40-45*)

1. How hard we worked
   a. . **b.** ! **c.** ?

2. Which kite is Tom's
   a. . **b.** ! **c.** ?

B. Write the letter of the sentence that has one line under the complete subject and two lines under the complete predicate. (*pages 46-51*)

3. **a.** The kite sails high.
   b. The tail flutters.
   c. A box kite falls.

4. **a.** Ida made a model.
   b. The wing is blue.
   c. The plane flew fast.

5. **a.** The kite string breaks.
   b. The children shout.
   c. The kite flies away.

6. **a.** The plane landed.
   b. Ida chased the plane.
   c. Betty ran quickly.

C. Write the letter of the words that are nouns. (*pages 78-79*)

7. The animals hunt for some food.
   a. animals, some **b.** hunt, food **c.** animals, food

8. The lion waits in the tall grass.
   a. lion, tall **b.** lion, grass **c.** waits, grass

D. Write the letter of the correct plural noun. (*pages 80-83*)

9. berry **a.** berry **b.** berries **c.** berrys **d.** berryes
10. goose **a.** gooses **b.** geeses **c.** geese **d.** goosses

E. Write the letter that names each noun. (*pages 84-85*)

11. Kansas **a.** common noun **b.** proper noun
12. mountain **a.** common noun **b.** proper noun
13. Pacific Ocean **a.** common noun **b.** proper noun

F. Write the letter of the correct possessive. (*pages 86-89*)

14. women **a.** womens **b.** womens' **c.** women's
15. train **a.** trains **b.** train's **c.** trains'
16. trucks **a.** truck's **b.** trucks's **c.** trucks'

G. Write the letter of the verb. (*pages 128-129*)
    17. Sarah drops a penny.
        a. Sarah   **b.** drops   **c.** penny
    18. The penny rolls across the room.
        a. rolls   **b.** across   **c.** room

H. Write the letter of the correct present tense verb.
    (*pages 130-135*)
    19. Government workers ____ coins.
        a. make   **b.** makes
    20. An artist ____ a design for a new coin.
        a. draws   **b.** draw
    21. The coin ____ the picture.
        a. matchs   **b.** match   **c.** matches

I. Write the letter of the correct past tense verb.
    (*pages 136-139*)
    22. The Chinese ____ paper money long ago.
        a. printed   **b.** print
    23. Some people ____ shells for money.
        a. carryed   **b.** carried

J. Write the letter of the linking verb that belongs in each
    sentence. (*pages 164-165*)
    24. Silver dollars ____ heavy.   **25.** Paper money ____ green.
        a. is   **b.** am   **c.** are   **a.** are   **b.** is   **c.** am

K. Write the letter of the correct main verb. (*pages 166-169*)
    26. A machine has ____ a new dime.
        a. stamp   **b.** stamps   **c.** stamped
    27. The boys have ____ an old coin.
        a. saw   **b.** seed   **c.** seen

L. Write the letter of the correct contraction. (*pages 170-171*)
    28. is not   **a.** isnt   **b.** isn't   **c.** is'nt
    29. were not   **a.** weren't   **b.** were'nt   **c.** wern't

M. Write the letter of the words that are correctly capitalized and punctuated. (*pages 200-201*)

30. **a.** Maple Avenue
    b. orchard street
    c. Park avenue
31. **a.** Yours truly
    b. love,
    c. Your friend,

32. **a.** Dear uncle Fred
    b. dear mom,
    c. Dear Joyce,
33. **a.** August, 8 1989
    b. July 4, 1988
    c. October 19 1991

N. Write the letter of the correct pronoun. (*pages 206-211*)

34. Tim plays the piano. ____ played for us today.
    a. He **b.** We **c.** They **d.** She
35. The girls sing in the chorus. ____ learned a new song.
    a. She **b.** You **c.** They **d.** We
36. Lucille and I wrote a play. ____ read it to the class.
    a. I **b.** We **c.** They **d.** She
37. Jorge laughed at the play. He liked ____.
    a. him **b.** us **c.** it **d.** them
38. Carla plays the tuba. We heard ____ yesterday.
    a. them **b.** her **c.** us **d.** you
39. Julie and I play, too. The teacher taught ____.
    a. us **b.** her **c.** them **d.** him
40. The teacher took ____ on a field trip.
    a. I **b.** me
41. Warren and ____ took our instruments.
    a. I **b.** me

O. Write the letter of the possessive form of the pronoun to replace the underlined possessive. (*pages 212-213*)

42. Lucille's mother came with the class.
    a. His **b.** Our **c.** Her **d.** My
43. The boys' sister lives in Washington.
    a. Our **b.** His **c.** My **d.** Their

P. Write the letter of the correct contraction. (*pages 214-215*)

44. I am   **a.** Im   **b.** I'm   **c.** Im'   **d.** Ia'm

45. they are   **a.** they're   **b.** theyr'e   **c.** theyar   **d.** they'ar

46. you will   **a.** youll   **b.** you'wll   **c.** you'll   **d.** youw'll

Q. Write the letter of the word that is an adjective.
(*pages 244-247*)

47. Weeds have long roots.
   a. Weeds   **b.** have   **c.** long   **d.** roots

48. Sharp thorns protect roses.
   a. Sharp   **b.** thorns   **c.** protect   **d.** roses

49. A plant takes in water through thin roots.
   a. plant   **b.** takes   **c.** water   **d.** thin

50. The stem contains a thick liquid.
   a. stem   **b.** contains   **c.** thick   **d.** liquid

51. Some vegetables grow underground.
   a. Some   **b.** vegetables   **c.** grow   **d.** ground

52. Juanita picked seven oranges from the tree.
   a. picked   **b.** seven   **c.** oranges   **d.** tree

R. Write the letter of the correct adjective. (*pages 248-251*)

53. She gave ___ oranges to her grandmother.
   a. an   **b.** the

54. Grandmother had ___ idea.
   a. a   **b.** an

55. She and Juanita went on ___ picnic.
   a. a   **b.** an

56. A melon is ___ than an orange.
   a. large   **b.** larger   **c.** largest

57. A lemon is the ___ of the three fruits.
   a. smaller   **b.** smallest   **c.** small

58. Strawberries are ___ than grapefruit.
   a. sweetest   **b.** sweet   **c.** sweeter

59. The redwood is the ___ tree of all.
   a. tall   **b.** tallest   **c.** taller

PART FOUR

Other Times and Other Places

Our history sings of centuries
Such varying songs it sings!
It starts with winds, slow moving sails,
It ends with skies and wings.

"Our History"
by Catherine Cate Coblentz

Learning about people in other times and other places can be very exciting. You never know what will happen! In these two units, think about what life would be like in other times and other places.

Descriptive Writing

◆

Adverbs

What Do You Know?

"I feel as if I'd been there!"

Even if you've never left your hometown, you can get a feeling about what other places are like by just listening to someone tell about them. You can also imagine places by reading about them. One sentence can tell you what it's like to stand on the hot, dry, Arizona desert. Another may describe the icy, green waters of the Pacific Ocean. A writer can describe the smell of fresh bread from a bakery. A good writer can give you all the details of a certain place—the colors, the smells and the sounds.

Descriptive writing includes details that tell about how things look, sound, feel, smell, and taste. Writers use these details to create word pictures for readers.

Thinking About Descriptive Writing

What is Descriptive Writing?

Descriptive writing has these features:

- It tells about a particular person, place, or thing.
- It uses sensory words to describe. Sensory words tell how something looks, feels, sounds, tastes, or smells.
- It paints a picture with colorful words.

Clear descriptions can improve almost any kind of writing. Descriptions in a letter might help a pen pal imagine the sights and sounds of your town. A short story may describe the rolling hills of an imaginary land. A newspaper description may take you to a baseball stadium or the foot of a volcano. By using descriptive writing, you can help a reader imagine what other places, persons, and times are like.

Discussion

1. What faraway places have you read about?
2. What places or things have you described to someone recently?
3. What are three words you would use to describe your neighborhood?

Reading Descriptive Writing

The following example of descriptive writing comes from the book *In Coal Country* by Judith Hendershot. This story is told by a woman who is remembering her childhood. She was the daughter of a coal miner and lived in a coal mining town. In the following passage she tells about both the ordinary days and the special holidays in her home.

In the summer, when it was hot, the Company Row kids often climbed the hills above the grove. We cooled ourselves by standing under Bernice Falls. The water flowed from a natural spring in the ridge above. It was cool and clean and tasted so sweet.

Here the writer describes how spring water feels and tastes.

We walked the red-dog road to the Company Store. Anything the miners' families needed, from matches to pongee dresses, could be found there. Every payday Papa treated us to an Eskimo Pie.

The Company Row kids played hopscotch in the dirt. Our favorite game was mumbletypeg. In the evenings we built bonfires along the creek and roasted potatoes on willow sticks.

The writer describes how the hills look in autumn.

In the autumn the hills were ablaze with color. We gathered hickory nuts and butternuts and dragged them home in *burlap* sacks. Papa shelled them and spread them on the porch roof to dry. Mama used the nutmeats in cookies at holiday time.

In the winter we climbed from the hollow to Baker's Ridge. Our sleds were made from leftover tin used for roofs, and we rode them down through the woods by moonlight. When the black creek was frozen, we snared a few skates and everyone took a turn. When we got home, we hung our wet clothes over the stove to dry and warmed ourselves in Mama's kitchen.

Christmas in the row was the best time of the year. Papa cut a fresh tree up on the ridge, and we pulled it home on a tin sled. Mama placed a candle on the end of each branch. The tree was lighted once, on Christmas Eve. Papa spent the whole day basting the roast goose for Mama. Our stockings bulged with *tangerines* and nuts and hard cinnamon candies. The house smelled of Christmas tree and roast goose and all the good things that Mama had made. No whistle called Papa to the mine. Everything felt so special. And it was.

The writer describes the smell of the house during the holidays.

The following poem is also an example of descriptive writing. It describes a trip through the country.

The Little Road
by Nancy Byrd Turner

A little road was straying
   Across a little hill.
I asked, "May I go with you, Road?"
   It answered, "If you will."
'Twas travel-stained and shabby,
   And dust was on its face.
Said I: "How fine to wander free
   To every lovely place!"
"O, if you're off to mountains
   Or if you're off to sea,
Or if you're bound across the world,
   It's all the same to me."

The writer describes a road.

The writer describes her feelings about traveling.

The writer uses comparisons to describe the color of the sky and the feel of the wind.

We loitered in the sunlight,
  We journeyed on together;
The sky was like a bluebird's wing,
  The wind was like a feather.

We passed a ruddy robin
  Who called, "How do you do?"
Some daisies shook their bonnets back
  And begged, "Ah, take us too!"
A squirrel briefly joined us,
  A brook came hurrying down.
We wandered through a meadow green
  And by a busy town.
When dusky twilight met us,
  No feet so slow as mine.
"Why, there's a little house," I said,
  "With windows all ashine.
"Perhaps, since night is nearing,
  I'd rather rest than roam."
"I knew you would," said Little Road.
  "That's why I brought you home."

Understanding What You've Read

Answer these questions about the story and the poem.

1. What sensory details does the writer of "In Coal Country" use to describe home at Christmastime?
2. What kind of mood, or feeling, does the writer set in her description of Christmastime in her home?
3. How is the little road in the poem described?
4. In the poem, what do comparisons tell you about the sky and the wind?
5. How do you think the road in the poem is similar to the road in the mining town?

Writing Assignment

The writer of "In Coal Country" describes life in a place that was very special to her. Imagine that you want to tell your friends about a place that is special to you. In this unit, you will learn to write a description. You will also learn to use descriptive language in a poem.

Your **audience** will be your teacher and classmates. Your **purpose** will be to describe a place that is special to you.

Choose a Place

Before you write, choose a place to describe. Write down an idea from the list below or think of an idea of your own. Save your work for the next lesson.

> What special place would be fun to write about?

a tree house   a forest
an old attic   the ocean

Organizing Sensory Details

One student, Wendy, wanted to write about her grandparents' living room. She wanted her readers to get a feeling of what it was like to be there.

To help plan the description, Wendy tried to think of all the things that made her grandparents' living room special to her. She remembered everything that she could see, hear, smell, taste, and touch in the room. She organized these details in the cluster map below.

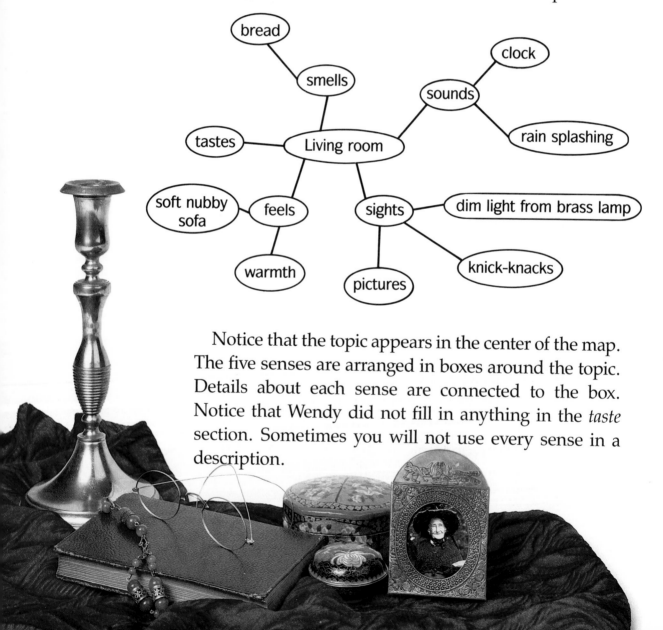

Notice that the topic appears in the center of the map. The five senses are arranged in boxes around the topic. Details about each sense are connected to the box. Notice that Wendy did not fill in anything in the *taste* section. Sometimes you will not use every sense in a description.

Practice

A. Copy the cluster map below onto your paper. Complete it with details relating to the senses that are shown.

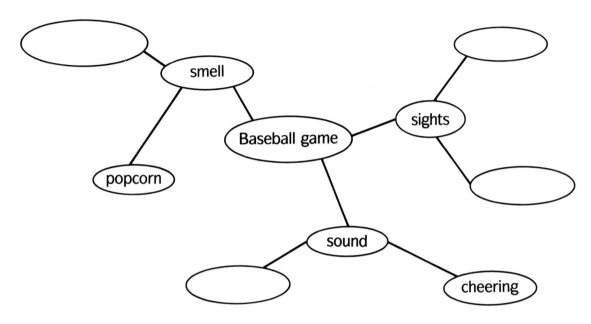

B. Imagine you are bicycling along a dusty country road in the fall. Make a cluster map with the words *country road* in the center. Then list the five senses in boxes around the topic. For each sense, give two details you might include.

Organize Your Topic

Think about the place you chose to write about. Use all of your senses. Think of words and phrases that describe your place. Make a cluster map to organize your details. Save your work for the next lesson. Later you will also use your cluster map to write a poem.

Using Precise Details

Wendy wanted to describe the lamp in her grandparents' living room. She wanted her readers to be able to imagine it in their minds. Wendy decided to choose exact words to show how that lamp was different from other lamps.

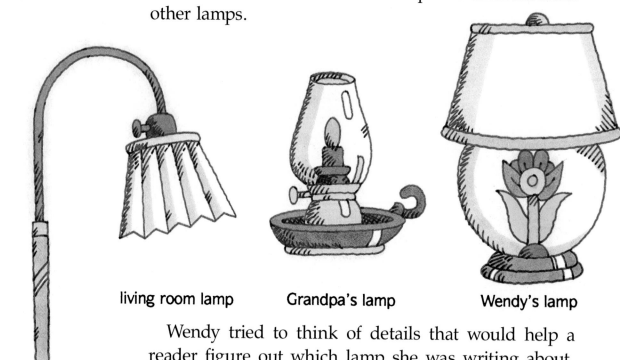

living room lamp   Grandpa's lamp   Wendy's lamp

Wendy tried to think of details that would help a reader figure out which lamp she was writing about. Her grandpa's lamp was very old. It was small and made out of brass. A glass chimney was placed over the bulb, which rested on a short base. The base was connected to a dish. A handle was attached to the side of the base. That lamp was quite a bit different from Wendy's bedroom lamp. Her lamp had a big round glass base with a flower painted on it. The shade was white. Wendy's living room lamp was a floor lamp. It was tall and thin, and bent over at the top. The lamp shade had folds in it.

By using precise details, Wendy can tell how her grandpa's lamp is different from other lamps.

276

Practice

Look at both pictures in each pair. Write a description of both objects. Use specific details to show how the objects in each pair are different.

1.

2.

3.

Add Precise Details

Look back at your cluster map. See if you can find words that will describe your place more precisely. Add the precise details to your cluster map. Save your work to use in both your story and poem.

APPLY
STEP BY STEP

Comparisons and Sound Words

Writers often use comparisons to make descriptions more interesting. A **comparison** tells how two different things are alike. One way to compare things is to use the words *like* or *as*.

The sun was <u>like</u> an oven, baking the land.
Michael was <u>as</u> quick <u>as</u> a rabbit.

Wendy wrote this comparison to make a detail from her cluster map more colorful.

The pictures that fill the fireplace mantle are <u>like</u> a group of old friends.

Another way to improve some descriptions is to include some **sound words**. These words imitate or suggest sounds. Words such as *boom, whir, ring, tick-tock,* and *thud* are sound words.

The air <u>hissed</u> out of the balloon.
The egg <u>sizzled</u> in the pan.

Wendy used a sound word to describe the sound of the clock.

In the corner, the big clock <u>ticks</u> loudly.

Practice

A. Use a sound word from the Word Box to complete each sentence.

1. Mud ____ my coat.
2. The little car ____ all over town.
3. He ____ at all my jokes.
4. Mickey ____ his soup.
5. After a cold, she ____.
6. The bottle ____ open.

WORD BOX

spattered
slurped
zips
giggles
popped
wheezes

B. Make a comparison to finish each sentence.

7. The sky was as blue as ____.
8. His smile was like the ____.
9. The TV show was as boring as ____.
10. Jill was as fast as a ____.
11. The car's headlights were like a ____.
12. The house was as messy as ____.
13. The baby's hair was like ____.

APPLY STEP BY STEP

Use Comparisons and Sound Words

Look at the details in your cluster map. Find places where comparison or sound words would make your description more colorful and unusual. Write the comparisons or sound words that you think of on another piece of paper. Save your work.

Writing a First Draft

Read the first draft of Wendy's descriptive paragraph. She wasn't worried about making it perfect. It will be changed later.

> There is not a more special place than my grandparents living room. It always feels warm and cozey. I love sitting on the soft, nubby sofa. Grandpas small brass lamp casts a dim yellow beam. The smell of freshly baked bread comes out from the kitchen. In the corner, the big clock ticks loudly the pictures that fill the fireplace mantle are like a group of old friends. They are just a few more reasons I feel so at home there.

Write Your First Draft

Use details from your cluster map to write about the place you chose. Write your draft on every other line. Save your work.

Discussing a First Draft

Wendy finished her first draft. She wanted to make it better so she talked it over with her classmate Edward. He had some suggestions for her.

Discussion Strategy: If you do not understand something your partner has written, it may be because the idea is not expressed clearly. Ask for an explanation. Use this Content Checklist to discuss Wendy's paragraph with your class.

Content Checklist

- ✔ Does the paragraph tell about one particular place?
- ✔ Does it tell how the place looks, smells, sounds, feels, or tastes?
- ✔ Does it paint a clear picture with colorful words?

APPLY STEP BY STEP

Revise Your First Draft for Content

To the Reader: Exchange papers with a classmate. Try to imagine the place being described. If you can't picture it in your mind, discuss details that might help give a clearer picture.

To the Writer: Listen to your partner's suggestions. Then revise your draft. Save your work.

Using a Thesaurus

Edward thought that some of the words in Wendy's paragraph could be more colorful. One place to find new words is a thesaurus. A **thesaurus** is a book that lists words in alphabetical order. For each word, a list of **synonyms,** words with the same or similar meaning, is given.

Here is a list of synonyms for the word *group* from Wendy's thesaurus.

> group: bunch, cluster, collection, crowd, gathering, set,
> team

Here is how a sentence with the word *group* can be improved using a thesaurus.

Walter has a <u>group</u> of toy cars.
Walter has a <u>collection</u> of toy cars.

Here is the list of synonyms for *small*.

> small: short, tiny, undersized, unimportant, weak

Here is how a sentence with the word *small* can be changed.

It's silly to get upset over <u>small</u> things.
It's silly to get upset over <u>unimportant</u> things.

Wendy used her thesaurus to make this change.

> The pictures that fill the fireplace mantle are
> like a ~~group~~ of old friends.
>   *crowd*

Practice

A. Read the synonyms in the thesaurus for *give*. Then write each sentence and replace *give* with the best word from the thesaurus.

> **give** (verb) donate grant award assign
> hand allow present

1. My teachers give homework every day.
2. The judges give prizes to the top singers.
3. Please give money to build a new gym.
4. The good fairy will give you three wishes.
5. Please give me the dishcloth.
6. I will give you thirty minutes to play.
7. John will give the award.

B. Read this thesaurus entry for *take*. Write a sentence for each synonym. **take** (verb) nab, receive, grab, capture, steal, gather

Revising Checklist
✔ Have I included all the features of descriptive writing?
✔ Can I combine subjects and predicates to make new sentences? (p. 32)
✔ Can I vary my sentence beginnings? (p. 198)
✔ Where can I use a thesaurus to make my language more descriptive?

Revise Your First Draft for Style

Check your descriptive paragraph for items on the Revising Checklist. You can use the thesaurus on page 357 for help finding interesting words. Mark corrections on your draft. Save your work.

Using Apostrophes

Wendy noticed that she forgot to use apostrophes in her paragraph. She knew that both possessives and contractions are written with apostrophes. Remember, a possessive is a word that tells who or what has something. A contraction uses an apostrophe to show where letters have been left out. Here is a chart Wendy found that explained the rules for using apostrophes.

Rule	Example
To make the possessive form of a singular noun, add an apostrophe and s.	friend ⟶ friend's cat ⟶ cat's cup ⟶ cup's
To make the possessive form of most plural nouns, add an apostrophe at the end of the word.	musicians ⟶ musicians' teams ⟶ teams' stores ⟶ stores'
Use an apostrophe to show where letters have been left out in a contraction. Some contractions are formed with the word *not*.	is not ⟶ isn't have not ⟶ haven't had not ⟶ hadn't was not ⟶ wasn't did not ⟶ didn't does not ⟶ doesn't

24 STUDIES IN ALL THE MAJOR AND MINOR KEYS · Flute

Op. 21.

SCHIRMER'S
OF MUSICAL

Vol. 1671

OTTO LUENING

FIFTH SUITE

ANDERSEN

Practice

A. Write each sentence. Write the correct possessive form of the underlined word.

1. My parents travel agency is quite small.
2. My mom uncle sold it to her five years ago.
3. My parents plan all of their customers trips.

B. Write each sentence. Write the correct contraction for the underlined words.

4. I have not been on any long trips yet.
5. At first I did not think that was fair.
6. Since I will not be old enough for a while, my parents decided to take me on their next trip.

Proofreading Marks

- ^ add
- take away
- ¶ indent
- ≡ capitalize
- / small letter
- check spelling
- ∿ transpose

Proofreading Checklist

- Did I indent the first sentence of each paragraph? (p. 34)
- Did I begin each sentence with a capital letter? (p. 34)
- Did I use apostrophes correctly?
- Have I used the correct form of an adjective to compare two or more nouns?

APPLY STEP BY STEP

Proofread Your Description

Check your description for correct punctuation. Use the Proofreading Checklist. Make corrections on your draft. Save your work.

Checking Spelling/Writing a Final Copy

Spelling Strategy

Knowing letter patterns can help you spell many words. Here are some words with an *at* pattern:

bat   cat   fat   hat

Here is Wendy's revised paragraph.

---

isn't
There is not a more special place than my grandparents living room. It always feels warm and ~~cozey~~ *cozy*. I love sitting on the soft. nubby sofa. Grandpa's small brass lamp casts a dim yellow beam. The smell of freshly baked bread comes out from the kitchen. In the corner. the big clock ticks loudly. the pictures that fill the fireplace mantle are like a ~~group~~ *crowd* of old friends. They are just a few more reasons I feel so at home there.

Check Your Spelling

Correct any spelling errors. Add any misspelled words to your spelling log. Then, write a neat, final copy. Be sure to proofread your work and save it for later.

Learning About Poetry

Read the descriptive paragraph and the poem.

In the strange city, it was hard to get to sleep. I could still feel the crowds pushing me through the streets. The light from the skyscrapers poured through the thin curtains. Trucks rumbled by many feet below. I thought of the green fields at home and began to drift off. Then I heard the deep moan of a foghorn in the bay and was up once again.

Foghorns
by Lilian Moore

The foghorns moaned
in the bay last night
so sad
so deep
I thought I heard the city
crying in its sleep.

The poem and the paragraph describe some of the same things. But the poem includes only a few images from the paragraph. The words that tell about these details stand out more clearly in the poem.

Writers have special ways of using sound words in poems. Words that have the same ending sound **rhyme.** Rhyming poems have rhyming words at the ends of lines. The word pairs deep and sleep are in both the poem and the paragraph. However, in this poem they are used at the end of lines. This gives the poem a sound pattern.

Read the rhyming poem below. Notice how the word pairs *by* and *sky* and *it* and *lit* have the same ending sound.

Firefly
by Elizabeth Madox Roberts

A little light is going by,
Is going up to see the sky,
A little light with wings.

I never could have thought it,
To have a little bug all lit
And made to go on wings.

Rhythm is the number of strong beats per line. Clap the strong beats as you read "Firefly" aloud. Notice that each line has four strong beats.

/   /   /   /
A little light is going by

Poets also use **sound words** such as *pop* and *ring* to make a poem fun to read. Sometimes, poets make up these words. Read the poem below. Watch for sound words that have been made up.

Our Washing Machine
by Patricia Hubbell

Our washing machine went whisity whirr
Whisity whisity whirr
One day at noon it went whisity click
Whisity whisity whisity click
Click grr click grr click grr click

Call the repairman
Fix it . . . Quick!

Practice

A. Tell whether each short poem shows *rhyme and rhythm, rhythm without rhyme,* or *sound words.*

1. The moon is not a silver globe.
The sun is not a ball of gold.
The stars are more than burning sparks.
They only look like that from here.

2. The clock clicks.
And ticks and tocks.
Twelve chimes ping.
Today again becomes tomorrow.

3. I love to spin my globe and see
The whole world turn in front of me.
I watch the seas and tiny lands
And hold a planet in my hands.

B. Choose the line that best completes each short poem with the correct rhyme and rhythm.

4. My city seems to grow and grow
With buildings high and buildings low.
This building here is very tall.
   a. When I can reach the top, I shall.
   b. I cannot see the top at all.

5. This park does not have lots of space
Or rides or slides or sights to see.
No, it's a very little place,
   a. But still, it's big enough for me.
   b. Just right for me.

Comparing in Poems

Earlier in this unit, you learned about comparisons. Comparisons are often used in poems.

Zebra
by Judith Thurman

white sun	morning
black	grazing like a zebra
fire escape,	outside my window.

Sunrise
by Frank Asch

| The city YAWNS | Like baking bread |
| And rubs its eyes, | about to rise. |

In the poem "Zebra," morning in a city is being compared to a zebra. The poet paints a picture of white sun coming through the black bars of a fire escape. She compares this picture to a zebra's stripes.

"Sunrise" also describes morning in a city. The poem compares the city to a person waking up and to bread rising.

Notice that while "Zebra" does not use rhyme or rhythm, "Sunrise" uses both. When you write a comparison poem, it is up to you to decide whether to use sound patterns.

290

Practice

A. Tell whether each poem is a comparison.

1. A city is like
a forest of stone
Like living trees,
Its gray buildings
Grow toward the
sun.

2. Red balloons rise
Like happy, round
birds
toward the clouds.

3. Traffic jam—
Car after car,
No room to move.
How loud they are!
Lights all turn red.
Then they turn
green.
Still nothing moves.
Oh, what a scene.

B. Look at each numbered subject below. Write a sentence comparing it to *one* of the lettered items.

4. a train
a. a snake **b.** a dragon **c.** thunder

5. the sun
a. a lamp **b.** a jewel **c.** a lion

Choose Your Topic for a Poem

Reread your paragraph and the cluster map you made for it. Choose a detail that you would like to write a poem about. Or choose a different subject, and make a cluster map for it. Think about what you could compare your subject to. Write down your ideas and save them.

What would I like to write a poem about?

291

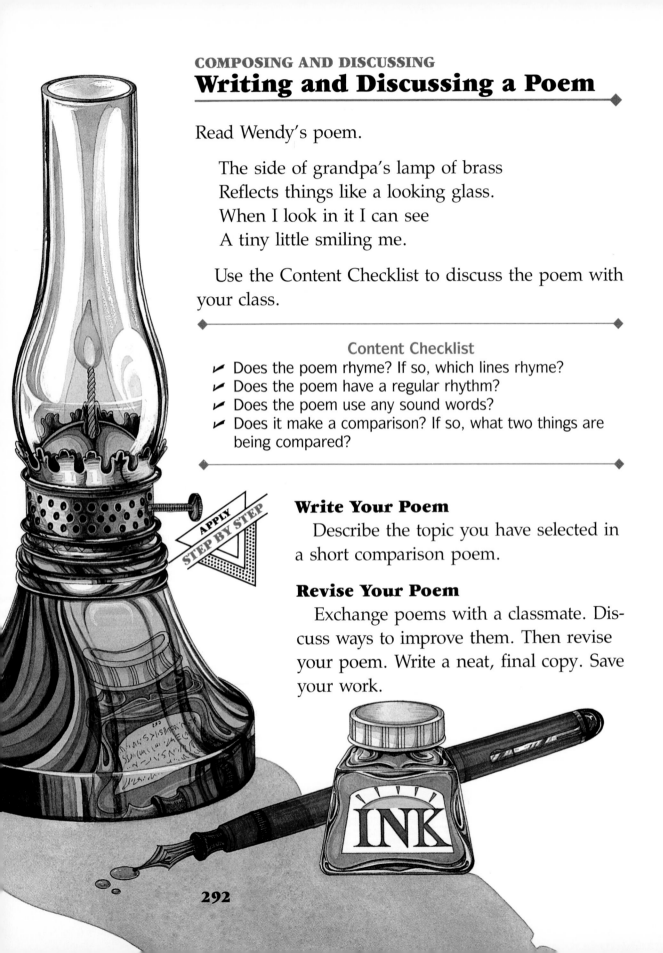

Writing and Discussing a Poem

Read Wendy's poem.

> The side of grandpa's lamp of brass
> Reflects things like a looking glass.
> When I look in it I can see
> A tiny little smiling me.

Use the Content Checklist to discuss the poem with your class.

Content Checklist
- ✔ Does the poem rhyme? If so, which lines rhyme?
- ✔ Does the poem have a regular rhythm?
- ✔ Does the poem use any sound words?
- ✔ Does it make a comparison? If so, what two things are being compared?

APPLY STEP BY STEP

Write Your Poem
Describe the topic you have selected in a short comparison poem.

Revise Your Poem
Exchange poems with a classmate. Discuss ways to improve them. Then revise your poem. Write a neat, final copy. Save your work.

INK

Sharing Your Descriptions

Speaking/Listening Strategy

While reading use your voice to show which words or phrases are most important. If you are in the audience, try to imagine what the speaker describes.

Choosing a Way to Share

Here are ways to share your descriptive writing.

Read Aloud   Read your descriptive writing to your classmates. You might want to add sound effects like tapping or the whoosh of wind blowing to your description.

Make a Place Book   Gather up everyone's poems and paragraphs and make a book of places. Students who enjoy drawing could make pictures for the book. Display your book in the class or school library.

Share Your Descriptive Writing
Choose a way to share your poem and paragraph. Present them to your class.

Add to your Learning Log
- Am I satisfied with my poem and paragraph?
- Which was more fun to write, the poem or the paragraph?
- What would I change about my descriptive poem or paragraph?

The Literature Connection: Adverbs

You do many things every day. You wake and go to school. You run and play. Do you do everything the same way each day? Of course not! You wake early or late. You play inside or outside. You run quickly or slowly.

Words that tell more about an action are called **adverbs.** An adverb helps you describe how, when, or where something is done.

The writer of this poem listened to a shell. Look for the words that tell how he listened.

The Shell
by
David McCord

I took away the ocean once,
Spiraled in a shell,
And happily for months and months
I heard it very well.

How is it then that I should hear
What months and months before
Had blown upon me sad and clear,
Down by the grainy shore?

Discussion

1. Did the poet listen to the shell in a happy or sad way? Name the word in the third line that tells you.
2. Did the poet hear the ocean well or poorly? Name the word in the fourth line that tells you.
3. Imagine you found a shell. What words could tell how you would listen to it?

The Writing Connection: Adverbs

You can use adverbs to make your own writing more exciting. Read this sentence below.

I played.

The sentence doesn't tell you much, does it? Adverbs can tell more about things you do.

I played yesterday.   I played quietly.
I played outdoors.   I played happily.

Can you see the difference? Use adverbs in your writing to paint a clear picture of how things happened.

Activity

Imagine you are at the beach. Write at least three sentences telling about what you are doing. Use a word ending in *ly* in each sentence. Your sentences can tell about these things:

- how the waves move to the shore
- how you run across the sand
- how the wind blows

You can write more sentences telling about what is going on in the picture above.

295

Adverbs Telling *How*

An **adverb** is a word that tells more about an action.

A. Some adverbs tell how an action is done. To find the adverb in a sentence, first find the verb. Then ask a question about the verb that starts with *how*.

> The camel plodded slowly. (How did the camel plod? slowly)
> The wind blew hard. (How did the wind blow? hard)

B. Many adverbs that tell *how* end in the letters *ly*.

brightly	coldly	quickly	rudely
safely	sharply	smoothly	warmly

Adverbs that tell *how* often follow the verb.

> The traveler arrived safely.

Strategy

When you look for the adverb in a sentence, the ending *ly* is a good clue. Be careful, though. Not all adverbs end in *ly*. Be sure to find the verb and ask a question about it starting with *how*.

Check Your Understanding

A. Write the letter of the question that shows you the adverb.
1. The waves rolled steadily.
   a. What rolled?　**b.** How did the waves roll?
2. The ship sailed smoothly.
   a. How did the ship sail?　**b.** What sailed?

B. Write the letter of the adverb.

   3. The young traveler packed rapidly.

      a. young   **b.** traveler   **c.** packed   **d.** rapidly

   4. The sun beamed brightly.

      a. The   **b.** sun   **c.** beamed   **d.** brightly

Practice

A. Write the answer to the question in parentheses.

   5. Marco Polo left eagerly. (How did Polo leave?)

   6. He traveled slowly. (How did he travel?)

   7. Dust rose quietly. (How did dust rise?)

   8. Polo stopped gladly. (How did Polo stop?)

B. Write each sentence. Put two lines under the adverb. The verb is already underlined to help you.

   9. The Chinese emperor spoke warmly.

  10. People stared curiously at Polo.

  11. Polo worked hard for the emperor.

  12. He learned quickly in China.

C. Mixed Practice Write each sentence. Put two lines under the adverb. The verb is already underlined.

  13. Chinese clerks wrote beautifully.

  14. Fireworks exploded brilliantly.

  15. Polo watched cheerfully.

  16. He returned wearily to Italy.

  17. Friends laughed loudly at his stories.

  18. Polo unpacked carefully.

  19. Suddenly jewels sparkled richly.

  20. People finally believed Polo's adventures.

Apply: Learning Log

In your learning log, tell the hardest part of this lesson. Write a plan for learning it.

Adverbs Telling *Where* or *When*

A. An adverb can tell *where* an action is done.

down	here	in	inside
out	outside	there	up

Hopis lived here. (Where did Hopis live? here)

B. An adverb can also tell *when* an action is done.

always	early	late	now		once
soon	then	today	tomorrow		yesterday

Hopis hunted then. (When did Hopis hunt? then)

An adverb may come at the beginning or the end of a sentence.

Today we read about the Hopi Indians.
We read about the Hopi Indians today.

Strategy

To find an adverb in a sentence, first look for the verb. Then ask *when?*, *where?*, or *how?* about the verb.

It's easy to find the adverb when you ask the right question!

Check Your Understanding

A. Write the letter of the question that shows you the adverb.

1. Weavers worked outside.
   a. How did weavers work? **b.** Where did weavers work?
2. She put the mat down.
   a. How did she put the mat down? **b.** Where did she put the mat?

B. Use the directions for Check Your Understanding A.

   3. The Hopis once built mud huts.

   a. Where did the Hopis build mud huts?

   b. When did the Hopis build mud huts?

   4. We visit the village now.

   a. Where do we visit?

   b. When do we visit?

Practice

A. Write the answer to the question in parentheses.

   5. Farmers work outside. (Where do farmers work?)

   6. They plant here. (Where do they plant?)

   7. Crops grow there. (Where do crops grow?)

B. Use the directions for Practice A.

   8. Hunters wake early. (When do hunters wake?)

   9. They always hide. (When do they hide?)

   10. They return late. (When do they return?)

C. Mixed Practice Write each sentence. Put two lines under the adverb. The verb is already underlined.

   11. Hopis <u>came</u> to the desert once.

   12. They <u>built</u> many houses then.

   13. Ladders <u>stood</u> outside.

   14. In times of danger, Hopis <u>climbed</u> up.

   15. All the villagers <u>came</u> in.

   16. Hopi leaders <u>talked</u> inside.

   17. Hopis often <u>met</u> there.

   18. Today Hopi children <u>go</u> to school nearby.

Apply: Test a Partner

   On a sheet of paper, write three adverbs that tell *where* and three adverbs that tell *when*. See if your partner can use each one correctly in a sentence.

Suffixes

A **base word** is a word to which other word parts can be added. A **suffix** is a word part that is added to the end of a base word.

A. Study the suffixes in the chart below.

Suffix	Meaning	Example
er	a person who	A <u>builder</u> is a person who builds.
or	a person who	A <u>sailor</u> is a person who sails.

B. Adding *er* or *or* changes the meaning of a base word. The new word names a person who does an action or a job.

work → work<u>er</u>   act → act<u>or</u>

If the base word ends in *e*, drop the *e*. Then add *er*.

skate → skat<u>er</u>   drive → driv<u>er</u>

Strategy

There is no rule to tell you whether to add *er* or *or*. To write a word that means a *person who*, remember the spelling. If you can't remember, look up the word in a dictionary.

Check Your Understanding

A. Write the letter of the word that correctly completes each sentence.

1. A ____ came to the fair.   **2.** A ____ put up a tent.

    a. visit   **b.** visitor   **a.** helper   **b.** help

B. Use the directions for Check Your Understanding A.

   3. The ⎯⎯ made a new machine.

       a. invention   **b.** invent   **c.** inventor

   4. That ⎯⎯ won the race.

       a. rider   **b.** ride   **c.** riding

Practice

A. Write each sentence. Put one line under the word with a suffix. Put two lines under the suffix.

   5. Our teacher told us about county fairs.

   6. Each farmer came to town.

   7. Every marcher walked in a grand parade.

   8. The leader carried a flag.

B. Write each sentence. Complete it by writing the meaning of the underlined word.

   9. A painter is a person who ⎯⎯.

   10. An actor is a person who ⎯⎯.

   11. A dreamer is a person who ⎯⎯.

   12. A helper is a person who ⎯⎯.

C. Mixed Practice Write each sentence. Underline each word with a suffix, and tell what it means.

   13. The town baker made dozens of pies.

   14. A speaker gave a long speech.

   15. A singer sang the Star Spangled Banner.

   16. A player started a baseball game.

   17. The pitcher threw the ball.

   18. The batter drove in a runner.

   19. The editor printed a story for the readers.

Apply: Exploring Language

Think of people who do jobs. How many words that describe these jobs end in *er* or *or*? Use five of them in sentences.

LANGUAGE IN ACTION

A Group Discussion

Your class wants to take a trip. You have a group discussion to decide where to go. What should you do?

Group discussions help people share ideas and solve problems. Here are some tips for group discussions.

- Be prepared. Plan what you want to say.
- Listen to what other people say. Consider their opinions.
- Be brief. Say what you want to say simply and quickly.
- Don't interrupt. Wait your turn to speak. If you think you'll forget what you wanted to say, write it down.
- Stick to the topic. You may want to talk about something besides the subject. It may be funny and interesting. Save it until the discussion is over.
- You may disagree with someone. Say so politely and pleasantly. Never raise your voice.

Practice

On a separate sheet of paper, answer the following questions.

1. What do you do when other people are speaking?
2. You disagree with someone. How should you say that you disagree?
3. How should you say what you want to say?
4. What do you do before the discussion begins?

Apply

Have a group discussion in your class. Ask your teacher to suggest a topic and to pick a discussion leader.

HISTORY OF LANGUAGE

British and American Spelling

Did you ever read a book from England, such as *Chitty Chitty Bang Bang*? If you did, maybe you noticed that some words were spelled "wrong."

The language we write and speak in America is American English. The language written and spoken in England is British English. The two are not exactly the same. One difference is how some words are spelled.

In British English, the word for the edge of the sidewalk is spelled *kerb*. In American English, we spell the same word *curb*. Both *kerb* and *curb* are pronounced the same. They both mean the same thing, too. Only the spelling is different.

Here are some words that are spelled differently in the two kinds of English.

British English	American English
colour	color
plough	plow
realise	realize

Activity

Rewrite this chart. Write the American spelling for each British English word. You can use a dictionary.

British spelling	American spelling
aeroplane	
draught	
flavour	
humour	
theatre	

UNIT REVIEW

Descriptive Writing *(page 269)*
1. On your paper, list three features of descriptive writing.

Using Comparisons *(pages 278-279)*
Make a comparison to finish each sentence. Write the sentence.
2. This flower feels as soft as ____.
3. The strong wind is like ____.
4. The sudden thunder sounded like ____.

Using Apostrophes *(pages 284-285)*
Write each sentence. Use the possessive form of the underlined word.
5. My school pet show was unusually exciting.
6. Many dogs leashes got tangled together.
7. My friend parrot would not keep quiet.

Learning About Poetry *(pages 287-291)*
Choose the line whose rhyme and rhythm best complete each short poem.
8. Bright green bird with yellow beak,
    This is Anna's brand new pet.
    Anna says that it can speak,
    a. But not yet.
    b. But I have not heard it yet.
9. Apples grown,
    Being thrown,
    Careless toss —
    a. Applesauce!
    b. Now the apples are applesauce!

Adverbs Telling *How*   (*pages 296-297*)

Write each sentence. Put two lines under the adverb that tells *how*. The verb is already underlined.

10. The day darkens gradually.

11. Snow falls softly.

12. The sled dogs run fast.

13. The driver shouts loudly.

14. The sled sinks rapidly into the snow.

15. A cold wind blows steadily.

16. Harness bells ring merrily.

17. The dogs pant eagerly.

Adverbs Telling *Where* or *When*   (*pages 298-299*)

Write each sentence. Put two lines under the adverb that tells *where* or *when*. The verb is already underlined.

18. The dog team wakes early.

19. The big dogs eat outside.

20. The driver hitches the dogs here.

21. Yesterday they traveled 30 miles.

22. The dogs finally finish the race.

23. The dogs always bark at wolves.

24. A river flows nearby.

25. The large dogs drink there.

Suffixes   (*pages 300-301*)

Write each sentence. Underline each word with a suffix. Then write the meaning of the word.

26. The driver shouts to the dogs.

27. A hunter rides the sled.

28. A builder puts up a log cabin.

29. A sailor lives in the cabin.

30. The governor meets with officials.

31. A director makes a movie about the book.

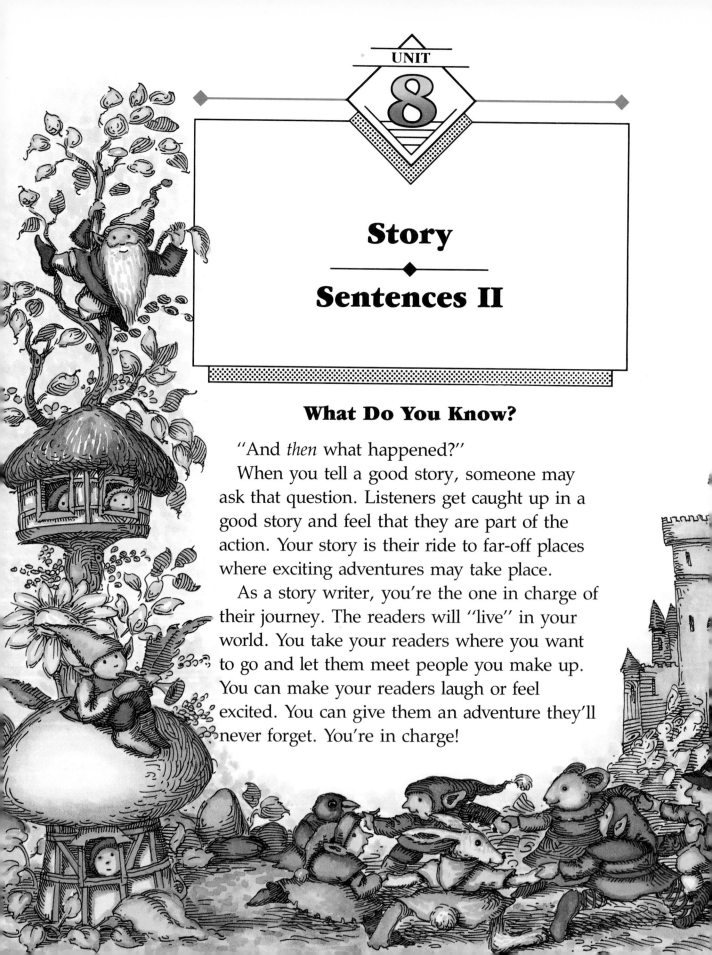

Story

Sentences II

What Do You Know?

"And *then* what happened?"

When you tell a good story, someone may ask that question. Listeners get caught up in a good story and feel that they are part of the action. Your story is their ride to far-off places where exciting adventures may take place.

As a story writer, you're the one in charge of their journey. The readers will "live" in your world. You take your readers where you want to go and let them meet people you make up. You can make your readers laugh or feel excited. You can give them an adventure they'll never forget. You're in charge!

Thinking About Stories

What Is a Story?

A **story** has these features:

- It has **characters,** people or animals in the story.
- It has a **setting,** the time and place of the story.
- It has a **plot,** the events that happen in the story.
- The **introduction** tells the setting and characters.
- The **solution attempts** are ways in which the characters try to solve the problem.
- The **outcome** tells how the problem is solved.

Stories are part of our everyday life. We tell stories to our classmates and see stories acted out in plays and on TV. We read stories in books and magazines. In stories we learn how characters in other places solve their problems. Indeed, stories are a great way to explore new places and meet new people without ever leaving your chair!

Discussion

1. What kind of story do you like best?
2. What interesting places have you read about recently?
3. What character do you like best in the stories you've read lately?

Reading a Story

The following story, "Yagua Days" by Cruz Martel, is about a New York boy who visits his parents' homeland of Puerto Rico. There he learns what yagua days are. Pay close attention to the different settings in the story. Notice, too, the main character and other characters.

Yagua Days
by Cruz Martel

The setting is described here.

It was drizzling steadily on the Lower East Side. From the doorway of his parents' *bodega*, Adan Riera watched a car splash the sidewalk.

School had ended for the summer two days ago, and for two days it had rained. Adan wanted to play in East River Park, but with so much rain about the only thing a boy could do was watch cars splash by.

The characters are introduced.

Of course he could help father. Adan enjoyed working in the bodega. He liked the smells of the fruits and the different colors of the vegetables, and he liked the way the mangos and *quenepas* felt in his hands.

But today he would rather be in the park. He watched another car spray past. The rain began to fall harder.

Mailman Jorge *sloshed* in, slapping water off his hat. He smiled. "*Qué pasa*, Adan? Why the long face?"

"Rainy days are terrible days."

"No—they're wonderful days. They're *yagua* days!"

"Stop teasing, Jorge. Yesterday you told me the vegetables and fruits in the bodega are grown in panel trucks. What's a yagua day?"

"*Muchacho, this* day is a yagua day. And Puerto Rican vegetables and fruits *are* grown in trucks. Why, I have a truck myself. Every day I water it!"

Adan's mother and father came in from the back.

"*Hola*, Jorge. You look wet."

"I *feel* wetter. But it's a wonderful feeling. It's a yagua-day feeling!"

His mother and father liked Jorge. They had all grown up together in Puerto Rico.

"So you've been telling Adan about yagua days?"

"*Sí. Mira*! Here's a letter for you from *Corral Viejo*, where we all had some of the best yagua days."

Adan's father read the letter. "Good news! My brother Ulise wants *Mami*, Adan, and me to visit him on his *finca* for two weeks."

"You haven't been to Puerto Rico in years," said Mailman Jorge.

"Adan's *never* been there," replied his mother. "We can ask my brother to take care of the bodega. Adan will meet his family in the mountains at last."

Adan clapped his hands. "Puerto Rico! Who cares about the rain!"

Mailman Jorge smiled. "Maybe you'll even have a few yagua days. *Hasta luego. Y que gocen mucho!*"

Tío Ulise met them at the airport in *Ponce*. "Welcome to Puerto Rico, Adan."

Stocky Uncle Ulise had tiny blue eyes in a round, red face, and big, strong arms, but Adan, excited after his first plane ride, hugged Uncle Ulise even harder than Uncle Ulise hugged him.

"Come, we'll drive to Corral Viejo." He winked at Adan's father. I'm sorry you didn't arrive yesterday. Yesterday was a wonderful yagua day."

"You know about yagua days too, Tío Ulise?"

"Sure. They're my favorite days."

"But wouldn't today be a good yagua day?"

"The worst. The sun's out!"

In an old jeep, they wound up into the mountains.

"Look!" said Uncle Ulise, pointing at a river jumping rocks. "Your mother and father,

310

Mailman Jorge, and I played in that river when we were children."

They bounced up a hill to a cluster of bright houses. Many people were outside.

"This is your family, Adan," said Uncle Ulise.

Everyone crowded around the jeep. Old and young people. Blond-, brown-, and black-haired people. Dark-skinned and light-skinned people. Blue-eyed, brown-eyed, and green-eyed people. Adan had not known there were so many people in his family.

Uncle Ulise's wife Carmen hugged Adan and kissed both his cheeks. Taller than Uncle Ulise and very thin, she carried herself like a soldier. Her straight mouth never smiled—but her eyes did.

The whole family sat under wide trees and ate rice, roast pork, and avocado and tomato salad.

311

Adan talked and sang until his voice turned to a squeak. He ate until his stomach almost popped a pants button.

Afterward he fell asleep under a big mosquito net before the sun had gone down behind the mountains.

In the morning Uncle Ulise called out, "Adan, everyone ate all the food in the house. Let's get more."

"From a bodega?"

"No, *mi amor*. From my finca on the mountain."

"You drive a tractor and plow on the mountain?"

Tía Carmen smiled with her eyes. "We don't need tractors and plows on our finca."

"I don't understand."

"*Vente*. You will."

Adan and his parents, Aunt Carmen, and Uncle Ulise hiked up the mountain beside a splashy stream.

Near the top they walked through groves of fruit trees.

"Long ago your grandfather planted these trees," Adan's mother said. "Now Aunt Carmen and Uncle Ulise pick what they need for themselves or want to give away or sell in Ponce."

"Let's work!" said Aunt Carmen.

Sitting on his father's shoulders, Adan picked oranges. Swinging a hooked stick, he pulled down mangos. Finally, gripping a very long pole, he struck down coconuts.

"How do we get all the food down the mountain?" he asked.

"Watch," said Aunt Carmen. She whistled loudly.

Adan saw a patch of white moving in the trees. A horse with a golden mane appeared.

Uncle Ulise fed him a *guanábana*. The horse twitched his ears and munched loudly.

"Palomo will help us carry all the fruit and vegetables we've picked," Adan's mother said.

Back at the house, Adan gave Palomo another guanábana.

"He'll go back up to the finca now," his father said. "He's got all he wants to eat there."

Uncle Ulise rubbed his knee.

"*Que te pasa?*" asked Adan's mother.

"My knee. It always hurts just before rain comes."

Adan looked at the cloudless sky. "But it's not going to rain."

"Yes, it will. My knee never lies. It'll rain tonight. Maybe tomorrow. Say! When it does, it will be a yagua day!"

In the morning Adan, waking up cozy under his mosquito net, heard banging on the metal roof and *coquies* beeping tiny car horns.

He jumped out of bed and got a big surprise. His mother and father, Uncle Ulise, and Aunt Carmen were on the porch wearing bathing suits.

"*Vámonos*, Adan," his father said. "It's a wonderful yagua day. Put on your bathing suit!"

In the forest he heard shouts and swishing noises in the rain.

Racing into a clearing, he saw boys and girls shooting down a runway of grass, then disappearing over a rock ledge.

Uncle Ulise picked up a canoelike object from the grass. "This is a yagua, Adan. It fell from this palm tree."

"And this is what we do with it," said his father. He ran, then belly-flopped on the yagua. He skimmed down the grass, sailed up into the air, and vanished over the ledge. His mother found another yagua and did the same.

"*Papi!* Mami!"

Uncle Ulise laughed. "Don't worry, Adan. They won't hurt themselves. The river is down there. It pools beneath the ledge. The rain turns the grass butter-slick so you can zip into the water. That's what makes it a yagua day! Come and join us!"

That day Adan found out what fun a yagua day is!

Two weeks later Adan lifted a box of mangos off the panel truck back in New York.

"Hola, muchacho! Welcome home! "

Adan smiled at Mailman Jorge. "You look sad, *compadre*."

"Too much mail! Too much sun!"

"What you need is a yagua day."

"So you know what a yagua day is?"

"I had six yagua days in Puerto Rico."

"You went over the ledge?"

"Of course."

"Into the river?"

"Sí! Sí! Into the river. Sliding on yaguas!"

"Two-wheeled or four-wheeled yaguas?"

Adan laughed. "Yaguas don't have wheels. They come from palm trees."

"I thought they came from panel trucks like mine."

"Nothing grows in trucks, Jorge. These mangos and oranges come from trees. Compadre, wake up. Don't *you* know?"

Mailman Jorge laughed. "Come, *campesino*, let's talk with your parents. I want to hear all about your visit to Corral Viejo!"

Understanding What You've Read

Write the answers to these question.

1. What time of year does the story take place?
2. Where is the opening setting?
3. What do you think Adan thinks of Puerto Rico?
4. What might Adan think of when it rains at home?
5. If you were Adan, how would you feel when you met all those members of your family in Puerto Rico?

Writing Assignment

Suppose your town library is having a Story Hour. The theme is "Other Places." You are going to write a story and read it at the story hour. In this unit, you will learn to write a story. You will also see how another student, Ming, develops her story.

Your **audience** for your story will be your classmates. Your **purpose** will be to entertain and interest your readers.

Choose an Event

Think about an event that might make a good story. It may be based on a real experience or it could be made up. It should include a problem that a person could overcome. For example, you might write about fighting with a friend or losing something that meant a lot to you. Jot down some notes about the plot, characters, and setting of this event. Save your work for the next lesson.

Writing a Character Sketch

Every story has characters. They are the people and animals whom the story tells about. Interesting characters make a story more fun to read.

Making up characters takes careful planning. You should answer these questions about each important character in the story:

Is the character male or female?
What is the character's name?
How old is the character?
What does the character do?

Also, you must know what each character is like. Is the person shy? Knowing about your characters will make writing easier.

To get to know your character, it's helpful to prepare a *character sketch*—a list of notes describing the person. A character sketch tells what the character is like. It can also tell the character's interests—his or her likes and dislikes. Here is a character sketch Ming wrote for the main character in her story.

> — girl named Mona
> — twelve years old
> — active and curious
> — likes adventures
> — values her friends

Practice

A. Answer these questions about the character sketch that Ming wrote.

   1. What is the name of the character?
   2. How old is the person?
   3. What kind of friend is she?
   4. What is she like?
   5. What other details could you add to the sketch to make the character even more interesting?

B. The character sketch below is for an imaginary character. Copy the sketch on your paper. Fill in notes to complete the sketch. Make the character as interesting as possible.

boy named _____
_____ years old
favorite subject in school is _____
very good at _____
often goes to _____

Write a Character Sketch

Think about who the most important characters in your story are. Prepare a character sketch for at least two characters. Include details that tell who the character is and what the character is like. Save your sketches for the next lesson.

Who are my characters? What are they like?

Planning the Parts of a Story

Knowing your characters is very important in writing a story. However, you must also figure out your setting and plot.

The **setting** is the time and place of your story. The events that happen are the plot. The plot has four parts. In the *introduction*, the main characters and setting are told. Later, one or more characters face a *problem* that comes up. The *solution attempts* are the ways the characters try to solve their problem. The final part of the story, or *outcome*, tells how the story ends.

Ming made a chart of her story like the one below.

Characters:	Mona, Dar the Dragon, Homer the Knight		
Setting:	outside the dragon's cave in a fairy tale		
Plot:			
Introduction	**Problem**	**Solution Attempts**	**Outcome**
Mona dreams that she is part or a fairy tale to help Homer fight Dar the dragon.	She learns that the dragon is nice and the knight is mean.	Mona helps the dragon chase away the knight.	Mona helps Dar chase away the knight.

Practice

A. Answer these questions about Ming's chart.
1. What is the setting in the story?
2. Who are the other characters besides Mona?
3. What problem does Mona face in the story?
4. Why do you think Mona helps Dar?
5. What other outcome can you think of that would have solved the problem?

B. The chart below is for an imaginary story. Copy the chart. Fill in the missing parts with details that will make the story interesting.

Characters:	Ernie Pickens and _____		
Setting:	a toy factory after closing		
Plot:			
Introduction	**Problem**	**Solution Attempts**	**Outcome**
Ernie has gotten lost in the toy factory while on a school tour.	Ernie can't find his way out, and he's getting very scared by the unfinished toys.	Ernie finds _____ in a hidden work room. This person helps Ernie by _____.	Ernie finds his way out and decides _____.

Plan the Parts of Your Story

Decide on the setting and plot for your story. Make a chart that lists each part. Include the introduction, problem, solution attempts, and outcome of the plot. Save your chart for the next lesson.

Writing a First Draft

Read the first draft of Ming's story. She wasn't worried about making it perfect. It will be changed later.

Mona always wished that she could be in her favorite fairy tale. Then, she got her wish. Mona was in the story, "The Dragon's Last Laugh." She knew the story well. The story's hero was Homer, the brave knight. Mona was always thrilled by the way Homer beat Dar, the mean dragon. Now, Mona was next to Homer. They were in front of the dragon's cave.

Homer looked at Mona and frowned. it's you, he said. "Can't you leave us alone?" Then he said, "You can stand there. You can sit. Just don't be a pest

Dar the dragon peaked out of the cave. He saw Mona and smiled. "I've wantted to meet you for so long," he said happily Then he sighed. "You can watch Homer beat me again Homer laughed meanly.

Mona knew what she had to do. She picked up a sword. She helped Dar chase away homer. Mona was glad to be Dar's friend.

Write Your First draft

Use the character sketches and the story chart you made to help you write your story. Begin with the introduction. Then describe the problem, solution attempts, and the outcome.

Discussing a First Draft

One way to improve your first draft is to discuss it with a classmate.

Discussion Strategy

Before you begin the discussion, make sure you have read carefully what is being discussed. For example, if you were talking about a short story, read the story at least two times before you start talking about it.

Use the Content Checklist to discuss Ming's story with your class.

Content Checklist
- ✔ Are the characters described well?
- ✔ Is the setting stated in the story?
- ✔ Does the plot have an introduction, problem, solution attempts, and an outcome?

Revise Your First Draft for Content

To the Reader: Exchange stories with a classmate. Read your partner's story. Look for the characters and setting. Pay close attention to the parts of the plot. Discuss ways to make the characters more interesting or the problem and outcome better. Use Content Checklist and Discussion Strategy for help.

To the Writer: Listen to your partner's comments. Then revise your draft for content. Save your work.

Combining Sentences for Style
◆

Sometimes the ideas in two sentences go together. You can use the words *and*, *or*, and *but* to join the two sentences. Put a comma *before* these words when joining two complete thoughts.

Use the word *and* to add one idea to another.
I jumped high. I ran fast.
I jumped high, <u>and</u> I ran fast.
Use the word *but* to show contrast.
I look weak. I am strong.
I look weak, <u>but</u> I am strong.
Use the word *or* to show choice.
You may have an apple. You may have a pear.
You may have an apple, <u>or</u> you may have a pear.

Here is how Ming combined sentences.

Homer looked at Mona and frowned. it's you. he said. Can't you leave us alone?" Then he said. "You can stand there, or You can sit. Just don't be a pest

Dar the dragon peaked out of the cave. He saw Mona and smiled. "I've wantted to meet you for so long." he said happily Then he sighed. "You can watch Homer beat me again Homer laughed meanly.

Mona knew what she had to do. She picked up a sword, and She helped chase away homer Mona was glad to be Dar's friend.

Practice

A. Read each pair of sentences. Use the word in parentheses to join them. Then write the new sentence. Be sure to use a comma.

   1. My plane took off late. My plane landed on time. (but)

   2. You can take a bus. You can ride a train. (or)

   3. The restaurant is downstairs. The rooms are upstairs. (and)

B. Use *and*, *or*, or *but* to join the sentences. Then write the new sentence.

   4. I tried to get a hotel room. The hotel was full.

   5. You can stay in a room. You can rent a cabin.

   6. I went to the clerk. I paid the bill.

◆━━━━━━━━━━━━━━━━━━━━━━━━━━━━━◆

Revising Checklist
✔ Have I included all of the features of a story?
✔ Can I combine sentences with the same subjects or predicates to make new sentences? (p. 32)
✔ Have I used exact language? (p. 70)
✔ Can I add descriptive language? (p. 120)
✔ Can I add information to make my work complete? (p. 156)
✔ Can I vary my sentence beginnings? (p. 198)
✔ Where can I combine sentences using *and*, *or*, or *but*?

◆━━━━━━━━━━━━━━━━━━━━━━━━━━━━━◆

Revise Your First Draft For Style
Check the items on the revising checklist. Mark your changes on the draft. Save your work.

Using Quotations

Ming wanted to make sure she punctuated her quotations correctly. She found a chart that explained the rules for using quotation marks. Here is the chart she found:

Rule	Example
Use quotation marks (") to show the exact words spoken by the speaker.	"Hurray for Hollywood!" cried the star as he stepped into the wet cement.
Use a comma to separate the quotation from the rest of the sentence.	Cynthia rubbed her eyes and said, "I'm going to bed now."
Begin the quotation with a capital letter.	Mrs. Horvath drew a strange creature on the blackboard and said, "Who would like to name this little guy?"
Put the end punctuation of the quotation inside the quotation marks when the quote is at the end of the sentence.	Maria sneezed and said, "I hate having a summer cold!"

Practice

Rewrite the sentences below on another piece of paper using the correct punctuation.

(1)My sister told me that our attic is an amazing place (2)in it are clues to what Mom and Dad were like when they were young" she said. (3)When i looked, I discovered tap shoes, old comic books, and some dusty photographs of them in high school.

(4)Oh yes, I was an artist once" my mom said when I found a stack of paintings up there. (5)"and did you know your dad was a musician" (6)Sure enough, when I looked, there was an old trombone with my dad's name scratched on it

Proofreading Checklist

- Did I indent the first sentence of each paragraph? (p. 34)
- Did I begin each sentence with a capital letter? (p. 34)
- Did I put the correct end mark at the end of each sentence? (p. 34)
- Did I use commas correctly? (p. 72)
- Did I capitalize proper nouns, initials, and titles? (p. 238)
- Did I use apostrophes correctly? (p. 284)
- Did I use quotation marks correctly?
- Did I use adverbs to tell *where* and *when* about an action?

Proofreading Marks	
∧	add
⌁	take away
¶	indent
≡	capitalize
/	small letter
⬯	check spelling
∿	transpose

Proofread Your Story

Use the proofreading checklist to help you check for punctuation and capitalization. Make corrections on your draft. Save your work.

Checking Spelling/Writing a Final Copy

Spelling Strategy

Many words can be broken into parts. Knowing word parts can help you spell entire words.

These words start with the word part *re*

reheat, rewrite, repaint

What other words with this word part can you spell?
Here is part of Ming's revised and proofread story.

> Homer looked at Mona and frowned. "it's you," he said. "Can't you leave us alone?"
> Then he said. "You can stand there. You can sit. Just don't be a pest."
>   Dar the dragon ~~peaked~~ peeked out of the cave. He saw Mona and smiled. "I've ~~wantted~~ wanted to meet you for so long," he said happily. Then he sighed. "You can watch Homer beat me again."
> Homer laughed meanly.
>   Mona knew what she had to do. She picked up a sword, and She helped chase away homer.
> Mona was glad to be Dar's friend.

Check Your Spelling

Use the proofreading marks to correct spelling mistakes. Then write a neat, final copy of your story. Save your work.

Sharing Your Story

Speaking/Listening Strategy

As a speaker, use your voice to create excitement. Show feeling when reading the high point of your story. If you are in the audience, listen for words that will help you picture what is being read.

Choosing a Way to Share

Here are some ways to share your story with others.

Presenting a Play   Have students perform your story. As you read aloud, have classmates act out the events that you are describing. Let them read any parts where the characters actually speak.

Making a Story Book   Design a book cover for your story and staple it to your work. Place all the stories together in a box or folder titled *Kids' Classics*.

Share Your Story

Choose a way to share your story.

Add to Your Learning Log

- Am I proud of this story? Explain.
- What part of doing this story was the most fun?
- If I could write my story over, what things might I change?

The Literature Connection: Sentences

Poems and stories are special kinds of writing. They may tell about people and places of today or of long ago. Sometimes they tell what makes people happy or sad. Writers use many kinds of sentences to tell about their feelings. Some sentences are long, and others may be short. The sentences work together to express what the writer imagined.

The poem below tells how the poet feels about mud. Does the poem make you feel the same way, too?

Mud
by
Polly Chase Boyden

Mud is very nice to feel
All squishy-squash between the toes!
I'd rather wade in wiggly mud
Than smell a yellow rose.

Nobody else but the rosebush knows
How nice mud feels
Between the toes.

Discussion

1. Does mud make the writer feel good or bad? Tell what sentences in the poem show this.
2. You won't find the word "squishy-squash" in a dictionary. Even so, you probably know what it means. What kind of picture forms in your mind when you read the word?
3. What other things, besides mud, may make people feel good?

The Writing Connection: Sentences

When you write, you can tell about your feelings. You can tell what makes you happy and sad. The sentences you write let readers know more about you.

Read these sentences.

I am happy when I read a new book.
I am happy when I play after school.

I am sad when I have to take a bath.
I am sad when it rains all afternoon.

Activity

Think of things that make you happy. You can look at the picture to get ideas.

- Write sentences that tell what makes you happy. Your sentences should begin like the one below.
  I am happy when ____.
- Then write sentences that tell what makes you sad. Your sentences should begin like this one.
  I am sad when ____.
- Share your sentences with others in your class. Learn what makes your classmates happy and sad.

Nouns in Sentences

A. You have already learned that a sentence has a complete subject.

The **complete subject** tells whom or what the sentence is about.

The complete subject can have one word or several words. The complete subject is shown in red.

> Most Chinese people work on farms.

B. You have learned that a noun is a word that names a person, place, or thing. The main word in the subject part of a sentence is often a noun.

> The world's highest mountain is in China.

Sometimes the complete subject is only one noun.

> Farmers work many hours each day.

Strategy

The complete subject is usually found in the first part of a sentence. The noun may not be the first word.

Check Your Understanding

A. Write the letter of the complete subject.
   1. Farmers build houses from bricks or mud.
      a. Farmers   **b.** build house   **c.** from bricks
   2. Many Chinese people live in cities.
      a. Chinese   **b.** cities   **c.** Many Chinese people

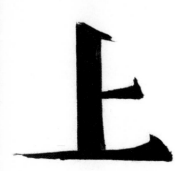

B. Write the letter of the noun in the subject part of the sentence. The complete subject is underlined.

    3. <u>Powerful families</u> once ruled China.
        a. Powerful   **b.** families
    4. <u>Many fine artists</u> painted pictures.
        a. Many   **b.** artists

Practice

A. Write each sentence. Circle the complete subject.

    5. Families grow their own food.
    6. All the children help on the farm.
    7. Rice is a main crop.

B. Write each sentence. Draw two lines under the noun in the subject. The complete subject is underlined.

    8. <u>People</u> grow rice in the south.
    9. <u>Wheat</u> grows in the north.
   10. <u>Chinese cooks</u> use bits of meat.

C. Mixed Practice Write each sentence. Put one line under the complete subject. Put two lines under the noun in the subject.

   11. Volleyball is also a popular sport.
   12. Little children dress in bright clothes.
   13. Adults wear dark clothes.
   14. Many people work in factories.
   15. Some large factories make steel.
   16. Both men and women work in factories.
   17. Has your mother visited China?

Apply: Learning Log

In your learning log, tell what was most difficult about this lesson. What can you do to learn it?

Verbs in Sentences

A. You have learned that a sentence has a complete subject and a complete predicate.

The **complete predicate** tells what the subject of the sentence is or what it does.

The complete predicate can be one word or a group of words. The complete predicate is shown in blue.

The Nile River flowed.

It flooded the fields every year.

B. You know that a verb is a word that tells what the subject part of the sentence is or does. The main word in the complete predicate is the verb. The verb can be an action verb or a form of the verb *be*.

Many small boats sailed on the Nile.

The Nile is a mighty river.

Strategy

To find the complete predicate, look for the complete subject. The complete predicate usually follows. The verb is often the first word in the complete predicate. Sometimes the complete predicate is only the verb.

Check Your Understanding

A. Write the letter of the complete predicate.
  1. A hot wind blew.
   a. wind   **b.** wind blew   **c.** blew
  2. Sand covered old statues.
   a. Sand   **b.** covered   **c.** covered old statues

B. Write the letter of the verb in each predicate. The complete predicate is already underlined.

3. Egypt <u>is a dry land.</u> **a.** Egypt **b.** is **c.** dry
4. Rain <u>falls in the desert.</u> **a.** rain **b.** falls **c.** desert

Practice

A. Write each sentence. Put one line under the complete predicate.

5. The Nile River flooded.
6. It brought water for crops.
7. Ditches carried water to the fields.

B. Write each sentence. Draw two lines under the verb. The complete predicate is already underlined.

8. Powerful kings <u>built great palaces.</u>
9. Thousands of people <u>worked.</u>
10. They <u>dragged huge blocks of stone.</u>

C. Mixed Practice Write each sentence. Draw one line under the complete predicate. Draw two lines under the verb.

11. Egyptians wrote with pictures.
12. Some Egyptian books are in museums.
13. Egyptians studied the stars.
14. They made a very good calendar.
15. Egyptians used many medicines.
16. Egyptian rulers fought and traded.
17. Many students have read about the Egyptians.

Apply: Test a Partner

Write five complete subjects. Trade papers with a partner and finish each sentence. Circle the complete predicates. Put a line under the verbs. Check your work.

Compound Sentences

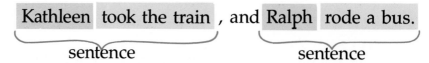

A **compound sentence** is made up of two sentences joined by the word *and*.

A. Read the following compound sentence.

Kathleen took the train , and Ralph rode a bus.

sentence   sentence

Each part has a subject and a predicate and could be a sentence by itself. Both parts make a compound sentence.

B. A compound sentence usually joins two ideas that go together. Read the following examples.

Kangaroos hop. Koala bears climb.

These sentences can be joined with a comma (,) and the word *and* to form a compound sentence.

Kangaroos hop , and koala bears climb.

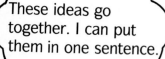

These ideas go together. I can put them in one sentence.

Strategy

It's easy to recognize a compound sentence. Look for two separate sentences joined by a comma and the word *and*. Does each part have a subject and predicate? If it does, it is a compound sentence.

Check Your Understanding

A. Write the letter that names each sentence.

1. Daniella and Laura visit different places.

    a. compound   **b.** not compound

2. She lives in Peru, and we live in Ireland.

    a. compound   **b.** not compound

B. Write the letter of the correct compound sentence.

    3. a. Some people swim and others play tennis.

       b. Some people swim, and others play tennis.

    4. a. The sun shines, and a cloud passes.

       b. The sun shines and, a cloud passes.

Practice

A. Write each sentence. Then write whether it is *compound* or *not compound*.

    5. Farms are large, and cities are far apart.

    6. Farmers grow wheat, and ranchers raise sheep.

    7. Many Australians eat lamb for dinner.

B. Join the pairs of sentences with a comma and the word *and* to form compound sentences.

    8. Planes fly to Australia. Ships sail there.

    9. The mountains are cool. The desert is hot.

  10. Bart lives in Sydney. June lives in Perth.

C. Mixed Practice Write each sentence. Write *compound* or *not compound*. If it is compound, underline the two parts from which it is formed.

  11. Ranchers sell wool, and factories make cloth.

  12. Children travel many miles to school.

  13. Students study by mail, and they learn by radio.

  14. Farmers often see kangaroos.

  15. Kangaroos eat plants, and koalas like leaves.

  16. Kangaroos jump high and run fast.

  17. The air is cool and damp, and wind blows.

Apply: Journal

Write two short sentences about three different topics. Join each pair with a comma and the word *and*.

Reviewing Parts of Speech

You have learned about nouns, pronouns, verbs, adjectives, and adverbs. They are called **parts of speech**.

A. Words can name things or tell about actions.

A **noun** is a word that names a person, place, or thing.

Ester flew to California on a plane.

A **pronoun** is a word that takes the place of a noun.

Cesar comes from Haiti. He comes from Haiti.

An **action verb** is a word that tells what someone or something does.

Geraldo drives a truck. The motor roars.

The **verb be** joins the subject of a sentence with words that name or describe it.

Aiko is my sister. I am happy.

B. Adjectives and adverbs describe other words.

An **adjective** is a word that tells more about a noun.

Sarita wore a blue dress. It is a pretty color.

An **adverb** is a word that tells more about an action.

Yesterday Hillary walked quickly.

Strategy

Words in a sentence are like actors in a play. Each one plays a part. To tell what part of speech a word is, use the definitions in this lesson.

Check Your Understanding

A. Write the letter that names the underlined word.
1. They <u>came</u> here. **a.** noun **b.** verb **c.** pronoun
2. <u>We</u> grew crops. **a.** noun **b.** verb **c.** pronoun

B. Use the directions for Check Your Understanding A.
3. They built a <u>tall</u> fort. **a.** adjective **b.** adverb
4. A river ran <u>nearby</u>. **a.** adjective **b.** adverb

Practice

A. Write each sentence. Write the part of speech that names each underlined word.
5. My <u>mother</u> came from the <u>Philippines</u>.
6. <u>She</u> <u>is</u> a doctor.
7. <u>My</u> uncle <u>sent</u> us a letter.

B. Follow the directions for Practice A.
8. Hiroki plays an instrument with <u>five</u> strings.
9. Her fingers move <u>quickly</u>.
10. She played <u>yesterday</u>.

C. Mixed Practice Write each sentence. Write the part of speech that names each underlined word.
11. <u>Asians</u> brought different ways of life.
12. <u>Many</u> Chinese sailed to California.
13. <u>They</u> <u>worked</u> hard.
14. <u>Some</u> Chinese <u>built</u> railroads.
15. <u>Today</u> farmers <u>grow</u> vegetables <u>outside</u>.
16. Yo Yo Ma <u>is</u> a <u>famous</u> <u>musician</u>.

Apply: Work with a Group

Work with your group to make a poster about the parts of speech you learned. Show what each part is.

Homographs

Homographs are words that are spelled alike but have different meanings.

A. Some words have the same spelling but different meanings. They are called homographs. Many homographs sound alike.

> The child's <u>top</u> spins merrily. (*Top* is a toy.)
> I stood on <u>top</u> of a hill. (*Top* is the highest place.)

Some homographs are pronounced differently.

> I <u>close</u> the door. (*Close* means shut.)
> Stand <u>close</u> to me. (*Close* means near.)

B. You can often tell what a homograph means from the way it is used in a sentence.

> A <u>bat</u> flew out of the cave.
> She brought her <u>bat</u> and ball.

In which sentence does *bat* mean a kind of animal? In which one does *bat* mean a wooden club?

Strategy

Homographs can be confusing. If you don't know how to say or spell a homograph, look in a dictionary.

Check Your Understanding

A. Write the letter of the homograph.
1. I saw a movie. We cut the wood with a saw.
   a. saw   **b.** cut   **c.** wood   **d.** with
2. The dogs bark. Peel the bark from the log.
   a. dogs   **b.** peel   **c.** bark   **d.** log

B. Write the letter that tells the meaning of the underlined word.

    3. She put a <u>bow</u> in her hair.

        a. bend from the waist   **b.** a knot with loops

    4. He writes with his <u>left</u> hand.

        a. opposite of right   **b.** went away from

Practice

A. Write the sentences. Underline the homographs.

    5. Wagons roll on wheels. I ate a buttered roll.

    6. Sailors row a boat. Ten trees stood in a row.

    7. I fed a pig in a pen. My pen ran out of ink.

B. Write each sentence. Write the meaning of the
underlined homograph. Use the words in parentheses.

    8. <u>Wind</u> lifts the kite. (roll up; air that moves)

    9. I <u>wind</u> the kite string. (roll up; air that moves)

   10. A <u>duck</u> quacks. (water bird; lower the body)

   11. We <u>duck</u> our heads. (water bird; lower the body)

C. Mixed Practice Write each pair of sentences. Underline the homographs. Write the meaning of each.

   12. He put a ring on his finger. Alarm clocks ring.
(make a bell sound; band of metal)

   13. Leaves turn red in the fall. Then they fall. (drop;
season between summer and winter)

   14. A rock fell. We rock the baby's cradle. (move
from side to side; piece of stone)

   15. Camels live in the desert. Sailors desert the
sinking ship. (region without water; leave)

Apply: Exploring Language

See if you can write three sentences each using a pair
of homographs. What does each homograph mean?

LANGUAGE IN ACTION

Filling Out Forms

Imagine that you want a bicycle license. You must fill out a form. What should you do with it?

Here are some tips to help you fill out forms.

- Write neatly. Use your best handwriting. You might make a mistake. Cross it out neatly. If you make too many mistakes, ask for a new form.
- Answer every question. Some questions might not apply to you. If one doesn't, draw a line through the answer space.
- When finished, read everything over. Make sure your answers are correctly written in the right place.

Practice

On a separate sheet of paper, answer the following questions.

1. How should you write on a form?
2. What should you do if a question doesn't apply to you?
3. What should you do if you make a mistake?
4. What should you do if you make too many mistakes?
5. What should you do when you have finished filling out a form?

Apply

Choose a partner to work with. Make up a form to apply for something you want. Exchange papers and complete your partner's form.

TEST TAKING

Answering Test Questions with Sentences

In some tests, you will be asked to answer the questions with sentences. Here are some ways to help make writing sentence answers easier.

- **Think About the Question** Before you begin to write, think about what you are being asked. It may help to turn the question or direction into a sentence as the beginning of your answer. For example:
  Question: Why is soil important?
  Statement: Soil is important because . . .
- **Write and Check Your Answer** Make sure you stick to the subject. Read the sentence again to see if it answers the question.
- **Write Complete Sentences** Be sure your answer is a complete sentence. Check that each sentence starts with a capital letter and ends with a period.

Practice

Answer the following questions.

1. What can you do if you aren't quite sure what is being asked?
2. Why should you reread your answer after you've written it?
3. What should you check to see if you have written a complete sentence?

Apply

Learning Log Decide what things from this lesson will help you. Write them in your learning log.

UNIT REVIEW

Story   *(page 307)*

1. On your paper, list three features of a story.

Writing a Character Sketch   *(pages 318-319)*

Complete the character sketch below for an imaginary story character. Write the sketch on your paper.

   2. a girl named ___

   3. favorite sport is ___

   4. often goes to ___

Combining Sentences/Using Quotations
(pages 324-327)

Use *and*, *or*, or *but* to join each pair of sentences below. Write each new sentence.

   5. a. I can pitch well.   **b.** I cannot catch well at all.

   6. a. Should I play now?   **b.** Should I play later instead?

   7. a. The game is now over.   **b.** Everyone is leaving.

Write the sentences below. Punctuate quotations correctly.

   8. Kevin said Where are you going?

   9. We are on our way home Emma answered

   10. Kevin smiled and said I'd love a ride home in your car!

Nouns in Sentences   *(pages 332-333)*

Write each sentence. Put one line under the complete subject. Put two lines under the noun in the subject.

   11. People built castles long ago.

   12. Thick walls surrounded the castle.

   13. A deep ditch kept enemies away.

   14. Soldiers in armor entered the castle.

Verbs in Sentences *(pages 334-335)*

Write each sentence. Put one line under the complete predicate.
Put two lines under the verb.

15. The prince climbed toward the castle.

16. Workers walked to the fields.

17. Many villagers worked for the king.

18. They gave him part of their crops.

19. The king protected the people.

Compound Sentences *(pages 336-337)*

Write each sentence. Write *compound* or *not compound*. If it is
compound, underline the two parts from which it is made.

20. Wind once powered ships.

21. The sails filled, and the ropes creaked.

22. The captain shouted, and the crew obeyed.

23. Wind and waves made a loud roar.

24. Sailing ships were slow, and modern ships are fast.

Reviewing Parts of Speech *(pages 338-339)*

Write each sentence. Write the part of speech that names each
underlined word.

25. Planets travel around the sun.

26. Saturn is a planet.

27. We saw Saturn yesterday.

28. It is larger than Mercury.

29. The round moon rose into the sky.

Homographs *(pages 340-341)*

Write each pair of sentences. Underline the homographs. Write
the meaning of each.

30. We have a can of soup. Now we can eat lunch. (are able to;
metal container)

31. She rose from the chair. She watered the rose. (got up; kind
of flower)

32. Turn right at the corner. This is the right address. (opposite
of left; correct)

MAKING ALL THE
CONNECTIONS

You and several classmates will now write as a group a short play. What you have learned about describing characters, setting, and plot will help you in your writing.

You will do the following in your play:

♦ Include characters, setting, and plot
♦ Use conversation called *dialogue* to tell the plot

Reading a Play

Read the following play. The sidenotes tell the features of the play.

The setting tells where the events take place.
Dialogue is what the characters say.

Three friends are eating lunch at school. They talk about their plans for International Day.

MITA: What are you bringing to the fair, Cheryl?

CHERYL: A thumb piano. It's a musical instrument from Africa. What will you bring, Mita?

The characters have a problem to solve.

MITA: Nothing. I'm going to sing a song my mother learned when she was a girl in Peru.

CHERYL: That's a good idea, Mita. Marcos, what are you going to do?

The problem forms the plot of the play.

MARCOS: I don't know. I can't think of anything.

MITA: What are you eating, Marcos?

MARCOS: It's my dessert. In the Philippines, we call it kuchinta. I helped make it.

CHERYL: You could bring that to the fair.

MARCOS: Now I know what to do! Thank you, Cheryl.

The characters solve the problem.

Speaking and Listening

Work in a group. Talk about these questions.

1. In the play you read on page 346, who were the characters?

2. What problem did the characters face and how was the problem solved?

3. What did you learn about the characters and setting from the picture at the top of the page?

4. How do you think each character felt at the end?

Thinking

Brainstorming

Choose one person from your group to take notes. Then talk about these questions. Save your notes.

Organizing

MAKING ALL THE CONNECTIONS

When you are gathering ideas for a play, it is helpful to write down those ideas. Look at the chart below. It shows the ideas that were used in the play about International Day.

Meet with your group. Arrange your notes from brainstorming in a chart like the one below.

Characters: Cheryl, Mita, Marcos			
Setting: School lunchroom			
Plot Introduction	**Problem**	**Solution Attempts**	**Outcome**
Students plan International Day and what they will do.	Marcos can't decide what to bring.	The children discuss what he could do.	Marcos decides to bring kuchinta.

Writing a Play

Imagine that you and your group have been asked to write a play for school. Use the chart of ideas you made to write your play.

1. What special events have taken place at school?
2. Who took part in the event?
3. Where did the event take place?
4. What problems occurred? How were they solved?
5. How did the event turn out?

Planning

• Look at the chart you made as a group. Can you think of any other ideas to add to the chart?

- Talk about where the events will take place.
- Discuss what each character in the play will do.

Composing

- Work with your group to write a short play. Choose one person to write the first draft.
- Decide exactly how to describe the setting.
- Next, decide what each character will say to show the problem and how it is solved.
- Decide on the beginning, middle, and end of your play.

Revising

- With your group read over the play.
- Check that the plot is clear and easy to follow.
- Make sure that each character speaks naturally.
- Does the play have a beginning, middle, and end?

Proofreading

As a group, proofread your play. Choose one student to make the changes on your draft. Answer these questions:

- Is every sentence a complete thought with correct capitalization and punctuation?
- Did you use all nouns and verbs correctly?
- Are all the words spelled correctly?

Presenting

- Choose one group member to write a final copy.
- Read your play aloud to the rest of the class.

CUMULATIVE REVIEW

A. Write the letter of the group of words that is a sentence. (*pages 40-41*)

   1. a. Picks wild flowers.
      b. Yellow blossoms.
      c. Flowers grow tall.

   2. a. Some brown weeks.
      b. Bees land on flowers.
      c. Fell to the ground.

B. Write the letter of the correct punctuation to end each sentence. (*pages 42-45*)

   3. Did you find a rose
      a. .   **b.** !   **c.** ?

   4. The vase is new
      a. .   **b.** !   **c.** ?

C. Write the letter of the sentence that has one line under the complete subject and two lines under the complete predicate. (*pages 46-51*)

   5. a. Seeds become plants.
      b. Wind carries seeds.
      c. Birds eat seeds.

   6. a. Plants sprout early.
      b. New flowers unfold.
      c. Rain wets the ground.

D. Write the letter of the word that is a noun. (*pages 78-79*)

   7. A warm breeze blows.
      a. A   **b.** warm   **c.** breeze   **d.** blows

   8. All the children play nearby.
      a. the   **b.** children   **c.** play   **d.** nearby

E. Write the letter of the correct plural noun. (*pages 80-83*)

   9. Workers filled seven ____. (box)
      a. boxes   **b.** boxs   **c.** boxse   **d.** box

   10. The children found a few ____. (penny)
      a. penny   **b.** pennys   **c.** pennies   **d.** pennyes

F. Write the letter of the proper noun. (*pages 84-85*)

   11. a. boy   **b.** brother   **c.** Harold   **d.** house
   12. a. bridge   **b.** state   **c.** Lake City   **d.** doctor

G. Write the letter of the correct possessive. (*pages 86-89*)

13. driver   **a.** driver's   **b.** drivers   **c.** drivers'

14. mice   **a.** mices's   **b.** mice's   **c.** mices

H. Write the letter of the correct abbreviation. (*pages 90-93*)

15. a. Sun, Oct 7   **16. a.** mr. Eugene field

    b. Wed., Nov. 9   **b.** ms. henrietta fox

    c. Ths., Ap. 11   **c.** Dr. Maria Sanchez

I. Write the letter of the verb. (*pages 128-129*)

17. Carol dips a net into the pond.

    a. dips   **b.** net   **c.** the   **d.** pond

18. Several fish dart away.

    a. Several   **b.** fish   **c.** dart   **d.** away

J. Write the letter of the correct verb. (*pages 130-135*)

19. Luis ____ for insects. (search)

    a. searches   **b.** search   **c.** searchs

20. Betty ____ a cricket yesterday. (spot)

    a. spot   **b.** spotted   **c.** spoted

21. The cricket ____ under a log. (scurry)

    a. scurried   **b.** scurryed   **c.** scurryd

22. Luis ____ Betty a jar. (pass)

    a. pass   **b.** passd   **c.** passed

23. Betty ____ the cricket in the jar. (place)

    a. place   **b.** placed   **c.** placd

K. Write the letter of the correct linking verb. (*pages 164-165*)

24. Jays ____ noisy birds.   **25.** We ____ curious.

    a. is **b.** am **c.** are   **a.** was **b.** were

L. Write the letter of the correct main verb. (*pages 166-169*)

26. We have ____ several nests nearby.

    a. seen   **b.** saw   **c.** seed   **d.** see

27. Birds have ____ here every spring.

    a. came   **b.** comed   **c.** come

M. Write the letter of the correct contraction. (*pages 170-171*)

28. was not   **a.** wasnt   **b.** wasn't   **c.** was'nt
29. did not   **a.** didnot   **b.** didnt   **c.** didn't
30. had not   **a.** hadnt'   **b.** hadn't   **c.** had'nt

N. Write the letter of the correct pronoun to complete each sentence. (*pages 206-211*)

31. Laura visited the museum. ____ saw many pictures.
     a. She   **b.** We   **c.** They   **d.** You
32. Yolanda and Sue went. We met ____ at the museum.
     a. him   **b.** her   **c.** them   **d.** us
33. Leroy and ____ liked the African masks.
     a. I   **b.** me
34. The teacher asked Melba and ____ about the pictures.
     a. I   **b.** me

O. Write the letter of the possessive form of the pronoun to replace the underlined possessive. (*pages 212-213*)

35. We saw the <u>artists'</u> pictures.
     a. their   **b.** his   **c.** your   **d.** our
36. The <u>boy's</u> father works at the museum.
     a. Our   **b.** Your   **c.** Their   **d.** His

P. Write the letter of the correct contraction. (*pages 214-215*)

37. I have   **a.** Iv'e   **b.** I've   **c.** Ih've
38. she will   **a.** shell   **b.** shew'll   **c.** she'll
39. It is   **a.** its   **b.** it's   **c.** its'

Q. Write the letter of the word that is an adjective. (*pages 244-247*)

40. A yellow canary sang in its cage.
     a. yellow   **b.** canary   **c.** sang   **d.** its
41. The bird ate a tiny seed.
     a. bird   **b.** ate   **c.** tiny   **d.** seed.
42. The children saw many birds at the zoo.
     a. children   **b.** saw   **c.** many   **d.** birds

43. They spent two hours at the zoo.

    a. They   **b.** spent   **c.** two   **d.** zoo

R. Write the letter of the correct article. (*pages 248-249*)

44. Snow falls from ___ cloud.

    a. a   **b.** an

45. ___ icicle hangs from the roof.

    a. An   **b.** A

46. Snow soon covers ___ trees.

    a. a   **b.** an   **c.** the

47. Wind whistles through ___ orchard.

    a. an   **b.** a

S. Write the letter of the correct adjective. (*pages 250-251*)

48. The moon looks ___ than a star.

    a. bright   **b.** brightest   **c.** brighter

49. The sun is the ___ body of the three.

    a. brightest   **b.** brighter   **c.** bright

50. Jupiter is the ___ planet of all.

    a. large   **b.** larger   **c.** largest

51. A rocket is ___ than a plane.

    a. faster   **b.** fast   **c.** fastest

T. Write the letter of the adverb in each sentence.
(*pages 296-299*)

52. The dancer leaps gracefully.

    a. The   **b.** dancer   **c.** leaps   **d.** gracefully.

53. Her partner reaches up.

    a. Her   **b.** partner   **c.** reaches   **d.** up

54. Then he catches the dancer.

    a. Then   **b.** he   **c.** catches   **d.** the

55. The audience cheers loudly.

    a. The   **b.** audience   **c.** cheers   **d.** loudly

U. Write the letter of the line of conversation that is written correctly. (*pages 326-327*)

56. a. Kim asked "who has my notebook"?

  b. "I saw it on your desk," said Julia.

  c. Kim shook her head and said "It's not there."

57. a. Ms. Edelson said, "Look for the notebook."

  b. Wayne shouted "here it is"!

  c. "Thank you very much, Kim said"

V. Write the letter of the sentence that has the complete subject underlined. (*pages 332-333*)

  58. a. Brave <u>sailors</u> crossed the Atlantic Ocean.

  b. An Italian explorer <u>landed in Canada</u>.

  c. <u>The cold water</u> contained many fish.

  59. a. <u>French traders</u> roamed Canada.

  b. <u>Several Indian tribes</u> sold furs.

  c. Fur <u>hats</u> were very popular in Europe.

W. Write the letter of the sentence that has the main word in the complete subject underlined. (*pages 332-333*)

  60. a. The <u>king</u> of France wanted Canada.

  b. <u>Many French farmers</u> moved to the new land.

  c. The <u>new</u> settlement grew quickly.

  61. a. <u>A French trader</u> sailed down the Mississippi River.

  b. Other <u>brave men</u> explored the Great Lakes.

  c. Sturdy <u>forts</u> guarded the settlers.

X. Write the letter of the sentence that has the complete predicate underlined. (*pages 334-335*)

  62. a. Newspapers <u>tell about important events</u>.

  b. News <u>comes</u> from all over the world.

  c. Many <u>people</u> work for a large newspaper.

  63. a. Reporters <u>gather</u> many facts.

  b. They <u>write their stories later</u>.

  c. <u>Editors</u> check the facts.

Y. Write the letter of the sentence that has the main word in the complete predicate underlined. (*pages 334-335*)

64. a. Photographers take pictures.
   b. Cartoonists draw funny pictures.
   c. Newspapers contain more than words.
65. a. Workers deliver the newspapers.
   b. People read the paper at breakfast.
   c. Some people watch news on television.

Z. Write the letter of the compound sentence. (*pages 336-337*)
66. a. Cows eat grass, and lions eat meat.
   b. Chickens and ducks live on the farm.
   c. A family of cats lives in the barn.
67. a. Troy plays baseball and basketball.
   b. We raise wheat, and they grow corn.
   c. The children run in the playground.

AA. Write the letter of the word that names the part of speech of the underlined word. (*pages 338-339*)
68. James Marshall found gold in California.
   a. noun   **b.** pronoun   **c.** action verb   **d.** verb *be*
69. People soon heard about his discovery.
   a. verb *be*   **b.** adjective   **c.** pronoun   **d.** adverb
70. They rushed to California.
   a. verb   **b.** adjective   **c.** pronoun   **d.** noun
71. The trip was very long.
   a. adverb   **b.** verb *be*   **c.** action verb   **d.** pronoun
72. Towns sprang up suddenly.
   a. noun   **b.** adverb   **c.** pronoun   **d.** adjective
73. Miners searched for lumps of yellow metal.
   a. action verb   **b.** verb *be*   **c.** adjective   **d.** pronoun
74. People built stores there.
   a. adjective   **b.** adverb   **c.** noun   **d.** pronoun
75. We read about the gold rush in school.
   a. action verb   **b.** adjective   **c.** pronoun   **d.** verb *be*

Here is your thesaurus; it is like a dictionary. It lists words that are similar to one another. There is an entry for each main word. The main words are in heavy type and are listed in alphabetical order. Here is the entry for the word *give*:

part of speech

main word —— **give** *verb* Give an apple to your friend.
Similar words: *grant* a favor, *offer* a new idea, *bestow* a gift, *donate* some old clothes, *furnish* the food for a party, *sacrifice* spare time to help a friend.
Opposite words: seize, **take, keep,** hold. ——another main entry word

Most entries contain the following information: the main word, its part of speech, a sentence using the main word, phrases suggesting similar words, and words that mean the opposite of the main word. Some entries give you other information. For example, the entry for *boat* lists kinds of boats.

The thesaurus can be very helpful when you are writing. Use it to find a different word to replace a word you have used several times. You can also use it to look for a word you can't remember. Look up a similar word. Maybe you will find the word you are thinking of.

It isn't a good idea to use a word from the thesaurus if you don't already know it. You might not use the word in exactly the right way. If you find a word you don't know, look it up in a dictionary.

Thesaurus

A a

above *adverb* The stars shine above. *Similar words*: *on the heights* overlooking the city, *on top of* the shelf.

act *noun* The act of breaking a window will get you into trouble. *Similar words*: the *action* of running, a hero's brave *deeds*, a clever *feat*.

active *adjective* Owls are most active at night. *Similar words*: a *lively* dance, a *peppy* cheerleader, a *frisky* horse, a *busy* bee. *Opposite words*: unmoving, idle, lazy, dull.

again *adverb* The window was broken again—for the fourth time! *Similar words*: birds returned *once more*. *Opposite word*: never.

angry *adjective* I was angry when my bike was broken. *Similar words*: *annoyed* at being late, *fuming* when the secret diary was read, *furious* at being forgotten, *gruff* words, *grumpy* because it's raining, *indignant* at the mistake, *irritated* at losing a pencil, **mad** as a wet hen, *outraged* that there was nothing to eat, *resentful* about losing the game, a *snarling* tiger, a *sulky* three-year-old baby, *upset* about burning the toast.

animal *noun* The panda is the most popular animal in the zoo. *Similar words*: a *beast* in the wild, a *creature* of nature, the *pest* that destroyed the crops, a family *pet*.

Some animals are ant, bear, bird, cat, chicken, cow, dog, elephant, gerbil, horse, lion, mouse, monkey, pig, tiger, whale, and zebra.

Some animal homes are barnyard, bird-house, burrow, cage, den, doghouse, farm, hive, jungle, nest, pasture, perch, ranch, range, stable, stall, web, the wild, and zoo.

Some animal sounds are bark, buzz, chirp, croak, crow, hiss, honk, hoot, howl, meow, moo, neigh, purr, quack, screech, squawk, and squeak.

answer *verb* A good student could answer that question. *Similar words*: *respond* to a question, *retort* sharply.

argue *verb* The two of them argue and can't agree about anything. *Similar words*: *bicker* over who was at fault, *debate* the pros and cons, *quarrel* about whose turn it is.

artist *noun* The artist formed the clay into a graceful, delicate shape. *Similar words*: the *craftsperson* made a clay pot, the *creator* of a work of art.

Some types of artists are actor, author, clown, composer, dancer, musician, painter, performer, photographer, poet, singer, and storyteller.

ashamed *adjective* He was ashamed about taking his brother's bike without asking. *Similar words*: a *sheepish* look, *embarrassed* at being discovered, *disgraced* for forgetting his report, *humiliated*.

ask *verb* Please ask for help if you need it. *Similar words*: *beg* for mercy, *quiz* a contestant, *invite* a friend to dinner, *plead* with the judge, *inquire* about their decision, reporter who *interviews* the movie star, *question* the reasons, *request* more money.

attractive *adjective* The jar of jam was attractive to the bees and the bear. *Similar words*: an *appealing* puppy, *magnetic* personality.

awful *adjective* The *rotten* apple smells awful. *Similar words*: a *disgusting* movie, a *dreadful* painting, a *terrible* story.

B b

bad *adjective* She gave a bad performance, full of mistakes. *Similar words*: an ***awful*** headache, an *evil* villain in the movie, a *harmful* act, a *fake* message, a *worn-out* tool, a *nasty* surprise, a *terrible* dragon, *unfit* to eat, a *villainous* plot, a *wicked* person, a *naughty* child. *Opposite words*: **good**, excellent, pure.

band *noun* The band played several marches. *Similar words*: many musicians in the *orchestra*, the conductor of the *symphony*.

bang *verb* Use this hammer to bang the nail in. *Similar words*: *beat* the drum, *clang* the bell, pots and pans *clatter* in the kitchen, *knock* on the door, *slam* the door, *thump* on the piano, *pound* on the table.

beach *noun* I spent the day at the beach playing in the sand and the water. *Similar words*: drive along the *coast*, swim close to *shore*, a fish market on the *waterfront*.

believe *verb* I believe your story is true. *Similar words*: *be of the opinion* that people are basically good, *trust* your friends.

below *adverb* The mountain climber looked at the valley below. *Similar words*: the submarine went ***under***, someone digs *underneath*, the toys *underfoot*. *Opposite words*: **above**, over.

bend *verb* Bend at the waist to touch your toes. *Similar words*: *flex* a muscle, *crook* a finger at a friend, *fold* the pages back.

better *adjective* Water would be better for you than that drink full of sugar. *Similar words*: a good student with a *superior* test score, new and *improved* flavor.

big *adjective* There is much more shade under that big chestnut tree. *Similar words*: *giant* steps, *gigantic* skyscraper, *immense* body of water, *large* sum of money, *enormous* crowd, ***grand*** spectacle, *huge* whale, *mighty* wrestler, *bulky* package, *mammoth* year-end

Thesaurus

sale, *massive* statue, *monumental* decision, *vast* planet. *Opposite words:* **small**, tiny, **little**.

bigger *adjective* I need a bigger box for all these supplies. *Similar words: expanded* balloon; *increased* number of people, *magnified* pages; *multiplied* in numbers.

bite *verb* Bite into this crisp apple. *Similar words: chew* some gum, *gnaw* on the chicken bone, *nibble* snacks, dogs *nip* the sheep to herd them.

black *adjective* The black cat disappeared into the night. *Similar words:* a fancy purse with *jet* beads, white and *ebony* piano keys.

boat *noun* The sailor had to row the boat. *Similar words:* sailing *ship*, seagoing *vessel*.

> Some types of boats are tug, canoe, rowboat, ferry, freighter, raft, sailboat, steamer, and clipper.

bother *verb* Running fingernails across a chalkboard can bother me. *Similar words: annoy* me with that noise, *pester* me with so many questions, *nag* your parents, *upset* a friend.

brave *adjective* The brave girl rescued her kitten from the tree. *Similar words: bold* action, *courageous* firefighter, *daring* leap to safety, **heroic** rescue, *plucky* speech, *fearless* leader. *Opposite words:* cautious, timid, wary.

break *verb* If you crawl out on that tree limb it might break. *Similar words: smash* an egg, *snap* the twigs, *shatter* the glass, *wreck* the car.

breathe *verb* Breathe deeply to relax. *Similar words: pant* like a dog, *puff* after running, *gasp* for breath, *sigh* after a big meal, *wheeze* because of a cold.

bright *adjective* She paid for her lunch with bright new coins. *Similar words: brilliant* sunshine, *shiny* new car, *glittering* jewels, *fiery* diamonds, *luminous* watch, *sparkling* water, *radiant* glow, *twinkling* eyes, *dazzling* snow. *Opposite words:* dull, faded, pale.

bring *verb* Please bring some fruit to the picnic. *Similar words: fetch* the stick, *carry* a meal to the table, *deliver* the mail.

building *noun* The doctor's office is located in that building. *Similar words:* a *shelter* from the cold, different rooms in the *house*.

> Parts of a building are attic, ceiling, cellar, chimney, closet, courtyard, door, fireplace, gate, gutter, hallway, lobby, loft, mailbox, platform, porch, office, rooms, sill, stairs, stairway, stoop, and window.

burn *verb* You'll burn the hot dog if it's that close to the fire. *Similar words:*

The campfire *blazes*, coals *smolder*, *kindle* a small flame.

C c

call *verb* Call my name if you need me. *Similar words*: **cry** out in surprise, **shout** at the top of your lungs, *summon* the guard.

calm *adjective* I want to spend a calm hour soaking in a warm bubble bath. *Similar words*: a *smooth* sea, a **quiet** answer, **peaceful** afternoon. *Opposite words*: **excited**, restless.

carry *verb* Can you carry the groceries up those stairs? *Similar words*: *lug* the bowling ball, *haul* the trash away, *tote* the wood, *bear* a heavy load.

catch *verb* Learning how to run and catch a football is fun. *Similar words*: *snare* the rabbit, *trap* a butterfly, *hook* a fish.

chair *noun* Find an empty chair. *Similar words*: park *bench*, best *seat* in the house, a queen on her *throne*, three-legged *stool*, comfortable *armchair*.

change *verb* Change your clothes before we go out to dinner. *Similar words*: *adapt* to your surroundings, *alter* your bad behavior, *substitute* an ingredient, *transform* into a butterfly, *vary* what you eat each day.

choice *noun* I have a choice between chicken and beef. *Similar words*: faced

with a difficult *dilemma*, the *vote* in the election.

city *noun* More and more people live in the city each year. *Similar words*: friendly people in the small *town*, a sleepy little *village*, the state *capital*, a growing *settlement*, a busy *community*.

clean *verb* Clean your room before the guests arrive. *Similar words*: *bathe* the dog, *wash* the socks, *scrub* the tile, *scour* the stove, *straighten* the messy closet.

clear *adjective* It was a clear day. *Similar words*: *pure* mountain stream, *cloudless* sky, *transparent* as glass.

climb *verb* It was hard work to climb that hill. *Similar words*: *ascend* the ladder, *mount* the horse, *scramble* up the cliff. *Opposite word*: descend.

cloth *noun* The cloth of this jacket is quite soft. *Similar words*: a stiff *fabric*, sew the *material*.

> Types of cloth are lace, silk, velvet, wool, burlap, denim, muslin, and jersey.

clothes *noun* You'll need warm clothes for the coming winter. *Similar words*: *costume* for the party, a stylish *outfit*, nurse's *uniform*, pile of dirty *laundry*.

cold *adjective* It's too cold outside to go swimming. *Similar words*: *cool* lemonade, *chilly* winter day, *icy* slopes, *frozen* lake, *wintry* weather, *unthawed* meat from the freezer. *Opposite words*: **hot**, heated.

color *noun* Your eyes are a lovely green color. *Similar words*: *dye* to color the cloth, *tint* in her hair, a reddish *hue*.

common *adjective* It's a common mistake made by many, many people. *Similar words*: at the *usual* time, an *ordinary-looking* person, a *familiar* friend, a *standard* model, *regular* guest on the show, a *typical* house. *Opposite words*: **special**, **rare**, **odd**, unusual.

complain *verb* The students will complain about getting so much homework over the weekend. *Similar words*: *criticize* her work, *grumble* about being late, *whine* over his homework.

complete *adjective* They will read the complete works of Dr. Seuss—every book. *Similar words*: an *entire* meal, a *total* wreck, the *whole* book.

compliment *verb* Let's compliment her on a job well done. *Similar words*: *congratulate* the winner, *applaud* the performance. *Opposite words*: **complain**, criticize.

confused *adjective* He was confused by all the flashing lights. *Similar words*: *dazed* by the flash of light, *dizzy* from spinning, *bewildered* by the riddle, *baffled* by the magician's tricks, *flustered* by everyone yelling at once.

cook *verb* Let's cook a delicious feast. *Similar words*: *bake* bread, *barbecue* the hamburgers, *boil* the eggs, *prepare* a meal, *broil* the fish, *fry* some chicken, *steam* the vegetables, *stew* the meat in its juices, *roast* the turkey.

copy *verb* She will copy her report onto a clean sheet of paper. *Similar words*: *duplicate* the results, *imitate* the sound of his voice.

craft *noun* Sewing is a difficult craft, but fun to learn. *Similar words*: a useful *skill*, learn my aunt's *trade*.

> Some of the people whose jobs are crafts are baker, barber, butcher, carpenter, cook, potter, printer, shoemaker, smith, tailor, and weaver.

cry *verb* She started to cry when she fell off the wall. *Similar words*: *groan* because of sore muscles, *moan* with pain, *sob* himself to sleep, *weep* for the loss, *whimper* and complain, *whine* like a tired child, *bawl* like a baby, *sniffle* into a handkerchief, *howl* at the moon, *wail* loudly at the sad movie.

curious *adjective* We were all curious to see what was inside the box. *Similar words*: *inquisitive* cat in the cupboard, a *nosy* reporter, a *snooping* spy.

cut *verb* The barber cut off all the baby's beautiful curls. *Similar words*: *carve* the turkey, *chip* the ice, *chop* the wood, *clip* the dog's nails, *crop* the bushes, *notch* the stick, *shred* the paper into strips, *slit* open the envelope, *snip* her bangs, *split* a log, *whittle* the soap, *saw* a board, *shave* the beard, *shear* the sheep, *slice* a lemon. *Opposite words*: **join**, fasten, connect.

D d

dangerous *adjective* Riding double on a bicycle is dangerous! *Similar words*: a *perilous* adventure, an *unsafe* toy, a *risky* dive into the shallow pool. *Opposite words*: **safe**, secure.

dark *adjective* Dark storm clouds gathered overhead. *Similar words*: reading by *dim* light, a *dull* and shapeless dress, *gloomy* gray day, *shadowy* hallway, *shady* side of the street. *Opposite words*: **light**, **bright**, lighted.

dead *adjective* Throw out that vase of dead flowers. *Similar words*: *extinct* volcano, *lifeless* performance. *Opposite words*: alive, existing.

different *adjective* You look quite different from your sister. *Similar words*: an **odd** group of characters, *various* things to see, *assorted* cheeses.

dig *verb* The tortoise will dig a hole to escape the heat. *Similar words*: *burrow* into the ground, *scoop* out the insides of the pumpkin.

dinner *noun* She had a healthy dinner of grains and vegetables. *Similar words*: a late *supper* after the movie, a filling *meal* of pasta, a tremendous *feast* of Mexican food, a *banquet* for the wedding, a *buffet* where you can help yourself.

dirty *adjective* I can't see a thing through these dirty windows. *Similar words*: an *untidy* desk, *dusty* old furniture, *filthy* kitchen, *hazy* city sky, *soiled* laundry, *sandy* floor of the beach house, *muddy* river bank, *murky* water, *grimy* stove, *grubby* clothes, *messy* room, *sticky* fingers. *Opposite words*: neat, tidy, spotless, sparkling.

do *verb* Do your homework before dinner. *Similar words*: *accomplish* a great work, *achieve* your goals, *arrange* for things to happen, *conduct* business wisely, *perform* in a play, *carry out* a plan, *finish* a task. *Opposite words*: neglect, ignore.

drink *verb* Be sure to drink plenty of water when the weather is hot. *Similar words*: *sip* a glass of water, *gulp* water, *chug* a carton of milk.

duty *noun* It is a privilege and a duty to vote. *Similar words*: *responsibility* to obey the law, carry out your given task.

E e

eat *verb* I like to eat lunch with my friends. *Similar words*: **bite** into the sandwich, *devour* a whole plateful, *dine* at a fine restaurant, *feast* on a delicious meal, *nibble* a snack, *munch*

Thesaurus

on popcorn, *chew* carefully and swallow, quickly *gobble* the seeds, *graze* on the grassy hill.

event *noun* The holiday parade was a big event in our tiny town. *Similar words*: birthday *celebration*, a serious *ceremony*, an important *occasion*, the rehearsal of the *program*, a live *performance* of the opera, a special *happening*, an elaborate *spectacle*.

excited *adjective* The children were excited to see their grandparents again. *Similar words*: *eager* for summer vacation, *enthusiastic* applause from the audience, *frantic* search for her lost pet, *frenzied* crowd at the football game, *thrilled* winner of the contest. *Opposite words*: **calm**, **quiet**, bored.

explore *verb* Let's explore our new town. *Similar words*: *examine* a leaf, *search* the woods for wildflowers.

F f

fair *adjective* Taking turns is fair. *Similar words*: *honest* and true friend, *proper* order of things, the umpire's *just* decision, an *accurate* summary. *Opposite words*: cheating, unjust, wrong, questionable.

fall *verb* Leaves fall from the trees. *Similar words*: *trip* on a crack in the sidewalk, *tumble* down the hill, *stumble* over the mess on the floor, the tall tower of blocks will *topple*, *drop* from the sky, sandcastles *collapse* easily.

false *adjective* It is false that the moon is made of green cheese. *Similar words*: a *fake* cure, a *wrong* idea, a *phony* story. *Opposite words*: true, sincere.

far *adjective* School is far from my house. *Similar words*: the *distant* mountains, *remote* part of the world.

fast *adjective* Horses are fast runners. *Similar words*: *quick* as a bunny, *speedy* as a roadrunner, *swift* water in the river, *rapid* trains, the *rushing* stream, eat a *hasty* meal, *instant* oatmeal, *prompt* answer to a question, a *sudden* ending, the *hurried* people pushing and running. *Opposite words*: **slow**, delayed.

feel *verb* Feel how cold the snow is. *Similar words*: **touch** the dog, *stroke* its fur, *pat* its head, *handle* the tool, *fumble* with the keys, *finger* the cloth, *press* the button.

feeling *noun* I have a good feeling when I get a hug. *Similar words*: good and bad *mood*, rising *spirits*, lion with a short *temper*, sunny *disposition*, artist known for *sensitivity*, *emotion* showing on their faces.

fight *verb* Boxers fight in a ring. *Similar words*: *battle* for first place, *argue* with the umpire, *struggle* to escape, *resist* being pulled, *quarrel* about who goes first, *wrestle* with a problem, push and *scuffle* with each other, *dispute* with him over the problem. *Opposite word*: surrender.

find *verb* Did you find the book you lost? *Similar words*: *discover* hidden treasure, *uncover* the reason, *learn* the answer to a puzzle, *locate* the missing key. *Opposite words*: **lose**, misplace.

fix *verb* Can you fix the broken clock? *Similar words*: *mend* the hole in the screen door, *patch* the rip in my pants, *prepare* lunch, *repair* a broken toy, *replace* a light bulb, *sharpen* a pencil, *correct* a mistake, *rebuild* the tower of blocks. *Opposite words*: **break**, shatter, demolish.

fly *verb* Airplanes fly above the clouds when they go across country. *Similar words*: gulls *soar* over the waves, little birds *flutter* about, hawks *swoop* down, *glide* in for a landing, startled pigeons *take wing*.

forever *adverb* The movie seemed to last forever. *Similar words*: I will be *eternally* grateful for your help, ocean tides move *endlessly*, *always* love someone.

free *adjective* Birds are free to fly anywhere. *Similar words*: the colonies declared they were *independent*, *at liberty* to do what you want.

funny *adjective* The funny clown made us laugh. *Similar words*: *comical* movie, *amusing* joke, *droll* comedian, *silly* tongue twisters, *humorous* cartoon, *ridiculous* rubber nose. *Opposite words*: **sad**, serious, humorless.

G g

game *verb* Our team won the soccer game. *Similar words*: a *contest* between two sides, our favorite *sport*, an enjoyable *activity*, a fun party.

gather *verb* Gather all the eggs in the hen house. *Similar words*: *collect* all the dishes, *pile* the leaves in a basket, *heap* your clothes on the bed. *Opposite words*: scatter, spread out.

get *verb* I will get my coat. *Similar words*: *receive* the letter, *acquire* a tan at the beach, *win* a prize, *catch* a cold, *earn* a salary.

give *verb* Give an apple to your friend. *Similar words*: *grant* a favor, *offer* a new idea, *bestow* a gift, *donate* some old clothes, *furnish* the food for a party, *sacrifice* spare time to help a friend. *Opposite words*: seize, **take**, **keep**, **hold**.

go *verb* We go to school every day. *Similar words*: *move* from place to place, *travel* by car, *advance* toward a goal, *leave* for a vacation, *scat*, you cat. *Opposite words*: come, **stop**, halt.

good *adjective* They did a good job of washing the dishes. *Similar words*: an *excellent* meal, a *skillful* mechanic, an *honest* person, a *kind* deed, water that is *pure* and safe to drink, *fine* weather for a picnic, an *enjoyable* movie.

365

grab *verb* She will grab the ball and run. *Similar words:* *seize* someone by the collar, *snatch* an apple from the tree.

grand *adjective* The queen looked grand in her crown. *Similar words:* *royal* robe, *noble* lion, *lordly* bearing, *splendid* palace, *majestic* mountain.

great *adjective* It is a great day for a party. *Similar words:* *glorious* morning, *wonderful* food at the party, *terrific* dancer, *superb* dinner, *important* achievement, *impressive* amount of money, *outstanding* grades, *spectacular* view. *Opposite words:* **ordinary,** terrible, horrible, **awful.**

group (of animals) *noun* Groups of animals are called different things. *Similar words:* a *herd* of cows or deer, a *flock* of chickens or sheep, a *pack* of wolves, a *swarm* of bees or wasps, a *school* of fish, a *pod* of whales or dolphins, a *pride* of lions.

group (of things) *noun* What do you call a group of things? *Similar words:* a *set* of books, a *bunch* of grapes, a *case* of cans, a first aid *kit*, a *collection* of bugs, a *cluster* of stars, a *fleet* of ships, a *batch* of muffins.

grown-up *adjective* A grown-up colt is a horse. *Similar words:* an *adult* decision, *mature* fruit.

guide *verb* The leaders *guide* us through the forest. *Similar words:* *steer* around the rocks, *navigate* down the river, *pilot* the airplane, *show* a visitor around town, *escort* the famous person, *lead* the team to victory.

H h

happen *verb* When did it happen? *Similar words:* *occur* later, *take place* at the beach.

happy *adjective* Everyone was happy to have a day off from school. *Similar words:* *glad* to hear it, *jolly* clown, *merry* party-goers, *joyful* song, *joyous* event, *overjoyed* expression on her face, singing and *rejoicing* voices, *cheerful* mood, *joking* storyteller, *contented* to read a good book, *gleeful* that the prank worked, in a *cheerful* mood. *Opposite words:* **sad,** gloomy.

hard (1) *adjective* The stale bread is hard. *Similar words:* *bony* fish, *crisp* crackers, *solid* ice, *sturdy* cardboard, *stiff* plastic, *rigid* pipe, *firm* vegetables, *stony* ground. *Opposite words:* **soft,** slack.

hard (2) *adjective* The test was very hard. *Similar words:* *difficult* spelling words, *puzzling* clues, *confusing* messages. *Opposite words:* easy, **simple,** a cinch.

hate *verb* We hate to get up in the morning, and we hate to go to bed at night. *Similar words:* *dislike* spinach, *despise* a boring movie, *detest* the color pink. *Opposite words:* **like,** admire, honor, cherish, treasure, prize.

help *verb* I will help you carry that big box. *Similar words*: *assist* in reaching a goal, *aid* people in trouble, *enable* them to go to college.

heroic *adjective* She was a heroic astronaut. *Similar words*: *bold* sailor, *daring* acrobat, *adventurous* mountain climber, *gallant* knight, *fearless* explorer. *Opposite words*: afraid, timid, cowardly, fearful.

hill *noun* That green hill is not very high. *Similar words*: low *foothills*, *mountains* covered with pine trees, snowy *mount* too tall for trees, birds flying around the *peak*, sand *dunes* at the beach, erupting *volcano*, *butte* that looked like a table of rock, steep *heights*, crumbling *cliff*, old burial *mound*. *Opposite words*: valley, pit, gully, crater, canyon.

hit *verb* You can hit the ball with that bat. *Similar words*: *paddle* the ping pong ball, *pound* the clay out flat, *punch* the pillow, *whack* the ball, *drive* a stake into the ground, *slap* a mosquito, *strike* the gong.

hold *verb* Hold your arms up over your head. *Similar words*: *grip* the bar before you climb higher, **grab** the cat, *clasp* the child in your arms, *clench* the bone in its teeth, vines *cling* to the tree.

holiday *noun* On this holiday we eat turkey. *Similar words*: *vacation* at the beach, birthday *celebration*, *carnival* time in New Orleans, fun at the *festival*.

hot *adjective* I felt too hot by the bonfire. *Similar words*: the *warm* jacket, *heated* air from the furnace, *molten* lava, *steaming* soup, *sizzling* bacon. *Opposite words*: **cold**, frozen, freezing.

house *noun* People live in this house. *Similar words*: log *cabin* in the mountains, wooden *cottage* by the beach, *farmhouse* with a front porch, the *hut* made of palm leaves, round *hogan* with one door.

hungry *adjective* I am hungry for a big dinner. *Similar words*: *starving* for something to eat, *empty* and could eat anything. *Opposite words*: fed, full.

hunt *verb* Go hunt for your missing sock. *Similar words*: *stalk* the prey, the cat *chases* the mouse, dogs *prowl* the alleys, *pursue* the thief, *seek* a lost treasure, *look* for a lost dog.

hurt (1) *verb* I hurt myself when I fell down. *Similar words*: *injure* someone in an accident, *wound* with a knife, *cut* his finger on broken glass, a stone *bruised* my foot, my head *aches*, *scratch* on a thorn. *Opposite words*: heal, cure, soothe, **help**, comfort.

hurt (2) *verb* Cold weather will hurt the crops. *Similar words*: rain will *spoil* the picnic, waves *destroy* the sand castle, wind *damages* the roof, *wreck* the automobile, a string of losses *ruins* the team's chances of victory. *Opposite words*: **fix**, repair, construct.

Thesaurus

I i

idea *noun* Whose idea was it to go for a ride? *Similar words*: a *theory* in science, *theme* of a story, *scheme* to get rich quick, a great *notion*.

important *adjective* The most important thing is to use your time well. *Similar words*: *serious* mistake, *weighty* decision, a *major* new invention. *Opposite words*: unimportant, minor.

interested *adjective* I am interested in collecting stamps. *Similar words*: *enchanted* by the view, *fascinated* by the kitten, *spellbound* by the music.

J j

job *noun* Most people make money doing a job. *Similar words*: the *chore* of washing dishes, my *task* for today, do office *work*, the **craft** of making rugs, a *career* may last a lifetime, using tools is a *skill*, put your heart into your **profession**.

Some types of jobs are **artist**, astronaut, attendant, cleaner, clerk, conductor, computer operator, custodian, diver, doctor, editor, electrician, farmer, firefighter, geologist, guide, housekeeper, inspector, librarian, manager, mechanic, messenger, nurse, pilot, photographer, plumber, police officer, reporter, sailor, sales clerk, scientist, secretary, teacher, and zookeeper.

join *verb* The two friends join hands. *Similar words*: *attach* the papers with a paper clip, *braid* your hair, buttons *fasten* shirts, *glue* the pieces back together, *knit* the yarn, *knot* your shoelaces, *sew* up the rip, *tape* the picture to the wall, *tie* with ribbon, *combine* the two liquids. *Opposite words*: untie, **cut**, separate.

jump *verb* The dog will jump the fence and run away. *Similar words*: *leap* to catch the ball, *hop* like a bunny, *skip* down the street, *hurdle* the gate, cats *pounce* on mice, *dive* into the pool, *plunge* into the deep water, *somersault* over and over.

K k

keep *verb* Keep your money in a safe place. *Similar words*: *hold on* to the instructions, **save** the box tops, *preserve* a flower.

L l

laugh *verb* You will laugh at the clown. *Similar words*: *chuckle* about a funny story, smile and *giggle*, *chortle* to yourself, *guffaw* loudly, *snicker* to yourself.

leftovers *noun* We are eating leftovers from yesterday's turkey. *Similar words*: cold *ashes* in the fireplace, *scraps* of food, *remains* of an old car.

lie *verb* Don't lie about your mistakes. *Similar words*: *bluff* your way out of trouble, *not tell the truth*, big talkers *exaggerate*, foxes *deceive* the chickens.

lift *verb* Lift the box onto the shelf, please. *Similar words*: *raise* your hat to say hello, *hoist* the heavy pipe into place.

light *adjective* Light yellow flowers look white in the sunshine. *Similar words*: **bright** stars, *candlelit* jack-o-lanterns, *gleaming* teeth, *glowing* coals in the fire, *moonlit* nights, *shiny* new pennies, *sunlit* gardens, *white* sheets hanging on the clothesline, *shining* sun on the water, *pale* shade of green, *faded* blue jeans.

like *verb* I like to have new friends. *Similar words*: *enjoy* the movie, *fancy* some new shoes, *care* about your best friend, *be fond of* grandmother, *prefer* peaches to apples, *appreciate* a gift.

line *noun* The teacher drew a line across the bulletin board. *Similar words*: a skunk has a *stripe* down its back, there is a *streak* of red in the painting, the children stood in single *file*.

limp *verb* I limp because I have a sore foot. *Similar words*: *shuffle* in big shoes, *hobble* along with the help of a cane.

little *adjective* The little mouse ran under the door. *Similar words*: **small** helping of peas, *dainty* china cup, *tiny* baby. *Opposite words*: **big**, large.

look *verb* I look both ways before I cross the street. *Similar words*: *watch for* the green light, *peek* around a corner, *stare* at the television, *gaze* in the toy store window, *glance* at the mirror, *peer* into the dark, *examine* the bug, *search* for the right answer.

lose *verb* You will lose your money if you don't put it in your pocket. *Similar words*: *misplace* a pencil, *miss* the point of a joke, *be defeated* in a game. *Opposite words*: **find**, win.

lot *noun* I have a lot of toys. *Similar words*: did *much* to help, a *group* of singers, the butterfly *collection*, *plenty* of food, a *great deal* of time spent watching television.

M m

mad *adjective* I am mad at the person who took my pencil. *Similar words*: *angry* at losing the game, *cross* because your feelings got hurt, *upset* and yelling, *grumpy* and frowning, *gruff* voice, *disgusted* with stupid talk, *furious* with yourself, *irritated* by the ending of the book, a *snarling* wild animal, *sulky* and full of tears, *annoyed* by a fly, *huffy* at being ignored, *fuming* over the broken glass, *sullen* and sad, *outraged* and loud, became *indignant* over the mistake, *resentful* about waiting.

make (1) *verb* The children make paper airplanes. *Similar words*: *build* a doghouse, *form* a statue out of clay, *invent* a new machine, *compose* a song.

make (2) *verb* You can't make me change my mind. *Similar words*: *cause* an accident, *force* someone to agree, *persuade* her to come with us.

make-believe *adjective* The story took place in a make-believe country. *Similar words*: *imaginary* friend, a *magic* fairy, a *legendary* hero, a *mythical* dragon, a *fabulous* castle with golden towers.

many *adjective* There were many people at the parade. *Similar words*: *several* people on the bus, *countless* grains of sand, *numerous* reasons, *various* ideas.

mark *noun* There is a mark on the table where the bleach was spilled. *Similar words*: The report had a *smudge* from her dirty fingers, the dog had a brown *spot* on his ear, he has a *birthmark* on his chin, the apple has a *bruise* when it fell from the tree.

maybe *adverb* Maybe we can play after we finish the work. *Similar words*: *Perhaps* it will rain today. Can you *possibly* climb so high?

meal *noun* We ate a meal at the restaurant. *Similar words*: fancy food at the *banquet*, *feast* fit for a king and a queen, a *picnic* in the park, milk and crackers for a *snack*.

mean *adjective* A mean person took my lunch. *Similar words*: taking more than your part is *unfair*, a *low* trick, the *spiteful* cat scratched the chair, stepping on the bug was *cruel*, the *savage* lion, a *menacing* cat chasing the bird, a *selfish* child took it all, the *stingy* person did not share. *Opposite words*: generous, grateful, good-natured, merciful.

medicine *noun* The doctor used a new medicine to treat the disease. *Similar words*: a *cure* for chicken pox, a *remedy* for the cold.

messy *adjective* The messy house took hours to clean. *Similar words*: the *dusty* old attic; smoky, *polluted* air, paper blowing in the *littered* street, an *untidy* room, *grubby* hands that need to be washed, *sloppy* kitchen, *jumbled* clothes and shoes. *Opposite words*: neat, tidy.

money *noun* Put the money in the bank. *Similar words*: two dollars in *cash*, a handful of *coins*, great *wealth*, a fabulous *fortune*, the *riches* of Midas, *treasure* of gold and jewels.

more *adjective* You can have more dinner. *Similar words*: *additional* work, *greater* skill, *extra* help, an *added* person at the table.

move *verb* I will move the chair into the other room. *Similar words*: **push** the swing, **pull** the wagon, **turn** the page, *pass* the jelly, rivers *flow* to the ocean, children *rush* to school, *scatter* seeds in the garden, birds *migrate* south, the plane will *depart* soon, the mule would not *budge*, *shift* the books from the table to the shelf, brooms *whisk* away dust, *ease* in between the sheets, the wagon will **hit** the curb.

N n

near *adjective* The store is near my school. *Similar words:* the *nearby* library, a *neighboring* town, a *close* relative. *Opposite words:* **far**, distant.

new *adjective* I have shiny new shoes. *Similar words:* rockets are *modern* inventions, a *young* cow is called a calf, replaced with an *unused* part. *Opposite words:* **old**, ancient, antique.

news *noun* Did you hear the latest news on the radio? *Similar words:* the club's *bulletin*, a magazine *article*, *information* about an event, a *report* from the White House.

next *adjective* You are the next one in line to get a ticket. *Similar word:* Each *succeeding* person gets a turn. *Opposite words:* previous, former.

nice *adjective* It is nice to have a good friend. *Similar words: agreeable* about taking turns, *pleasant* to have warm milk, *cozy* kitchen, *charming* kitten, *delightful* day at the beach, *amiable* friends agree on everything, her *gracious* greeting made me feel welcome, *pleasing* manners, *likable* person. *Opposite words:* naughty, **awful**, dreadful, ghastly, horrid, hateful, fierce.

noise *noun* The plane's engine made a loud noise. *Similar words:* a terrible *racket*, an *uproar* over the unfair decision, the *blare* of the radio.

noisy *adjective* The noisy children didn't hear the teacher. *Similar words: loud* music, *deafening* jet plane, *shrill* sirens, *roaring* engine, *booming* drums, *crashing* cymbals, *blaring* television, *earsplitting* howl, *thunderous* clapping, *resounding* echoes. *Opposite words:* **quiet**, **calm**, **peaceful**.

now *adverb* I have to go to the store now. *Similar words:* Come here *immediately*. Do it *this instant*. We must cross the street *this moment*. *Presto*! and a rabbit appears. *Opposite words:* later, earlier, in the future, in the past.

O o

odd *adjective* The kitten looked odd among the puppies. *Similar words:* a **different** kind of string bean, an *unusual* purple bird, winning a million dollars is *unlikely*, *eerie* houses, *weird* sounds from the dark house, *unexpected* knock, *peculiar* smell in the closet, *unfamiliar* place. *Opposite words:* usual, **common**.

often *adverb* We often play together. *Similar words:* babies cry *frequently*, I *usually* eat at noon.

old *adjective* The old house had no paint on the walls. *Similar words:* the *aged* book was torn and faded, in an *ancient* castle, an *elderly* relative, *antique* furniture. *Opposite words:* modern, **new**.

open *verb* Please open the door and let me in. *Similar words*: *unlock* the box, *unfold* the letter, *unwrap* the gift.

order *verb* Order them to stop! *Similar words*: *command* the dog to speak, *bid* your grandfather goodbye, *tell* the students to study. *Opposite words*: **ask**, obey.

ordinary *adjective* It was an ordinary school day. *Similar words*: *standard* way of doing things, *routine* check for homework, *customary* greetings. *Opposite words*: **odd**, strange, unusual.

outdoors *noun* The outdoors is beautiful. *Similar words*: a hike through the *wilderness*, walking in the *countryside*, animals in *nature*. *Opposite word*: indoors.

P p

part *noun* Please, could I have part of your sandwich? *Similar words*: a **piece** of the puzzle, a *portion* of the pie, main *ingredient* in the soup, an *element* in the mixture.

peaceful *adjective* The quiet garden was peaceful. *Similar words*: the *smooth*, **calm** bay, *safe* in mother's arms, a *secure* way of life. *Opposite words*: **noisy**, **dangerous**.

person *noun* She is the person I met yesterday. *Similar words*: a *human* being talks and thinks, the *character* in the movie.

picture *noun* The picture was hanging on the wall. *Similar words*: crayon *drawing* of a house and flowers, *doodle* of lines and circles, *photograph* of my mom, T-shirt *design*, *portrait* that looked just like her, *diagram* showing how things fit together.

piece *noun* I would like a piece of paper. *Similar words*: a *shred* of lettuce, a *slice* of bread, a *patch* to cover the small hole, a *strip* of tape, a *scrap* of metal, a *lump* of butter. *Opposite words*: whole, total.

plane *noun* The plane is taking off from the runway. *Similar words*: *jets* fly high, the *rocket* blasted into space, the old-timers' *flying machines*.

plant *noun* I watered the tomato plant. *Similar words*: trim the *shrub*, acorns grow on oak *trees*, a rose *bush*, green *shoots*, tulips are one kind of *flower*, ivy is a *vine*, growth of *weeds*.

Some plant parts are bloom, branch, bud, bulb, flower, fruit, leaf, petal, root, seed, stalk, stem, and twig.

Some places where plants grow are forest, garden, **swamp**, jungle, lawn, meadow, prairie, yard, grove, nursery, orchard, and underbrush.

---

plod *verb* We plod down the long, long road. *Similar words*: *slouch* down the alley, bears *lumber* through the forest, ducklings *straggle* after their mother, *shuffle* along in big shoes, *trudge* through deep snowdrifts.

police officer *noun* A police officer directs traffic. *Similar words*: the *detective* searching for clues, the *guard* watching the gate, the *state trooper* stopped the speeding car.

praise *verb* The teacher will praise my good work. *Similar words*: your kind words *flatter* me, we *cheer* the team.

pretty *adjective* It is a pretty flower. *Similar words*: *cute* puppy, *beautiful* rose, the *elegant* swans, *glamorous* movie stars. *Opposite words*: plain, **ugly**.

profession *noun* A profession takes a long time to learn. *Similar words*: get a **job** as a librarian, her *work* takes her to Europe, he has been in this *business* for many years.

promise *verb* I promise to do a good job. *Similar words*: *swear* to tell the truth, *vow* to do all my work, *assure* the scared child that everything will be fine.

proud *adjective* She is the proud owner of a new bicycle. *Similar words*: a **happy** winner, a *pleased* parent, a *dignified* judge. *Opposite words*: humble, modest.

public *adjective* There are public meetings at city hall. *Similar words*: *open* hearings, *known* leader, *widely* known movie stars. *Opposite words*: **secret**, hidden, private, closed.

pull *verb* The horses pull the wagon. *Similar words*: *drag* out that old rug, *jerk* the handle, *pluck* the flower, don't *yank* his hair, the car will *tow* the trailer. *Opposite words*: **push**, shove.

push *verb* Push the chair closer to the table. *Similar words*: *shove* a box into the corner, *press* the button, *nudge* the ball with your foot, motors *propel* the boat, *poke* it with your finger. *Opposite word*: **pull**.

Q q

quiet *adjective* With all the children gone, the house was quiet. *Similar words*: as *silent* as a mouse, speaking in *hushed* tones, *muffled* voices through the closed door, *subdued* child on a chair, *mute* radio that was turned off, *speechless* with surprise, *noiseless*, empty room. *Opposite words*: **noisy**, loud, roaring.

quit *verb* You quit hitting me! *Similar words*: *end* the game, *give up* your job, **stop** making noise. *Opposite words*: start, begin, continue.

R r

rain *noun* The rain fell from dark clouds. *Similar words*: a fine *mist*, a brief *shower*, *cloudburst* after the thunder. *Opposite words*: drought, dry spell.

Thesaurus

rare *adjective* This blue parrot is a rare bird. *Similar words*: *unusual* events, the *unexpected* surprise, *uncommon* amount of rain, a *special* treat. *Opposite words*: usual, **common**, **ordinary**.

real *adjective* This is a real diamond, not a fake one. *Similar words*: the *actual* reason, a *true* story, a *factual* movie, *genuine* leather. *Opposite words*: fake, unreal, imaginary.

red *adjective* The red fire engine raced through the town. *Similar word*: The boy's cheeks were *rosy* from the cold.

> Some shades of red are pink, scarlet, magenta, ruby, cherry, cardinal, carmine, crimson, and beet-red.

refuse *verb* I refuse to go out in the rain. *Similar words*: *turn down* a second helping, *veto* the plan. *Opposite words*: agree, accept.

road *noun* The road goes right by my house. *Similar words*: a winding country *lane*, the *alley* between the tall buildings, zoom along the *highway*, the main *route* across the country, a *trail* through the woods, the *course* for the race, the *path* by the side of the river, busy *avenue* full of cars.

rock *noun* A rock lay on the path. *Similar words*: the heavy *stone*, a lot of little *pebbles*, on top of the big *boulder*, *gravel* crunching under foot, a rock made of a shiny *mineral*, flat sides of a *crystal*.

round *adjective* Colombus said the earth was round. *Similar words*: the toy train ran on a *circular* track, the marble is *spherical*, the road isn't straight but *curved*, the football is *oval*, some squash are *egg-shaped*. *Opposite words*: straight, flat, angular, pointed, sharp.

rule *verb* Wise leaders rule the country. *Similar words*: *govern* the city, *control* the team of horses, *lead* an army, *direct* the actors, *head* the team. *Opposite words*: obey, follow.

run *verb* I like to run on the beach. *Similar words*: *jog* around the block, *dash* for the bus, hummingbirds *dart* to the feeder, horses *gallop* in the field, cars *race* around the track, rockets *zoom* into space, the mice *scurry* to their holes, cattle *stampede* across the range, ponies *trot* in front of the cart, bears *lope* into the forest, *flee* from danger, bunnies *scamper* in the garden, crabs *scuttle* across the beach, runners *sprint* down the hill.

S s

sad *adjective* The boy was sad when his good friend moved away. *Similar words*: *gloomy* players who lost a game, *unhappy* with a report card, *miserable* stray dog, *disappointed* when I couldn't go to the zoo, *sorrowful* event.

said *verb* I said, "No!"
see **say**

374

save *verb* I like to save stamps. *Similar words*: **keep** test papers to study later, *protect* the wild animals, *rescue* the whales, *defend* your country from attack.

say *verb* Did you say you like school? *Similar words*: **cry** in a loud voice, **ask** a question, **complain** about the test grade, **laugh** at the joke, **whisper** softly, *announce* to the audience, *declare* a state of emergency, *demand* quiet in the theater, *discuss* the weather, **tell** a story to the class, *pronounce* each sound carefully, *boast* of high grades.

saying *noun* The early bird gets the worm, as the old saying goes. *Similar words*: an advertising *slogan*, a state *motto*, the *moral* of the story.

scared *adjective* Scared by the monsters, I left the movie. *Similar words*: *afraid* of the dark, *fearful* of the large dog, *frightened* by a grizzly bear, *nervous* about a spelling test, *startled* by a loud noise, *timid* speaking in front of the class, *dreading* to see my report card, *worried* about sickness, *terrified* by the lion. *Opposite words*: **brave**, courageous.

sea *noun* The ship sailed across the sea. *Similar words*: dive into the *ocean*, stormy *waters*, a protected *gulf*, a *bay* with a good harbor.

search *verb* He searched for the lost book. *Similar words*: *look for* clues to solve the mystery, *examine* the room for a secret entrance, **hunt** for buried treasure. *Opposite words*: **find**, discover.

secret *adjective* The secret trap door is hidden under the rug. *Similar words*: *buried* treasure, *hidden* presents for a surprise party, *private* papers in the safe, *mysterious* symbol on the map, the *puzzling* code, *undiscovered* gold in the hills, *concealed* entrance, *disguised* face, *stealthy* actions. *Opposite words*: **public**, frank, above-board.

see *verb* I can see the ocean from my room. *Similar words*: *notice* the sentences on the chalkboard, *sight* an airplane, hunters *spot* deer, *observe* the animals at the zoo, *view* a movie, *gaze at* the stars, *understand* what they are trying to say.

send *verb* We send letters to our friends. *Similar words*: *shoo* the chickens off the porch, *throw* the ball to third base, *dismiss* from the room, *mail* a package, *give off* an odor.

sense *verb* I sense a growing interest in health. *Similar words*: *detect* a breeze, **feel** a person's mood, *grasp* the problem, *be aware of* danger.

serious *adjective* He read a serious book about President Lincoln. *Similar words*: a *grave* mistake, a *solemn* promise, an *earnest* plea for help, a *sober* decision.

Thesaurus

shake *verb* The ground shakes during an earthquake. *Similar words: shiver* from the cold, *vibrate* like a violin string, **wiggle** your foot, *wobble* before they fall over, flowers *sway* in the breeze, *waver* between two choices, *quiver* like a leaf in a breeze, *totter* across the street, *tremble* with excitement.

shout *verb* People shout at the ball game. *Similar words:* **call** for help, *cheer* the team, *exclaim* in excitement, *scream* in fear, *yell* in anger. *Opposite words:* **whisper**, mutter.

show *verb* Show me how to bake bread. *Similar words: indicate* the correct answer, *reveal* the secret, *point out* how it works, *display* the paintings.

shy *adjective* Shy animals are easily frightened. *Similar words: timid* at the party, *bashful* among adults, *modest* about receiving the award, *uneasy* in front of an audience. *Opposite words:* confident, boastful.

sick *adjective* I was sick and stayed home. *Similar words: ill* after eating too much, *feverish* with the flu, an *aching* tooth, a *diseased* plant, *ailing* for a long time, *stricken* with a virus. *Opposite words:* healthy, well, **strong,** vigorous.

simple *adjective* She wrote a simple letter of thanks. *Similar words: plain* blue jeans, *basic* design, *elementary* words, *unadorned* clothing, *natural*

beauty. *Opposite words:* fancy, fussy, elaborate.

slide *verb* We began to slide on the ice. *Similar words: glide* across the dance floor, *slip* on a banana peel, *slither* through the weeds, *skid* on gravel.

slow *adjective* The slow runner lost the race. *Similar words: gradual* rise in temperature, *unhurried* trip. *Opposite words:* rapid, quick, speedy, **fast**.

small *adjective* A new baby is very small. *Similar words:* **little** rock by the big boulder, *narrow* pass between the mountains, *short* stem on the apple, *slim* chance, *thin* sheet of paper, *tiny* seed, *dainty* glove, *miniature* cars, *skinny* stray dog, *slender* dancers, *slight* change in the weather, *wee* drop of flavoring. *Opposite words:* **big**, huge, giant, enormous.

smaller *adjective* The smaller basket was easier to hold. *Similar words: dwindling* supply of paper, *ebbing* tide, *reduced* price, *finer* print, *waning* moon. *Opposite words:* **bigger**, increasing, expanding.

smart *adjective* The smart student reads many books. *Similar words: intelligent* answer, *clever* solution, *brainy* young genius, *wise* teacher.

smell *noun* The smell of a pine forest is pleasant. *Similar words: perfume* of flowers, *scent* of a rose, *odor* of baking bread.

soak *verb* Soak your tired feet in the warm water. *Similar words*: *seep* through the ground, *wet* the clothes. Heavy rain *drenched* the garden.

soft *adjective* The rabbit's fur was soft. *Similar words*: *fluffy* clouds, *gentle* sound, *mild* weather, *slack* muscles. *Opposite words*: **hard**, firm, rocky.

some *adjective* Some people were waiting for the bus. *Similar words*: a *few* drops of rain, *several* pages of words, a *handful* of raisins, a *number* of people.

song *noun* My favorite song is about animals. *Similar words*: *music* I can sing, play a *tune* on the piano, whistle a *melody*, sing a *carol*, a *chant* sung over and over, *lullaby* for a baby.

special *adjective* As a special treat, we got to stay up late. *Similar words*: *rare* stamp collection, *choice* seats at the theater, *unusual* talent, *precious* diamond ring. *Opposite words*: **common**, everyday, **ordinary.**

stop *verb* Stop at the corner. *Similar words*: *brake* the car at a stop sign, *halt* the march for a rest, *pause* for a drink of water, *hesitate* before writing the answer, *quit* making the same mistake, cars *stall* on a steep hill, *end* the performance, *cease* making a noise, *interrupt* the program, *prevent* tooth decay, *delay* the game because of rain. *Opposite words*: start, begin.

strict *adjective* Our town has strict laws against littering. *Similar words*: *harsh* rules to obey, *stern* commands of the leader, *severe* expression.

string *noun* Tie the package with a piece of string. *Similar words*: the *cord* that pulls the curtains, tie with *twine*, wool *yarn*, sewing *thread*, a cowboy's *rope*.

strong *adjective* Exercise builds strong muscles. *Similar words*: a *hardy* plant, a *muscular* athlete. *Opposite words*: feeble, fragile, weak.

stupid *adjective* The stupid act caused a wreck. *Similar words*: a *foolish* decision, a *silly* idea, a *pointless* joke, an *idiotic* phrase.

sure *adjective* Are you sure you've done the best you know how to do? *Similar words*: *certain* to get the job, *determined* runner in the race, *steady* pace, *firm* ground, *safe* plan.

surprised *adjective* Surprised by the start of the story, I read it all. *Similar words*: *amazed* winner, *astonished* audience, *shocked* expression, *startled* rabbit.

surprising *adjective* The taste of the new food was surprising. *Similar words*: the *unforeseen* result, an *unexpected* visitor, the *unpredicted* storm.

swamp *noun* Cypress trees may grow in a swamp. *Similar words*: cranberry *bog*, birds in a *marsh*, *mud flats* by the ocean.

377

Thesaurus

swim *verb* It is fun to swim in the ocean. *Similar words*: *float* on an inner tube, *paddle* across the pond, *bob* up and down in the pool, *wade* in the shallow water, *tread water*.

T t

take *verb* How many oranges did they take? *Similar words*: **grab** a handful of leaves, *get hold of* a new book, *seize* control, **carry** the groceries home.

talk *verb* He likes to talk with children about their hobbies. *Similar words*: *chat* with my friend before class, *chatter* without listening, *gossip* about the neighbors, *speak* a few words, *recite* poetry out loud, *lecture* about grizzly bears, *babble* like a baby, **whisper** so no one else can hear.

tasty *adjective* That was a tasty sandwich. *Similar words*: *delicious* homemade bread, *flavorful* salad, *yummy* pizza. *Opposite words*: bitter, stale.

tease *verb* The cartoon mice tease the cat. *Similar words*: *mock* the villain in the story, crows *taunt* the scarecrow, *jeer* at each other, *sneer* at the new invention.

tell *verb* The teacher could tell many interesting stories. *Similar words*: *report* the news, *state* the facts, **say** what you mean, *express* your ideas, *recite* a story.

thing *noun* What kinds of things did you find in the attic? *Similar words*: that strange *object*, kitchen *utensil* for cooking, *artifact* in a museum, *article* of clothing, an *item* for sale.

throw *verb* The pitcher will throw the ball to the catcher. *Similar words*: *toss* me an apple, *pitch* the baseball, *chuck* a log into the fireplace, *lob* a basketball, *fling* a handful of pebbles.

tired *adjective* The runners are tired after a race. *Similar words*: *worn out* by the swim, *exhausted* after a hike, *weary* after work. *Opposite words*: brisk, frisky.

together *adverb* We saluted the flag together. *Similar words*: *united* in marriage, sing in *unison*.

tool *noun* A drill is a handy tool for making holes. *Similar words*: *equipment* used by carpenters, *machine* for making lenses, *gears* to move machinery, *instrument* to measure distance, a *device* to make work easier.

touch *verb* The runner did not touch base. *Similar words*: *brush* close to another person, *rub* a sore back, *pat* on the head, *tag* the runner, *tap* on the shoulder, *tickle* to make laugh, *handle* a snake, *stroke* a purring kitten, *nudge* with your elbow.

trip *noun* We took a trip to the mountains. *Similar words*: a slow *journey* across the desert, an early morning *flight* in the plane, a *tour* of the city, a *voyage* across the ocean, a *cruise* on a ship.

try *verb* Try to do your best work. *Similar words: attempt* to read a hard book, *aim* to please, *seek* to win the game, *strive* to get a good grade.

turn *verb* Turn to look behind you. *Similar words: twirl* around and around, *crank* the wheel to start the motor, *twist* the dial, *wring* the water out of your socks, *spin* the top, *whirl* overhead, the earth *revolves* around the sun and *rotates* on its axis.

two *adjective* Use two hands to hold on. *Similar words: both* animals, *double-decker* bus, an egg with a *double* yolk, *twin* sheep.

U u

ugly *adjective* The ugly building was unpainted and ready to fall down. *Similar words:* a *bad-looking* cut on a finger, the *hideous* beast. *Opposite words:* handsome, **pretty**.

under *adverb* The divers went under. *Similar words:* anyone age sixteen and **below**, lift the lid and look *beneath*, found it *underneath*. *Opposite words:* **above**, over, overhead.

V v

vain *adjective* Vain people admire themselves all the time. *Similar word: conceited* people bragging about what they do.

very *adverb* A whale is very big. *Similar words:* a *truly* good player, *extremely* happy, *especially* strong, *deeply* ashamed, *terribly* funny.

W w

wait *verb* I will wait for the next bus. *Similar words: stand* in line, *rest* in the chair, *be still* and listen, *perch* on the fence, *settle* in for the winter, *remain* at your desk.

walk *verb* Let's walk, not drive, to the park. *Similar words:* soldiers *march* in step, *strut* like a proud peacock, dress up and *parade* around the room, tigers *pace* back and forth, *crawl* like a baby, *creep* under the bushes, **limp** with a sore foot, **plod** along at the end of the day, *tiptoe* quietly, *hike* for three miles, horses *prance* about, kittens *skitter* across the floor, *tread* heavily, *stride* with long steps.

wander *verb* Did the child wander into the street without looking? *Similar words: drift* without plan or purpose, *roam* across the open spaces, *stray* away from home, *dawdle* behind the other children, *stroll* around the neighborhood, *amble* down the street in no hurry.

want *verb* Do you want to check a book out of the library? *Similar words: desire* a long and happy life, *hope* for a new bicycle, *long for* a vacation, *yearn* for a bedroom of my own. *Opposite words:* refuse, have, **hate**.

Thesaurus

water *noun* I drank a glass of water. *Similar words*: the *flood* destroying the bridge, *rain* that showered the earth, *snow* on my mittens, *steam* out of the hot teakettle, *tides* coming in and going out, *waves* on the ocean, only a *trickle* out of the broken faucet, *stream* flowing to the *lake*.

wet *adjective* The wet dog shook himself. *Similar words*: mist making my clothes *damp*, *melting* snow and ice, *moist* from the fog, rain on *slippery* streets, the garden *muddy* from the rain. *Opposite words*: dry, waterproof.

whisper *verb* I will whisper a secret in your ear. *Similar words*: *mumble* the answer, *mutter* to myself. *Opposite words*: **shout**, yell, scream, roar.

white *adjective* Puffy white clouds floated in the sky. *Similar words*: *ivory* keys on the piano, *pearly* teeth.

wiggle *verb* Children wiggle their toes in the water. *Similar words*: *squirm* in your seat, *wriggle* out of wet clothes.

wind *noun* The leaves were scattered by the blowing wind. *Similar words*: the gentle *breeze* at the shore, sudden *gust* blowing the hat off, *twister* destroying many homes, *whirlwind* uprooting the tree, *cyclone* carrying off the roof.

winning *adjective* We cheered the winning team. *Similar words*: the *successful* student, hail the *conquering* hero, the *victorious* team, the *triumphant* band marching proudly. *Opposite words*: beaten, failing, defeated, losing.

wipe *verb* Wipe up the milk spilled on the desk. *Similar words*: *shine* your shoes with a brush, *polish* silver with a soft cloth, *mop* the floor, *rub* with a towel, *swab* the deck.

wonderful *adjective* There was a wonderful dinosaur exhibit at the museum. *Similar words*: *marvelous* time at the zoo, *fantastic* concert, an *excellent* book.

wood *noun* It is fun to make a box out of wood. *Similar words*: wide *beam* on the roof, sawed a *board* for the picnic table, bark of an oak tree, *log* floated down the river to the sawmill, a round *peg* in the hole, tall telephone *pole*.

worried *adjective* The child was worried about losing lunch money. *Similar words*: *concerned* citizens, *alarmed* children crying, *anxious* to get test results, *dismayed* about the smashed bike, *distressed* by news reports, *fretful* babies. *Opposite words*: relieved, carefree.

wrap *verb* Wrap the birthday presents. *Similar words*: *drape* the table with a cloth, *encase* the gems in a velvet box, *enclose* the money in a card, *bundle* yourself in a warm coat, *bind* the stack of newspapers.

Type of Writing: Personal Story

A **personal story** is a story with these features:

◆ It tells a story that involved the writer. The story can be true or made-up.
◆ The writer uses the words *I*, *me*, or *my* in the story.
◆ It tells about the time, place, and people in the story.
◆ It may tell about the events in the order in which they happened.
◆ It shows the writer's feelings about the experience.

Writers of personal stories tell about themselves or others. They may tell about something that really happened or about something they imagine. The writer describes the events and the feelings people have about the events. A personal story makes a clear point about a story that matters to the writer.

Writing About Personal Stories

1. Imagine telling a story about a slumber party you went to at your cousin's house. Would you tell the story to your dentist the same way you would tell it to one of your friends? Explain your answer in a few sentences.
2. A list of important moments in your life may provide ideas for personal stories. To begin such a list, finish each of the statements below:
    a. I am proudest of the time that I . . .
    b. I had a real adventure when . . .
    c. It felt as if everything went wrong when . . .
    d. I was really happy the day I . . .

3. Sometimes it's fun to look at what happens in your life through the eyes of someone or something else. Pretend you are an umbrella. Think about how it feels when it is out in the rain. What do you think it's like to go out only on rainy days. Write a few sentences telling what it's like to be an umbrella.

4. Suppose you could pick anyone in the world to tell about in a story. First, tell who it would be. Next, write one sentence to explain why you picked this person. Then, in a sentence or two, tell about something that happened to this person that would make an interesting personal story.

Reading More Personal Stories

It's fun to read about other people's lives. Sometimes, it's almost as if you can share how they feel and understand what they think.

Dear Daddy by Philippe Dupasquier

Sophie's father is in the Navy. She misses him and wants to tell him about her life. On each page, words and pictures show what Sophie is doing and also what her father is doing on his ship at sea.

Koko's Kitten by Francine Patterson

This is the true story of Koko, a gorilla. Koko is a gentle animal who loves her kitten, All Ball.

Pelé by Julian May

This book tells about Pelé's early life in Brazil and also tells about his success as a soccer player when he grows up.

Type of Writing: How-To Paragraph

A **how-to paragraph** has these features:

- A **topic sentence** names the job to be done.
- It names the materials needed.
- **Detail sentences** tell each step to be followed.
- The steps are presented in their correct order.

"How-to" writing is important in daily life. People sometimes need instructions about such things as how to put together a toy or how to bake a cake.

Writing About How-To Paragraphs

1. A phone book is an example of a kind of book that is used in a special way. Think of another book that is also used in a special way, and write directions for using it.
2. Write what kind of book would tell you how to do each activity below:
   - **a.** growing tomatoes
   - **b.** making pizza
   - **c.** fixing a leaky faucet
   - **d.** multiplying

Reading More How-To Books

The Boomerang Book by M.J. Hansen
   This fascinating book tells you the history of the boomerang. It also tells you how to make one and how to fly it.

In My Garden: A Child's Gardening Book by Helen Oechsli
   Would you like to grow your own vegetables? This book tells you how to prepare the soil, plant the seeds, and take care of the plants. It also tells when your vegetables are ready to pick.

Type of Writing: Book Report

A **book report** has these features:

- It names the title and the author.
- It lists the main characters.
- It tells the **plot**, the main events in the story, without giving away the ending.
- It tells why the writer of the book report liked or disliked the book.

What makes a book good? What makes a book one that others should also read? The writer of a book report learns to answer these questions. Knowing how to judge a book makes reading more enjoyable. It also helps guide other readers to books that they will learn from and enjoy.

Writing About Book Reports

1. What kinds of books do you enjoy reading? For example, do you like books with talking animals, books with characters who are your own age, or books that are funny? List two kinds of books you like. Then write one or two sentences to explain why you like each kind of book.

2. Suppose a character in a book you read could leave the book and spend a day with you. What character would you most like to spend a day with? Name the character. Tell what book the character is from. Then write a few sentences telling why you picked this character and what you would do during the day you spent together.

3. You have been asked to choose a book to put in a time capsule. The time capsule will not be opened for 100 years. You have been asked to pick a book that you think readers your age will enjoy no matter what year it is. Choose a book you have already read. Write a few sentences about why you would put that book in the time capsule.

Reading for a Book Report

Each of the following books has been judged by writers to be a book good enough to recommend to others. Perhaps you would enjoy using one of them for a book report of your own.

Small Wolf by Nathaniel Benchley
In New York, in the early pioneer days, a Native American boy tries to be friends with the Dutch settlers. Because they don't understand each other's languages or customs, misunderstandings arise.

The Velveteen Rabbit by Margery Williams
At first he was a new, fresh toy rabbit, arriving in a Christmas stocking. The boy loved him so much he wore the velveteen away. Then the old, tired toy was thrown away—until something special happened.

The Picture Life of Martin Luther King, Jr.
by Margaret Young
Through words and pictures, this book shows you why Martin Luther King, Jr. was an important person. The book also explains how the civil–rights movement affected the lives of black people in America.

Type of Writing: Directions

Directions tell you how to get from one place to another.

- They name the place where you are and the place where you are going.
- They are divided into simple steps.
- The steps are given in order.
- They include landmarks that make them easy to follow.
- A landmark is something easy to spot, such as a firehouse or a radio tower.
- The directions are clear and exact.

One type of practical writing used in everyday life is writing directions. Phrases similar to, "First you go three blocks," "Next you . . . ," and "After that, you . . ." help the reader follow the directions.

Writing About Directions

1. Do you think a person could still reach the right place if the writer of the directions left out a street or forgot to say where to turn? Why? Write your answer in one or two complete sentences.

Reading More Directions

How to Read a Highway Map by Dorothy Rhodes
This book has all the information you need to become a good navigator on unfamiliar roads.

Type of Writing: Letters

A **friendly letter** has these features:

- It shares news with a friend or family member.
- It is written in a friendly way.
- It has a **heading**, a **greeting**, a **body**, a **closing**, and a **signature**.

A letter is a way of sharing thoughts with friends or relatives who are far away.

Writing About Letters

1. Write a good closing for a friendly letter to each of the following people:
   - **a.** your favorite uncle
   - **c.** your teacher
   - **b.** your best friend
   - **d.** your sister at camp
2. Some people write friendly letters to friends who have moved away. Others write to share important news or send holiday greetings. In one or two complete sentences, tell when you write letters.

Reading More Letters

More Stories Julian Tells by Ann Cameron
   Julian sends messages in bottles, tries to be brave, and makes bets with friends.

Etiquette: Your Ticket to Good Times by Helen Hoke
   The chapter on letters gives examples of thank-you notes, invitations, and acceptance letters.

Type of Writing: Research Report

A **research report** has these features:

- It gives information on a topic you have looked up and researched.
- The topic may be divided into two or more **main ideas**.
- Each main idea is supported with facts.
- All information in the report is true. It does not contain opinions.

The writer of a research report is like a detective. The writer hunts for information, then writes about the topic in his or her own way.

Writing About Research Reports

1. List four topics you would like to know more about. Then tell where you think you could find information about each topic.

Reading for Research Reports

Killer Fish by Russell Freedman

This is a good book for research on the dangerous creatures in the ocean. You'll find facts on marine animals that bite, sting, or shock when attacked.

The Sky, the Moon and the Stars by Mae Freeman

This book describes the sun, moon, planets, and stars. It includes experiments you can do and information about space, time, and distance.

Type of Writing: Descriptive Writing

Descriptive writing has these features:

- It tells about a particular person, place, or thing.
- It uses **sensory words** to describe. Sensory words tell how something looks, feels, sounds, tastes, or smells.
- It paints a picture with colorful words.

Descriptive writing lets readers "see" a person, place, event, or object. The use of details about sight, sound, smell, taste, and touch paints word pictures for readers. With the best descriptive writing, readers feel as if they were right there in the scene with the subject.

Writing About Descriptive Writing

1. Sometimes you can describe things by comparing them to other things. Example: Lying in the sun at the beach is like being a sausage in a frying pan. Finish each sentence below. Use your imagination.
   a. My hair feels like . . .
   b. The moon at night is like . . .
   c. Brushing my teeth is like . . .
   d. Milk tastes like . . .

2. Write a description of an apple that focuses on the five senses. Write one sentence about an apple for each of these senses:
   a. sight   **c.** smell   **e.** taste
   b. sound   **d.** touch or texture

3. Colors are important words of description. A description of a city on a rainy day, for example, might include the words *silver puddles of water*. Give one color detail to describe each of the following scenes:

a. a field of pumpkins on a sunny day

b. the sky just before a thunderstorm

c. the vegetable counter of a supermarket

Reading More Descriptive Writing

In novels, biographies, stories, and poems, writers describe real and imaginary worlds. The more you read, the easier it will be for you to describe your own special world.

Belinda's Hurricane by Elizabeth Winthrop

The author describes a ferocious hurricane that takes place while Belinda is visiting her grandmother. Belinda rescues a dog from the storm and makes friends with the dog's owner, Mr. Fletcher.

They Put on Masks by Byrd Baylor

During traditional dances and ceremonies, Native Americans wear interesting masks. The author describes dances that are about food, the earth, and the seasons.

The Trek by Ann Jonas

A girl uses her imagination to turn her daily walk to school into a jungle trek. Chimneys become giraffes and garbage cans become rhinos. Through the author's exact and colorful descriptions, you also see this magical world.

Type of Writing: Story

A **story** has these features:

- It has **characters**, people or animals in the story.
- It has a **setting**, the time and place of the story.
- It has a **plot**, the events that happen in the story.
- The **introduction** tells the setting and characters.
- The **solution attempts** are ways the characters try to solve the problem.
- The **outcome** tells how the problem is solved.

Writers of stories invent their own worlds. They can use characters and situations from their imaginations.

Writing About Stories

1. In a story, a character usually faces a problem. For example, a child wants a pet but is allergic to cat and dog hair. Write three other problems that you could use in a story.

2. The ending of a story is important. Here are some story outlines. Tell in a few sentences how you would end each story:

   a. Claude's sister and brother are playing on opposite teams in an important soccer match. Which team does he cheer for?

   b. The morning of the school play Karen spills grape juice on her costume. What does she do?

   c. Ed promised to go to a friend's birthday party. His parents surprised him with tickets to the circus for the same day. What will he do?

3. Think of a story you have read and would like to change. Pretend you could become part of the story. Name the story. Then write a few sentences telling what character you would be and how you would change what happens.

Reading More Stories

Does your library have a story hour? If so, listening to stories at story hour is a good way to learn to become a storyteller. In the short-story collections listed below, you may find stories you'd enjoy telling to someone else.

The Adventures of Ali Baba Bernstein by Johanna Hurwitz
David Bernstein is eight. To make himself different, he changes his name to Ali Baba. Through seven separate adventures, he keeps his new name. Then he invites every David Bernstein in the phone book to his ninth birthday party. What do you think he learns?

The Knee-High Man and Other Tales by Julius Lester
In "The Knee-High Man," a short man seeks advice on how to grow taller. In "The Farmer and the Snake," a farmer puts a frozen snake in his coat to thaw. In all these stories, a character learns a lesson about how to avoid trouble.

Super Sleuth: Twelve Solve-It-Yourself Mysteries by Jackie Vivelo
Stories include "The Pizza Puzzle," "Stop Thief!" and "The Big Diamond Robbery." Along with Ellen and Beagle, you are a detective.

Steps of Writing: When Time Matters

Even when your writing time is limited, you use the steps of writing. You simply spend less time on each step.

Planning Your Time

Know how much time you have. Decide how to divide it. For example, if you have 30 minutes, spend 5-10 minutes planning. Spend 15-20 minutes drafting. Spend 5-10 minutes revising and proofreading.

Understanding the Directions

First, read the directions carefully. Pay attention to words that tell your audience and purpose such as "describe," and "tell your classmates how to." Also, notice the words that tell your topic.

Planning

It is especially important to think carefully before doing a timed writing. You will have time to write only one draft. Choose the best way to get ideas quickly about your topic. Perhaps you can do clustering or draw a cartoon strip. Then look at your work and decide which part should come first, next, and last.

Composing

When you write, remember your purpose and your audience. The beginning should make the subject clear. The middle should give exact details. The ending should complete your topic. If you get stuck, look back at your notes for ideas.

Revising and Proofreading

Read over your work and ask yourself, "Will my reader know what I mean?" If you need to, add or take away words or groups of words to make sentences clearer. Check punctuation, spelling, and capitalization. Correct any errors.

A. Practice

Write a friendly letter in 30 minutes. First read the directions below. Then follow the steps described.

Directions: Write a friendly letter to a relative in another city. Tell about something that happened recently to you or to someone you know. It may be something you saw or did. It might include other people. Use exact words. Explain clearly what you mean.

1. Notice the important words in the directions. They are "friendly letter," "exact words," "relative," and "something that happened to you."
2. Decide on something that happened to you or to someone you know. Now, brainstorm about your topic. Use a word cluster, list, or word map. Think of sight, sound, smell, taste, or touch words. Spend about five minutes on this step.
3. Write your letter. Try not to stop writing too often. If you get stuck, take an idea from the brainstorming you've done.
4. Spend the last five minutes reading your letter. Will it make sense to the reader? Add words or take out words if you need to. Correct any errors in punctuation, spelling, or capitalization.

B. Practice

Directions: Write a paragraph for your classmates that describes something you use every day. For example, it may be your toothbrush. It could be your bicycle. It might be a spoon or fork. Tell what it is. Tell how you use it. Describe it completely. You have 30 minutes.

Steps of Writing: When You Use a Computer

Writing on a computer is special. It is fun to see your words appear on the screen. The steps of writing are still important when you write on a computer.

You can do your brainstorming on a computer. It is easy to move words around or take them out. You can see your ideas as you play with the words. You may want to group ideas that go together in different places on the screen. This helps you get organized. When you finish gathering ideas and planning your writing, save your work. You may want to print it to use later.

Writing your draft is easier on a computer. You never have to worry about messy handwriting. You can put your ideas down very quickly. If you need to, look back at your notes while you are writing.

When you have finished your draft, read it to make sure the meaning is clear. It may help to have a classmate read your draft on the screen or after you print it. If you need to add or remove words, it will be easy on the computer. Make sure your capitalization, punctuation, and spelling are correct. Then you can print your work.

Letter Forms

Friendly Letters

> heading   1636 Santa Cruz Avenue
> San Diego, California 92101
> August 14, 19--
>
> Dear Jeanne,   greeting
> It has been so much fun to stay at the beach
> and play in the waves. Maybe next summer we
> can take you along and leave my brother at home.
>
> closing   Sincerely,
> signature   Maria

A **friendly letter** has these features:

- The **heading** gives the writer's address and the date. There is a comma between the city and state. A comma is also used between the day and the year.
- The **greeting** begins with a capital letter and is followed by a comma.
- The **body** of the letter contains the writer's message. Each paragraph of the body is indented.
- The **closing** begins with a capital letter and is followed by a comma.
- The **signature** is the writer's signed name.

Practice: Write a friendly letter to someone you know. Label the heading, greeting, body, closing, and signature of your letter.

Envelopes

Maria Salerno
1636 Santa Cruz Avenue   return address
San Diego, CA 92101

                    Jeanne Clark
receiver's address *163 Emerald Court*
                    Grapevine, TX 76051

An **addressed envelope** has these features:

• The **return address** gives the writer's name and address. The return address appears in the upper left-hand corner.

• The **receiver's address** gives the name and address of the person who is receiving the letter. The receiver's address appears in the middle of the envelope.

Practice: Draw an envelope on your paper. Use this information to address the envelope.
To: List Fox 153 Willis Street Utica, New York 13505
From: Mike Collins 800 River Vista Drive Brooksville, Florida 33573

Thank You Notes

A **thank-you note** has the same features as a friendly letter. Here is the body of a thank-you note.

> *Thank you for the beautiful bouquet of balloons you sent to my party. I let each of my guests take one balloon home.*

Invitations

> To: *Jenny Wilson*
> Please come to: *A Skateboard Club Meeting*
> Where: *835 Northport Place*
> Date: *Friday, May 19th*
> Time: *4:00 to 5:00 p.m.*
> From: *your friend, Michael*

An **invitation** is a short letter, form, or note that invites someone to an event. The invitation should tell what the event is, the time and place it will be held, and the name of the sender.

Practice: Read the invitation above. Write the answers to these questions:
1. What event has Jenny been invited to?
2. Where is it being held?
3. What time does it begin?

Spelling Strategies

1. You can learn how to spell in different ways. Which ways work best for you?

+ **Look at the word**. See the letters in it. Picture the word in your mind, remembering the order of its letters.
+ **Say the word aloud**. Hear the sounds in it. What letter or letters make each sound?
+ **Write the word**. Practice making the letters. You can also write the words you misspell in a notebook. Write the words correctly. Make the notebook like a dictionary by using one page for each letter of the alphabet. Review your words each week.

2. Always check your spelling when you proofread. Follow these steps:

+ Circle each word you think is misspelled.
+ Write the word again. Does it look right to you?
+ Check in a dictionary if you are not sure.

3. Some words share the same letter pattern. By knowing a pattern, you can spell many words.

+ Some words with the *and* pattern include
    band   hand   land   sand   stand
+ Some words with the *eat* pattern include
    beat   feat   heat   meat   seat

What other spelling patterns do you know?

4. Many words can be broken into parts. Knowing word parts can help you spell entire words.

• These words start with the word part *re*:

reheat   rewrite   repaint

• These words end with the word part *ly*:

finally   lonely   quickly

What other word parts do you know?

Commonly Misspelled Words		
1. again	18. heard	35. some
2. another	19. into	36. sure
3. answer	20. laugh	37. surprise
4. beautiful	21. lose	38. their
5. busy	22. meant	39. there
6. chief	23. minute	40. though
7. come	24. money	41. thought
8. country	25. most	42. threw
9. course	26. neighbor	43. through
10. does	27. nothing	44. too
11. early	28. once	45. two
12. enough	29. only	46. Wednesday
13. every	30. people	47. who
14. friend	31. piece	48. wild
15. gone	32. quiet	49. woman
16. great	33. said	50. you're
17. hear	34. sign	

Handwriting Model

When you write to someone, it is important that they are able to understand and enjoy what you say. This handwriting is clear and neat. It's a good model for your own writing.

GRAMMAR DEFINITIONS AND PRACTICE

Sentences I

- A **sentence** is a group of words that tells a complete thought. A sentence starts with a capital letter and ends with an end mark. (*page 40*)

  <u>A</u> nurse helps sick people<u>.</u>

Practice Write *sentence* or *not a sentence* next to each group of words.

   1. A busy hospital.
   2. Brings a bandage.
   3. Nurses work hard.
   4. A tray with dinner on it.
   5. A doctor looks at the patient.

Practice Write each group of words that is a complete thought. Add capital letters and end marks as needed.

   7. ricardo is a nurse
   8. the kind nurse
   9. the man asks for a pillow
  10. a warm blanket
  11. ricardo helps
  12. people thank the nurse

- A **statement** is a sentence that tells something. Put a period at the end of a statement. (*page 42*)

  Florence Nightingale lived in England<u>.</u>
- A **question** is a sentence that asks for information. Put a question mark at the end of a question. (*page 42*)

  How did Florence help people<u>?</u>

Practice Write each sentence. Write *statement* or *question* next to each sentence.

  1. Did Florence become a nurse?

  2. Where did Florence study?

  3. The woman traveled to Paris.

  4. Florence worked in a hospital.

  5. Did Florence help soldiers?

  6. The nurse sailed to Turkey.

  7. The soldiers admired Florence.

Practice Write each sentence with the correct end mark. Write *statement* or *question* next to each sentence.

  8. Where is Turkey?

  9. The soldiers needed medicine.

10. What hospital did Florence work in?

11. Florence saved many lives.

12. Why did Florence become famous?

13. The children read about the nurse.

14. What did the students learn?

- A **command** is a sentence that tells somebody to do something. Put a period at the end of a command. (*page 44*)

    Please come here.

- An **exclamation** is a sentence that shows strong feeling or surprise. Put an exclamation mark at the end of an exclamation. (*page 44*)

    How tall that tree is!

Practice Write each sentence. Write *command* or *exclamation* next to each sentence.

  1. Take the children to the zoo.

  2. What a sunny day it is!

3. Take a picture of the moose.

4. Please feed the seals.

5. Wow, that seal swims fast!

6. What a lot of water the seals splash!

7. Stand behind the gate.

Practice Write each sentence with the correct end mark. Write *command* or *exclamation* next to each sentence.

8. Hand me a towel

9. Look at the elephant

10. What big ears the animal has

11. How long the trunk is

12. Show the class a film about elephants

13. Turn out the lights

◆ The complete subject of a sentence tells whom or what the sentence is about. (*page 48*)

Anna Orlov likes birthdays.

Practice Write each sentence. Underline the complete subject.

1. Anna gives a birthday party.

2. Many friends come to the party.

3. Balloons hang from the ceiling.

4. All the children wear party hats.

5. Anna's grandparents bring a gift.

6. The box is large.

7. Pretty blue paper covers the box.

8. A toy robot is inside.

9. The excited girl winds up the robot.
10. The funny machine scoots quickly.
11. The cat chases the robot.
12. Anna laughs.
13. Mother brings a cake to the table.
14. The special birthday cake has fruit on top.
15. The party makes Anna happy.
16. All the guests thank Anna.

⬩ The **complete predicate** of a sentence tells what the subject does. (*page 50*)

Abraham Lincoln came from Kentucky.

Practice Write each sentence. Underline the complete predicate.
1. The family moved to Indiana.
2. Young Abe lived in a log cabin.
3. Father plowed the fields.
4. The boy worked on the farm.
5. Abe studied at a small school.
6. All the students read aloud.
7. The teacher listened to their lessons.
8. Abe owned only a few books.
9. The boy wrote poems.
10. The curious boy read all the books.
11. Young Lincoln sailed a boat to New Orleans.
12. The boat carried food from the farm.
13. The river flowed.
14. Abe rowed.
15. Abe sold the food in a market.
16. The young man returned with many stories.

Nouns

- A **noun** is a word that names a person, place, or thing. (*page 78*)

    The <u>girl</u> rides a <u>bicycle</u> in the <u>park</u>.

Practice Write each sentence. Underline all the nouns.

1. Ducks swim on the pond.
2. A woman feeds the birds.
3. Julio went to school.
4. Many children played in the playground.
5. The bus turns at the corner.
6. Janet bought a new coat.
7. The doctor wears a white jacket.
8. The city has a large hospital.
9. Mom fixed the leaky faucet.
10. Several students ate lunch in the park.

- A **singular noun** is a word that names one person, place, or thing. (*page 80*)

    A <u>student</u> got one <u>book</u> at the <u>library</u>.

- A **plural noun** is a word that names more than one person, place, or thing. (*page 80*)

    The <u>students</u> read about <u>cities</u> in <u>books</u>.

Practice Write each sentence. Underline singular nouns once. Underline plural nouns twice.

1. One tree produces many bananas.
2. Workers cover each bunch.
3. Insects attack the trees.
4. The box contains apples.

5. The big tomato weighed four pounds.
6. Many farmers plant beets.
7. Ten cows eat in the barn.
8. The chickens lay several eggs.
9. A rake leans against the house.
10. A horse munches oats from a bag.

- Add *es* to form the plural of nouns that end in *s, ss, sh, ch,* or *x.* (*page 82*)

  classes   boxes   benches   dishes
- If a noun ends in a consonant and *y,* change the *y* to *i* and add *es* to form the plural. (*page 82*)

  family → families   berry → berries
- Some nouns do not follow rules. These nouns change their spelling to form the plural. (*page 82*)

  foot → feet   child → children

Practice Write the plural form of each singular noun.

1. cherry	**6.** story
2. man	**7.** mouse
3. ax	**8.** puppy
4. dish	**9.** branch
5. circus	**10.** bush

- A **common noun** names any person, place, or thing. A common noun begins with a small letter. (*page 84*)

  A person visits a city.
- A **proper noun** names a particular person, place, or thing. Capitalize the most important words in a proper noun. (*page 84*)

  Alonzo sees the Statue of Liberty.

Practice Write each sentence. Underline the common nouns. Capitalize the proper nouns.

1. theresa told about her trip to wyoming.
2. The family saw yellowstone national park.
3. Some of the park is in montana.
4. The highest point is eagle peak.
5. Several rivers flow from yellowstone lake.
6. People swim in the lake.
7. john colter discovered the park.
8. Visitors see many bears.
9. stephen visited the grand canyon.

♦ A **possessive** is a word that tells whom or what owns or has something. (*page 86*)

Kira has an apple. <u>Kira's</u> apple

Practice Find the noun in each sentence that owns or has something. Write that word as a possessive.

1. Chen owns a radio. _____ radio
2. The reporter has a pen. the _____ pen
3. The mayor has an office. the _____ office
4. Luisa owns a camera. _____ camera
5. Jorge owns a car. _____ car
6. The car has an engine. the _____ engine
7. The girl owns a kitten. the _____ kitten
8. The kitten has a bed. the _____ bed
9. Tyrone owns a football. _____ football

♦ A **plural possessive** shows that more than one person, place, or thing owns something. If a plural noun ends in *s*, add an apostrophe (') after the *s* to form the plural possessive. (*page 88*)

The students have a team. the <u>students'</u> team

◆ If a plural noun does *not* end in *s*, add *'s* to form the plural possessive. (*page 88*)

The women have a boat. the <u>women's</u> boat

Practice. Write each sentence. Write the noun in parentheses as a possessive.

1. The barber trimmed the (men) hair.
2. The (barbers) chairs were soft.
3. Many parents came to the (children) play.
4. The (players) music is loud.
5. The (girls) voices are clear.
6. Everyone liked the (boys) costumes.
7. The teacher collected the (students) papers.
8. The (neighbors) dogs bark loudly.
9. Janice joined the (women) track team.
10. Rita discovered the (mice) nest.

◆ Begin the names of people, places, titles, days, and months with a capital letter. The first letter of a name is called an **initial**. An initial that is used instead of a name is always capitalized and followed by a period. (*pages 90, 92*)

<u>Dr</u>. <u>H</u>enry <u>T</u>. <u>R</u>uiz   <u>M</u>onday, <u>J</u>une 3   <u>M</u>ills, <u>I</u>owa

Practice Write each name, title, or date. Use capital letters and periods where they are needed.

1. friday, march 2
2. mr. lucien rops
3. dr j t burns
4. beech drive
5. ms lucy m walters
6. tempe, arizona
7. tuesday, august 17
8. mrs cindy t williams
9. first avenue
10. saturday, july 4

Verbs I

- An **action verb** is a word that tells what someone or something does. (*page 128*)

    The engine <u>pulls</u> the train.

Practice Write each sentence. Underline each action verb.

1. The diver jumps into the pool.
2. The children swim to the other side.
3. The dog races around the pool.
4. Tony splashes Juan.
5. Jenny kicks with her feet.
6. Kristen slides down the hill.
7. The sled bumps into a bank of snow.
8. Kristen tumbles off the sled.
9. The girl brushes off the snow.
10. All the children laugh.
11. Muffy barks loudly.
12. The kitten climbs a tree.
13. Imelda reaches for the kitten.

- A verb in the **present tense** tells about an action that happens now. (*page 130*)

    Yolanda <u>points</u> to the moon.

Practice Write each sentence with the correct present tense verb in parentheses.

1. The children (make, makes) puppets today.
2. Bernice (draw, draws) an outline.
3. Janine (trace, traces) the design.
4. The girls (cut, cuts) the paper.
5. The students (paint, paints) the puppets.

6. Paul (snip, snips) cloth for the costumes.

7. Wayne (fasten, fastens) the cloth.

8. Melba (place, places) a hat on the puppet.

9. The children (laugh, laughs) at the funny hat.

10. The teacher (look, looks) at the puppets.

11. The students (write, writes) a short play.

12. The children (practice, practices) the play.

♦ If the main word in the subject part of a sentence is a singular noun, add *s* or *es* to the verb. Add *s* or *es* if the subject is *he*, *she*, or *it*. (*page 132*)

> The boy plays.   She joins the game.

♦ If the subject part of a sentence is a plural noun, do not add *s* or *es* to the verb. Do not add *s* or *es* if the subject is *I*, *you*, *we*, or *they*. (*page 132*)

> Monkeys chatter.   They swing through the trees.

Practice Write each sentence with the correct present tense of the verb in parentheses.

1. Farmers (raise, raises) turkeys.

2. A turkey (eat, eats) corn.

3. A tractor (pull, pulls) a plow.

4. Seeds (grow, grows) in the soil.

5. A truck (haul, hauls) milk to the dairy.

6. Storms (bring, brings) rain to the farm.

7. Workers (harvest, harvests) wheat.

8. The farmer (buy, buys) a cow.

9. The cow (give, gives) milk.

10. Several pigs (squeal, squeals) nearby.

11. Farmers (sell, sells) eggs.

12. A horse (sleep, sleeps) under a tree.

- If the present tense verb ends in *ch, s, sh, ss, x,* or *z,* you must add *es.* (*page 134*)

  march ⟶ marches   toss ⟶ tosses   fix ⟶ fixes

- If the present tense verb ends in a consonant and *y,* change the *y* to *i.* Then add *es.* (*page 134*)

  fly ⟶ flies   hurry ⟶ hurries

Practice Write each sentence with the correct form of the verb in the present tense.

1. The girl (toss) the ball.
2. The dog (fetch) the stick.
3. A fly (buzz) near the plate.
4. The cook (brush) the fly away.
5. The waiter (carry) the plate to the table.
6. Hal (fix) a sandwich.
7. Joline (try) the soup.
8. Raymond (hurry) to the table.
9. One person (mix) the batter.
10. Fernando (crush) the garlic.
11. The cook (cry) over the onions.
12. The chicken (fry) in a pan.
13. Brenda (pass) the salt.
14. Ted (wash) the dishes.

- A verb in the **past tense** tells about an action that already happened. Most past tense verbs end in *ed.* (*page 136*)

  The dog learned a new trick.

Practice Write each sentence. Change the underlined present tense verb into the past tense.

1. Ponce de Leon discovers Florida.
2. The Spaniard travels through swamps.

3. The Spanish king <u>owns</u> Florida.
4. American settlers <u>pour</u> into Florida.
5. Farmers <u>plant</u> orange trees there.
6. Some people <u>drain</u> the swamps.
7. Many people <u>visit</u> the state.
8. The visitors <u>need</u> hotels.
9. New schools <u>open</u> in many cities.
10. Scientists <u>launch</u> rockets at Cape Canaveral.

♦ To form the past tense of verbs ending in *e*, drop the *e* and add *ed*. (*page 138*)

   chase ⟶ chas<u>ed</u>   live ⟶ liv<u>ed</u>

♦ To form the past tense of verbs ending in a consonant and *y*, change the *y* to *i*. Then add *ed*. (*page 138*)

   carry ⟶ carr<u>ied</u>   scurry ⟶ scurr<u>ied</u>

♦ To form the past tense of verbs ending in one vowel and a consonant, double the last consonant. Then add *ed*. (*page 138*)

   hum ⟶ humm<u>ed</u>   flap ⟶ flapp<u>ed</u>

Practice Write each sentence. Use the correct form of the verb in the past tense.

1. Laura Ingalls (live) in Wisconsin.
2. The family (move) often.
3. A wagon (carry) the family.
4. The Ingalls (stop) in Kansas.
5. Laura (marry) Almanzo Wilder.
6. The woman (serve) as a newspaper editor.
7. Laura (plan) many stories.
8. People (like) the stories.
9. The class (study) about Laura Wilder.
10. The teacher (pin) a picture of Laura on the board.

Verbs II

◆ The verb *be* is a linking verb. A **linking verb** joins the subject of a sentence with words that name or describe it. (*page 164*)

Maya Angelou is a poet.
The poems are very beautiful.

Practice Write each sentence. Underline the verb. Write whether it is an *action verb* or a *linking verb*.

1. Some blind people walk with a cane.
2. Guide dogs lead blind people.
3. They are very helpful.
4. People taught the dogs commands.
5. The dogs were young.
6. The dog sits.
7. The dog crosses a busy street.
8. We are safe with the dog.
9. Rusty is a guide dog.
10. He was a smart puppy.
11. I am Rusty's owner.
12. Rusty stops at the corner.
13. Cars whiz past.
14. They are dangerous.
15. Guide dogs work hard.

◆ A **main verb** is the most important verb in a sentence. A **helping verb** helps the main verb tell about an action. Add *ed* to most main verbs that follow the helping verbs *have*, *has*, or *had*. (*page 166*)

Winston had worked at a store.

helping verb   main verb

Practice Write each sentence. Form the main verb correctly. Underline the helping verb.

1. Birds have _____ on the roof. (land)
2. Martha had _____ the birds yesterday. (watch)
3. The girl has _____ a sick bird. (help)
4. Martha has _____ the zoo. (call)
5. Workers have _____ the bird away. (carry)
6. Tony has _____ his bike. (fix)
7. Air had _____ from a tire. (leak)
8. The boy has _____ the tire. (patch)
9. The wheel had _____ into a rock. (bump)
10. Friends have _____ air into the tire. (pump)
11. The neighbors have _____ the house. (paint)
12. Mrs. Diaz has _____ a pretty color. (pick)
13. The children have _____ the paint. (mix)
14. Mr. Diaz has _____ the ladder. (raise)
15. The paint has _____ the house. (improve)

◆ **Irregular verbs** do not form the past tense by adding *ed*. (*page 168*)

  The children came home from school.
  Sheba ate a snack.
  The children went to the park.
  Sheba saw a family of squirrels.

Present	Past
come	came
do	did
eat	ate
go	went
run	ran
see	saw

415

◆ The main verb changes when it is used with the helping verbs *have, has,* and *had.* (*page 168*)

Present	Past with *have, has,* or *had*
come	(have, has, had) come
do	(have, has, had) done
eat	(have, has, had) eaten
go	(have, has, had) gone
run	(have, has, had) run
see	(have, has, had) seen

Practice Write each sentence with the correct form of the main verb in parentheses.

1. Settlers have _____ to California. (come)
2. They _____ from the east. (come)
3. The wagons _____ across a desert. (go)
4. The people have _____ tall mountains. (see)
5. They almost _____ out of food. (run)
6. Several pioneer families _____ squirrels for dinner. (eat)
7. Now they have _____ a big meal. (eat)
8. The pioneers have _____ something brave. (do)
9. Mr. Wilmot had _____ a mill in Ohio. (run)
10. A very big ship has _____ into the harbor. (come)
11. The sailors _____ the lighthouse. (see)
12. They _____ onto the deck. (run)
13. The men have _____ into town. (go)
14. The brave sailors _____ much work on the ship. (do)
15. They have _____ many beautiful places. (see)

♦ A **contraction** is a shortened form of two words. An apostrophe (') takes the place of the missing letters. Some verbs can be combined with the word *not* to form contractions. (*page 170*)

is + not ⟶ isn't	has + not ⟶ hasn't
are + not ⟶ aren't	had + not ⟶ hadn't
was + not ⟶ wasn't	do + not ⟶ don't
were + not ⟶ weren't	does + not ⟶ doesn't
have + not ⟶ haven't	did + not ⟶ didn't

♦ To write a contraction, join the verb with the word *not*. Replace the letter *o* in *not* with an apostrophe. (*page 170*)

was not ⟶ wasnot ⟶ wasn't

Practice Write each sentence. Form a contraction for the underlined words.

1. The train <u>has not</u> arrived.
2. The children <u>were not</u> there yet.
3. They <u>have not</u> packed their bags.
4. Jorge <u>did not</u> bring the dog.
5. The dog <u>does not</u> have a ticket.
6. There <u>are not</u> many people on the train.
7. The restaurant <u>is not</u> open.
8. The twins <u>do not</u> want any soup.
9. Josephine <u>was not</u> hungry.
10. The cook <u>had not</u> made enough food.
11. The eggs <u>were not</u> very large.
12. Candy <u>is not</u> good for teeth.
13. The dentist <u>did not</u> drill Bob's tooth.
14. Bob <u>has not</u> eaten many sweets.

Pronouns

- A **pronoun** is a word that takes the place of a noun. A **subject pronoun** takes the place of one or more nouns in the subject part of the sentence. The subject pronouns are *I, you, he, she, it, we,* and *they. (page 206)*

  Tricia plays ball.   She plays ball.
  The children choose teams.   They choose teams.

Practice Write each sentence. Replace each subject noun with a pronoun.

1. Christopher Columbus lived in Genoa.
2. Genoa was a busy port.
3. Ships crowded the harbor.
4. Felipa de Perestrello married Columbus.
5. Felipa and Christopher had a son.
6. Queen Isabella listened to Columbus's plan.
7. The plan promised great wealth.
8. The king and queen gave Columbus three ships for the voyage.
9. The man discovered America.
10. People cheered the brave sailors.
11. The students and I drew a map of the voyage.
12. Ms. Hernandez liked the map.

- An **object pronoun** takes the place of a noun after an action verb. It is found in the predicate part of a sentence. The object pronouns are *me, you, him, her, it, us,* and *them. (page 208)*

  Hiroki calls Tim.   Hiroki calls him.
  Tim answers the phone.   Tim answers it.

Practice Write each sentence. Replace the underlined words with the correct object pronoun.

1. Harriet Quimby flew <u>an airplane</u>.
2. Several pilots taught <u>Harriet</u>.
3. The young woman crossed <u>the English Channel</u>.
4. Fog covered <u>the airport</u>.
5. Harriet saw <u>houses</u> below.
6. Harriet Quimby also wrote <u>articles</u>.
7. Mom took <u>Judy and me</u> on an airplane.
8. We enjoyed <u>the trip</u>.
9. I told <u>dad</u> about the trip.
10. Betty builds <u>models</u>.
11. She won <u>a prize</u> for a model airplane.
12. Betty thanked <u>Mr. Wilde</u> for the prize.
13. Mr. Wilde told <u>Betty</u> about another contest.

♦ *I* is a subject pronoun. Use it in the subject part of a sentence. Always capitalize the pronoun *I*. (*page 210*)
   I need a new shirt.
♦ *Me* is an object pronoun. Use it in the predicate part of a sentence. (*page 210*)
   Dad took me to the store.
♦ When you write or speak, use *I* or *me* last to be polite. (*page 210*)
   Jerry invited Maxine and me to the party.
   Maxine and I wore new clothes.

Practice Write each sentence using the correct word to fill the blanks.

1. Barry and _____ played checkers. (I, me)
2. Mom taught _____. (I, me)

3. _____ made the first move. (I, me)
4. Barry and _____ played all afternoon. (I, me)
5. _____ captured Barry's king. (I, me)
6. Dad took Barry and _____ to a checkers match. (I, me)
7. Hannah told Barry and _____ about chess. (I, me)
8. Hannah and _____ played chess. (I, me)
9. Hannah beat _____ the first time. (I, me)
10. Hannah let _____ start first. (I, me)

◆ **Possessive forms of pronouns** tell whom or what owns or has something. They take the place of possessive nouns. The possessive forms of pronouns are *my, your, his, her, its, our,* and *their*. (*page 212*)

    Monica's scarf is very warm.
    Her scarf is very warm.

Practice Write each sentence. Replace the underlined possessives with possessive forms of pronouns.

1. Maine's state bird is the chickadee.
2. Thomas Edison's laboratory was in New Jersey.
3. We saw Jane Addams's home in Chicago.
4. The settlers' fort guarded Wichita.
5. I took a picture with dad's camera.
6. Chicago's famous zoo is Lincoln Park.
7. George Washington Carver's ideas helped farmers.
8. Roberta's and my trip was interesting.
9. I saw Roberta's snapshots.
10. We looked at the boys' pictures.
11. Mom's movies showed the Rocky Mountains.
12. Jim Bridge's camp was built there.

◆ A **contraction** is a shortened form of two words joined together. An apostrophe (') takes the place of the missing letter or letters in a contraction. Pronouns can be joined with the verbs *am*, *is*, and *are* to form contractions. (*page 214*)

Contraction	Meaning	Contraction	Meaning
I'm	I am	he's	he is
you're	you are	she's	she is
we're	we are	it's	it is
they're	they are		

◆ Pronouns can also be joined with the verbs *will* or *have* to form contractions. (*page 214*)

Contraction	Meaning	Contraction	Meaning
I'll	I will	we'll	we will
you'll	you will	they'll	they will
she'll	she will	I've	I have
he'll	he will	you've	you have

Practice Write each sentence. Use the correct contraction for the underlined words.

1. You have seen Winslow Homer's paintings.
2. They are very beautiful.
3. He is a famous American artist.
4. You will like the pictures.
5. I am interested in pictures of ships.
6. We will look at some pictures.
7. We have visited the museum.
8. It is very large.
9. She is our guide.
10. She will show us many pictures.

Adjectives

♦ An **adjective** is a word that tells about a noun. (*page 244*)

We saw a blue egg.

A bird sits in a round nest.

Practice Write each sentence. Put two lines under each adjective. Put one line under the noun it tells about.

 1. Valerie collects old stamps.

 2. She has a colorful collection.

 3. She keeps it in a large book.

 4. The book has a smooth cover.

 5. Valerie showed me a tiny stamp from Peru.

 6. The square stamp came from Canada.

 7. Mitos gave her a white envelope from Manila.

 8. Valerie loosens the stamp in warm water.

 9. She puts the stamp on a clean page.

10. Valerie looks at it with a happy smile.

♦ Some adjectives answer the question "how many" to tell about a noun. Numbers are special kinds of adjectives. (*page 246*)

I saw one truck with six wheels.

Practice Write each sentence. Underline the adjective that tells how many.

 1. John Glen circled the earth for four hours.

 2. A Russian walked in space for 10 minutes.

 3. Three astronauts traveled to the moon.

 4. The trip took eight days.

 5. The space shuttle is 122 feet long.

6. It has three sections.

7. One part is for the crew.

8. Two doors open at the top.

9. Rory made a model from four pieces of paper.

10. He flew his model seven times.

◆ Some adjectives tell how many without giving the exact number. Words such as *few, many, several,* and *some* all answer the question *how many? (page 246)*

    <u>Some</u> rain fell on a <u>few</u> people.

Practice Write each sentence. Underline each adjective that tells how many.

1. Cowhands herd many cattle.

2. Some cattle get lost.

3. Several cowhands ride after them.

4. The cowhands see a few rabbits.

5. They find several cows near a stream.

6. The animals drink some water.

7. The cowhands find the rest after many hours.

8. The cook has made many biscuits.

9. The cowhands eat some dinner.

10. A few men sing songs after dinner.

◆ The words *a, an,* and *the* are special adjectives. They are called **articles**. *A* and *an* are used only before singular nouns. *(page 248)*

    <u>A</u> student eats <u>an</u> orange.

Practice Write each sentence. Underline each article.

1. A rodeo is exciting.

2. The riders wear colorful outfits.

3. Here comes a clown.
4. The clown falls off his horse.
5. A bull charges into the ring.
6. A rider ropes an animal.
7. The audience cheers a brave rider.
8. The champion wins a medal.
9. The riders go to the next town.
10. The rodeo lasted an hour.

- Use *a* before nouns that begin with a consonant sound. (*page 248*)

   Eiko took a trip.
   She traveled for a year.
- Use *an* before nouns that begin with a vowel sound. (*page 248*)

   The travelers stayed at an inn.
   The prize was an honor.

Practice Write each sentence using the correct article.
1. We visited _____ lake in Africa. (a, an)
2. It is _____ home for many birds. (a, an)
3. We saw _____ animal by the shore. (a, an)
4. It was _____ antelope. (a, an)
5. _____ warthog came to feed by the beautiful lake. (A, An)
6. It ate for _____ hour. (a, an)
7. _____ family of baboons searched for the jungle food. (A, An)
8. They ran away from _____ leopard with large spots. (a, an)
9. _____ eagle landed in a nearby tree. (A, An)
10. The donkey ate _____ yam. (a, an)

- Adjectives can be used to compare two or more nouns. Add *er* to an adjective to compare two persons, places, or things. The word *than* follows an adjective ending in *er*. (*page 250*)

  The cat is small.

  The mouse is smaller than the cat.
- Add *est* to an adjective to compare three or more persons, places, or things. (*page 250*)

  A cow is large.

  A moose is larger than a cow.

  An elephant is the largest animal of the three.
- You also add *est* when the words *of all* are part of the sentence. (*page 250*)

  A whale is the largest animal of all.

Practice Write each sentence, using the correct form of the adjective in parentheses.

1. A drum is (loud) than a flute.
2. The Indian Ocean is (deep) than the Arctic Ocean.
3. The Atlantic is the (deep) ocean of the three.
4. The Pacific is the (deep) ocean of all.
5. Pluto is the (small) planet of all.
6. My little sister Lisa is (young) than my brother Willie.
7. Denise is the (young) child of the three children in our family.
8. My hands are (clean) than your hands.
9. Federico's desk is the (neat) desk of the three in the classroom.
10. Yesterday, Wednesday, was certainly the (rain) day of all.

Adverbs

- An **adverb** is a word that tells more about an action. (*page 296*)

    The train rushes <u>rapidly</u>.
- Some adverbs tell how an action is done. (*page 296*)

    Rain falls <u>steadily</u>.

    (How does the rain fall?   *steadily*)

Practice Write the answer to the question in parentheses.

1. Leaves drift lazily to the ground. (How do leaves drift?)
2. Jerry works hard. (How does Jerry work?)
3. Jerry rakes the leaves briskly. (How does Jerry rake?)
4. His mother calls to him loudly. (How does his mother call?)
5. Jerry runs eagerly to lunch. (How does Jerry run?)

Practice Write each sentence. Put two lines under the adverb. The verb is already underlined.

1. The sun <u>shone</u> brightly.
2. The water <u>sparkled</u> merrily.
3. Our ship <u>bobbed</u> gently on the waves.
4. The sails <u>flapped</u> briskly.
5. A gull <u>dived</u> swiftly.
6. The bird <u>lunged</u> suddenly for a fish.
7. Tina <u>jumped</u> quickly into the water.
8. She <u>swims</u> well.
9. The captain <u>steered</u> carefully.
10. The ship <u>returned</u> safely.

- An **adverb** can tell *where* an action is done. (*page 298*)

    The glider soars up.
- An adverb can also tell *when* an action is done. (*page 298*)

    The plane landed yesterday.

Practice Write the answer to the question in parentheses.

1. The pilot climbs in. (Where does the pilot climb?)
2. She starts the engine now. (When does she start the engine?)
3. She always tests the controls. (When does she test the controls?)
4. The plane lifts up. (Where does the plane lift?)
5. She lands the plane there. (Where does she land the plane?)
6. The pilot steps outside. (Where does the pilot step?)
7. She arrives early. (When does she arrive?)

Practice Write each sentence. Put two lines under the adverb. The verb is already underlined.

1. Miguel wakes early.
2. He looks outside.
3. The boy gazes up at the sky.
4. Fluffy clouds drift there.
5. Yesterday it rained.
6. Miguel played inside all day.
7. Today he goes to the park.
8. The boy soon eats breakfast.
9. He calls Tony later.
10. The boys dash out with their kite.

Sentences II

• The **complete subject** tells whom or what the sentence is about. (*page 332*)

Two brave Americans reached the North Pole.

Practice Write each sentence. Underline the complete subject.

1. Owls hunt at night.
2. The birds fly silently.
3. Dark feathers hide the owls at night.
4. Two large eyes peer from the owl's face.
5. Tiny mice scurry into holes.
6. Some owls eat insects.
7. Most owls live in trees.

• The main word in the subject part of a sentence is often a noun. (*page 332*)

Bright green feathers cover the parrot.

Practice Write each sentence. Put one line under the complete subject. Put two lines under the noun in the subject.

1. Many Indians made clothes from furs.
2. Some tribes wove cloth.
3. Many different plants provided food.
4. Young children gathered berries.
5. The whole family worked hard.
6. A few groups planted pumpkins.
7. Canoes carried fishermen.
8. Small wooden hooks dangled in the water.

- The **complete predicate** tells what the subject of the sentence is or what it does. (*page 334*)

  Hiroki is a potter.

  She makes things from clay.

Practice Write each sentence. Underline the complete predicate.
1. Hiroki takes a piece of clay.
2. She rolls it with her hands.
3. The clay is damp.
4. The potter feels the clay.
5. She presses the pieces of clay together.
6. The clay is round.
7. Hiroki scrapes the clay with a stick.
8. The sides of the pot are smooth.
9. She bakes the clay.

- The main word in the complete predicate is the verb. The verb can be an action verb or a form of the verb *be*. (*page 334*)

  Wilma Rudolph was an athlete.

  Wilma ran in the Olympics.

Practice Write each sentence. Put one line under the complete predicate. Put two lines under the verb.
1. Wilma came from Tennessee.
2. The little girl was very sick.
3. Her leg was weak.
4. Wilma played basketball with her brothers.
5. The girl ran.
6. Wilma studied at college.

7. The young woman won many races.
8. She received a gold medal.
9. She was 20 years old.
- A **compound sentence** is made up of two sentences joined by a comma (,) and the word *and*. (*page 336*)

  The stars shine, and the moon glows.

Practice Join the pairs of sentences with a comma and the word *and* to form compound sentences.
1. The car is red. The boat is blue.
2. Marsha paints. Wayne draws.
3. Apples grow on trees. Berries grow on shrubs.
4. Our trip ended. We returned to school.
5. The sky grew dark. Rain fell.
6. Ted dived in. He swam quickly.
7. The bell rang. The children came inside.
8. The lights dimmed. The movie began.
9. Lightning flashed. Thunder rumbled.

Practice Write each sentence. Then write whether it is *compound* or *not compound*. If it is compound, underline the two parts from which it is formed.
1. Some stars look yellow, and other stars look blue.
2. Stars and planets look different.
3. The sun is a star, and the earth is a planet.
4. The earth and the moon circle the sun.
5. The sun heats the air, and the air warms the earth.
6. The sun sets, and night begins.
7. The sun rises and sets.
8. Plants need sunlight, and animals need plants.
9. We like summer and winter.

◆ Nouns, pronouns, verbs, adjectives, and adverbs are called **parts of speech**. (*page 338*)

Practice Write each sentence. Write whether each underlined word is a *noun, verb,* or *pronoun.*
1. Indians built villages in cliffs.
2. They grew crops in fields.
3. Hunters caught deer.
4. The people ate squash.
5. Farmers harvested corn.
6. Paths led to the top of the cliff.
7. We visited an Indian village.

Practice Write each sentence. Write whether each underlined word is an *adjective* or *adverb.*
1. People use coal for many things.
2. Some coal comes from Pennsylvania.
3. Machines dig deep holes.
4. Workers drill there.
5. They hauled coal yesterday.
6. The dark coal burns brightly.
7. The huge coal truck has twelve wheels.

Practice Write each sentence. Write the part of speech that names each underlined word.
1. Our class studied spiders.
2. They have eight legs.
3. Some spiders eat fish.
4. The tiny spider spins a sticky web.
5. The spider drops down suddenly.
6. Tarantulas are the largest spiders of all.
7. Many tarantulas live in South America.

Mechanics Rules and Practice

Capitalization and End Marks

Capitalize the following	
the first letter of each sentence *(page 34)*	The bird sings.
each important word in a proper noun, such as people's names and titles, and specific places or things *(pages 84, 90, 92, 238)*	Mr, Sam Sterling *(pages 80, 238)* July *(page 92)* Ludlow Street *(pages 84, 238)* White Mountains *(pages 84, 238)*
the first word only in the closing of a letter *(page 200)*	Yours truly, Sincerely yours,
Use this end punctuation	
a period at the end of a statement *(page 42)*	The geese fly away.
a period at the end of a command *(page 44)*	Go to the store.
a question mark at the end of a question *(page 42)*	Where is my kite?
an exclamation mark at the end of an exclamation *(page 44)*	Wow, what a pretty flower!

A. Practice   Write each sentence. Correct the capitalization and the end punctuation.

1. have you seen the birdhouse at the zoo
2. no, I haven't
3. go see it
4. there are many different kinds of birds
5. what kinds of birds are there
6. the house has mockingbirds, parrots, peacocks, toucans, and many more
7. wow, I'd love to see them
8. take the bus directly to the zoo
9. how long is the trip
10. it takes one hour

B. Practice Write each sentence. Correct the capitalization.

11. Where I live, there are more fish in july and august than in december.
12. In june, many fish swim to cooler waters.
13. During november and december some fish swim to warmer waters.
14. The whitney museum is on madison avenue.
15. The center of chinatown is mott street.
16. The train station is on avenue of the americas.
17. hawaii is one of the united states.
18. The smithsonian institute is located in washington, d.c.
19. The capital of nebraska is lincoln.
20. The largest state in the united states is alaska.
21. The prudential tower is in boston.
22. You can see the statue of liberty in new york.
23. Have you read any books about mary poppins?
24. They were written by pamela travers.
25. My favorite books were written by frank baum.
26. He wrote the *wizard of oz.*
27. Last year I read the *cat in the hat comes back.*

C. Practice Write each short letter. Use correct capitalization.

28. dear peter
    Please get well soon.
        best wishes
        Your teammates

29. dear aunt minnie,
    It was wonderful to see you last week.
        love
        Yoko

Commas

Use a comma	
to set off the name of a person spoken to directly in a sentence *(page 72)*	Mindy, please come here. Please go there, John.
after *yes, no,* and *well* when they begin a sentence *(page 72)*	Yes, I can do it.
after a time order word when it begins a sentence *(page 72)*	First, fold the shirt. Then, put it in the closet.
to separate three or more items in a series *(page 72)*	I like eggs, ham, and cheese.
before the word *and* when you join two complete thoughts into a compound sentence *(page 72)*	I went to the library, and borrowed two books.
between the city and the state in an address *(page 200)*	Albany, New York
between the day and the year in a date *(page 200)*	June 23, 1957
after the greeting of a letter *(page 200)*	Dear Jacob,
after the closing of a letter *(page 200)*	Your friend, Love,

A. Practice   Write each sentence. Add commas where needed.

1. Lena where is your workbook?
2. Did you finish the last lesson Amy?
3. I finished it last night Abdul.
4. Please return the book Ann.
5. I'll return it tomorrow Mr. Filbert.
6. Jeff I met your cousin Lea.

7. Yes I heard that.
8. No I don't think it's true.
9. Yes I'll ask him tomorrow.
10. Well maybe he'll visit us.
11. No he doesn't live far away.
12. Well maybe they'll come with us.

13. I love the colors red orange and brown.
14. My hat scarf and mittens are red.
15. Dad's boots coats and hat are brown.
16. Mom Dad and I go out for a walk.

B. Practice   Write each sentence. Add a comma where necessary.

17. Chicago is the capital of Illinois and it is on Lake Michigan.
18. It has many tall buildings and my aunt and uncle live there.
19. I went to visit them and they took me up to the top of a very tall building.
20. It was the Sears Tower and it is the tallest office building in the world.
21. My ears popped in the elevator and I felt dizzy.
22. There was an observation deck at the top and we could see the whole city from there.
23. It was a clear day and we could see almost a hundred miles away.

C. Practice   Write each letter. Add commas where necessary.

24.   4 Madera Ave.
             Taft CA 93268
             June 17 1990
        Dear Aunt Julie
           Thank you for everything. Please say hi to Ana.
                Love
                   Paco

25.   17 Acorn Rd.
             Wall NJ 07719
             July 14 1990
        Dear Aziz
           I hope your party was fun. I'm sorry I missed it.
                Your friend
                   Amy

Apostrophes, Abbreviations, and Initials

Use an apostrophe	
to replace a missing letter or letters in a contraction (pages 170, 214, 284)	do not don't (pages 170, 284) she will she'll (pages 214, 284)
to make the possessive form of a singular noun or a plural noun that does not end in s, add an apostrophe and s. (pages 86, 284)	Anjou's records children's books
to make the possessive form of most plural nouns, add an apostrophe at the end of the word (pages 88, 284)	bears' lair elephants' trunks

When writing an abbreviation	
capitalize the first letter in abbreviations of proper nouns and addresses (pages 90, 92, 158)	Dr. Zipser, Ms. Lowe (page 90) Oak St., Grand Ave., (page 158) Jan., Feb., Mon., Tues. (pages 92, 158)
end most abbreviations with a period (pages 90, 92)	Mr. Green, Mrs. Slavin (page 90) Aug., Sept., Oct., Nov. (page 92)
for an initial in a person's name, use a capital letter followed by a period (pages 90, 238)	F. D. Roosevelt H. Doolittle
to abbreviate ordinal numbers write a numeral and an ending, but no period (page 158)	1st, 2nd, 3rd 31st, 25th, 43rd

A. Practice   Write each sentence. Make each underlined word possessive.

1. The post office delivers peoples mail.
2. Americas post office is one of the largest in the world.
3. The post offices equipment is fast and efficient.
4. The mail carrier picks up the days mail from boxes.
5. Stamp collectors groups meet regularly.
6. The groups members learn from each other.
7. Different members stamps are often exchanged.
8. People collect different countries stamps.

436

B. Practice Write each sentence. Write the contraction for each underlined word.

9. Please <u>dont</u> forget.
10. He <u>doesnt</u> have the time.
11. <u>Well</u> see you later.
12. <u>Theyve</u> a job to do.
13. <u>Im</u> happy to see you.
14. <u>Shes</u> coming later.
15. <u>Were</u> going there together.

C. Practice Write each abbreviation correctly.

16. <u>ms</u> Brown works on Apple <u>aven</u>, at the school.
17. Sam went to 86th <u>Str.</u> to see <u>doc.</u> Stein
18. On Hicks <u>av.</u> I saw <u>mr</u> and <u>mrs</u> Kane's car
19. Last. <u>frid</u> they went ice-skating.
20. On <u>thur.</u>, he brought a poster to school.
21. In <u>Decem</u>, we have our first long vacation.
22. In <u>Janu.</u> it often snows.
23. <u>e l</u> Konigsburg wrote *From the Mixed-Up Files of Mrs. Basil <u>e</u> Frankweiler*.
24. After <u>f. d.</u> Roosevelt, the next President was <u>h. s.</u> Truman.

D. Practice Write each sentence. Abbreviate each underlined word.

25. Pennsylvania was the <u>second</u> state to join the Union.
26. Connecticut was the <u>fifth</u> state to join the Union.
27. Illinois was the <u>twenty-first</u> state to join the Union.
28. Thomas Jefferson was our <u>third</u> President.

Writing Titles and Conversation

To write titles of works	
Capitalize the first word, the last word, and all important words *(page 122)*	*A Chair for My Mother* *The Wizard of Oz*
Underline book titles *(page 122)*	*The Little Prince*
Put short stories and poem titles in quotation marks *(page 122)*	"A Curve in the River" "Dandelion Magic"
To write conversation	
Enclose a speaker's exact words in quotation marks *(page 326)*	She said, "Hello, nice to meet you."
Begin a quotation with a capital letter *(page 326)*	He said, "See you later."
Separate a quotation from the rest of a sentence with a comma *(page 326)*	"Try again," said Dad.
Put the end marks inside the quotation marks when the quote is at the end of a sentence *(page 326)*	Sam replied, "I will." Aiko said, "Wow, it's great!"

A. Practice Write each book, story, and poem title correctly.

1. book: the little Prince
2. book: the cat in the hat
3. book: yertle the turtle
4. book: the wizard of oz

5. story: the tortoise and the hare
6. story: the three little pigs
7. story: snow white and the seven dwarfs
8. story: the adventurous sardine

9. poem: the owl and the pussycat
10. poem: walk at night
11. poem: city

B. Practice Write each sentence. Correct the capitalization and quotation marks if necessary.

12. Mario said, it's snowing outside.
13. Sue said, it looks like it won't stop.
14. I said, let's build a snowman.
15. Mike yelled look, it's a real storm!
16. Mr. Black said, you may all go home now.

C. Practice Write each sentence. Add commas where necessary.

17. "Last weekend we saw the marathon" Mary said.
18. "The race was 22 miles long" Al said.
19. Mom asked "Were there people watching?"
20. Mary said "Oh, yes, very many!"
21. Al said "Here is the program."

D. Practice Write each sentence. Put end punctuation marks at the end of each quote.

22. "Wow, look who just walked by" Tyreen said.
23. "Who is it" I asked.
24. "Don't you recognize him" Tyreen asked.
25. I said, "No, I don't"
26. "He is Jacques Cousteau, the famous oceanographer" he said.

E. Practice Write each sentence. Add proper capitalization and punctuation.

27. Mom called out, is there anyone home
28. I answered, I am, Mom
29. She yelled, where are you
30. I answered, over here in the kitchen

Troublesome Words

◆ Homophones are words that sound alike but have different spellings and different meanings. This chart shows several homophones that are easy to confuse.

Word	Meaning	Example
its	belonging to it	I have a new shirt. Its sleeves are long.
it's	it is	It's my favorite shirt.
their	belonging to them	The cats eat their lunch.
there	in or at that place	Put the food there.
they're	they are	They're friendly animals.

A. Practice   Write each sentence, using the correct word in parentheses.

1. The children put on ____ coats. (their, there)
2. ____ ready for the ballgame. (There, They're)
3. ____ very late. (Its, It's)
4. ____ is the dog. (Their, There, They're)
5. The tickets are in ____ mouth. (its, it's)
6. The dog runs here and ____. (their, there)
7. He thinks ____ a fun game. (its, it's)
8. The children catch ____ dog. (their, they're)

B. Practice   Use the directions for Practice A.

9. ____ is a baby bird. (Their, There, They're)
10. ____ lost. (Its, It's)
11. The boys find ____ father. (their, there)
12. ____ worried about the bird. (There, They're)
13. Where is ____ mother? (its, it's)
14. Father puts the baby in ____ nest. (its, it's)
15. The boys clap ____ hands. (their, there)
16. ____ happy now. (Their, There, They're)

♦ This chart shows other homophones that are easy to confuse.

Word	Meaning	Example
to	in the direction of	Hand the clay to Don.
too	also; more than enough	Lola wants some, too. She has too much clay.
two	the number 2	I have two lumps of clay.
your	belonging to you	Is this your sled?
you're	you are	You're on the sled.

A. Practice   Write each sentence, using the correct word in parentheses.

1. We go ___ the dentist. (to, too, two)
2. She cleans ___ teeth. (your, you're)
3. She cleans my teeth, ___. (to, too, two)
4. The baby has ___ teeth. (to, too, two)
5. Is this ___ toothbrush? (your, you're)
6. ___ ready for the dentist. (Your, You're)
7. We got here ___ early. (to, too, two)
8. You must wait for ___ turn. (your, you're)
9. The dentist points ___ the chair. (to, too, two)

B. Practice   Use the directions for Practice A.

10. Janet runs ___ first base. (to, too, two)
11. Bob swings the bat ___ times. (to, too, two)
12. Jill borrowed ___ glove. (your, you're)
13. She borrowed a hat, ___. (to, too, two)
14. She throws the ball ___ Jim. (to, too, two)
15. It's ___ turn at bat. (your, you're)
16. ___ a good batter. (Your, You're)
17. You made ___ runs. (to, too, two)
18. ___ a champion! (Your, You're)

441

Index

Illustrations: Teresa Anderko, 22, 40, 53, 78–80, 110–111, 172, 206–207, 244–245, 278–279, 290–291; Susan David, 48, 170–171, 337; Nancy Didion, 117, 209, 215, 238; Paul Harvey, 160, 195; Meryl Henderson, 46–47, 164–165; Steve Henry, 64, 74, 83, 133, 246–247, 321–326; John Killgrew, 148–149, 152, 157, 272; Linda Miamoto, 332, 334–335; Carl Molno, 276–277, 280–281; Sal Murdocca, 34–35, 118–119, 122–123; Jon O'Brien, 306–307; Diane Paterson, 26–27, 30, 71, 108–109, 115, 146–147, 188–189, 250; Jan Pyke, 20–21, 222–223; Claudia Sargent, 62–63, 67, 89, 94, 139, 190–191, 195, 200, 268–269, 271, 292, 299; Claire Schumaker, 39, 77, 101, 127, 163, 179, 205, 243, 259, 293, 305, 331, 347; Mou Tsientseng, 130, 224–225, 297; Lane Yerkes, 18–19, 25, 51, 128–129, 158, 168–169, 228–229, 234.

Photographs: 33 John Lei/Omni-Photo Communications, Inc.; **41** The Granger Collection; **68** John Lei/Omni-Photo Communications, Inc.; **72** Ken Karp/Omni-Photo Communications, Inc.; **86** Ken Karp/Omni-Photo Communications, Inc.; **93** NASA; **113** Ken Karp/Omni-Photo Communications, Inc.; **121** Ken Karp/Omni-Photo Communications, Inc.; **136** (both) UPI/Bettmann Newsphotos; **150 The Bettmann Archive; 154–155** John Lei/Omni-Photo Communications, Inc.; **197** John Lei/Omni-Photo Communications, Inc.; **199** Ken Karp/Omni-Photo Communications, Inc.; **210** John Lei/Omni-Photo Communications, Inc.; **227** John Lei/Omni-Photo Communications, Inc. Cosmo Map Series © Copyright 87-S-171 by Rand McNally & Company, R.L. 87-S-171; **249** The Granger Collection; **274** John Lei/Omni-Photo Communications, Inc.; **284–285** John Lei/Omni-Photo Communications, Inc.; **289** Ken Karp/Omni-Photo Communications, Inc. International World Map © Copyright 87-S-171 by Rand McNally & Company, R.L. Antique maps courtesy of Library of Congress; **325** John Lei/Omni-Photo Communications, Inc.

Acknowledgments

For permission to adapt and reprint copyrighted materials, grateful acknowledgment is made to the following publishers, authors, and other copyright holders:

Atheneum Publishers for "Our Washing Machine" from *The Apple Vendor's Fair* by Patricia Hubbell. Copyright ©1963 by Patricia Hubbell. Used by permission of Atheneum Publishers; for "Zebra" from *Flashlight and Other Poems* by Judith Thurman. Copyright ©1976 by Judith Thurman. Used by permission of Atheneum Publishers.

Children's Better Health Institute, Benjamin Franklin Literary & Medical Society, for "Where the Bear Went Over the Mountain." From *Child Life* magazine, copyright ©1973 by The Saturday Evening Post Company. Adapted by permission of Children's Better Health Institute, Benjamin Franklin Literary & Medical Society, Inc., Indianapolis, Indiana.

E. P. Dutton, for "Yagua Days" from *Yagua Days* by Cruz Martel. Copyright © 1976 by Cruz Martel. Used by permission of Dial Press, an imprint of E. P. Dutton.

Harcourt Brace Jovanovich, Inc., for "Feet" from *Whispers and Other Poems* by Myra Cohn Livingston. Copyright © 1958 by Myra Cohn Livingston. Used by permission of Harcourt Brace Jovanovich, Inc.; for "The Little Road" from *Magpie Lane* by Nancy Byrd Turner, copyright ©1927 by Harcourt Brace Jovanovich, Inc. and renewed 1955 by Nancy Byrd Turner, reprinted by permission of the publisher.

Harper & Row, Publishers, Inc., for "The Snake" from *Dogs & Dragons, Trees & Dreams* by Karla Kuskin. Copyright © 1980 by Karla Kuskin. Reprinted by permission of Harper & Row, Publishers, Inc.

Alfred A. Knopf, Inc., for "In Coal Country" excerpted from *In Coal Country* by Judith Hendershot, illustrations by Thomas B. Allen. Text copyright © 1987 by Judith Hendershot. Illustrations copyright © 1987 by Thomas B. Allen. Reprinted by permission of Alfred A. Knopf, Inc.

Little, Brown & Co., Inc., for "The Shell" from *One at a Time* by David McCord. Copyright © 1925, 1974 by David McCord. Used by permission of Little, Brown & Co., Inc.

Macmillan Publishing Co. for "The Little Turtle" from *Golden Whales* by Vachel Lindsay. Reprinted by permission of the publisher.

William Morrow & Co. for "Sunrise" from *City Sandwich* by Frank Asch. Copyright © 1978 by Frank Asch. Reprinted by permission of William Morrow & Co.

G. P. Putnam's Sons for "Blum" from *All Together* by Dorothy Aldis. Copyright © 1925, © 1952 by Dorothy Aldis. Reprinted with permission of G. P. Putnam's Sons; for "Little" from *All Together* by Dorothy Aldis. Copyright ©1925, © 1952 by Dorothy Aldis. Reprinted with permission of G. P. Putnam's Sons; for "My Nose" from *All Together* by Dorothy Aldis. Copyright © 1925, © 1952 by Dorothy Aldis. Reprinted with permission of G. P. Putnam's Sons.

Random House, Inc., for "Mud" by Polly Chase Boyden.

Marian Reiner, Literary Agent, for "Foghorns" from *I Thought I Heard the City* by Lilian Moore. Copyright © 1969 by Lilian Moore. Used by permission of Marian Reiner.

Viking Penguin, Inc., for "Firefly" from *Under the Tree* by Elizabeth Madox Roberts. Copyright ©1930 by The Viking Press, Inc. Copyright renewed 1958 by Ivor S. Roberts. Reprinted by permission of Viking Penguin, Inc.

Highlights

Hidden Pictures
Halloween Puffy Sticker Playscenes

**Find 8 hidden objects in each scene.
Then use your stickers to decorate!**

Illustrated by Mattia Cerato, Mike Dammer,
Kelly Kennedy, James Loram, and Mike Moran

HIGHLIGHTS PRESS
Honesdale, Pennsylvania

Back to School

It's Harry's first day of school. Say cheese!

Objects to Find

Egg

Balloon

Dish

Pinecone

Spaceship

Football

Watermelon

Paper Clip

Imagine and Draw

What is Harry having for lunch? Draw a picture of it here.

Fall Fun

The more leaves that fall now, the bigger the pile to jump in later!

Objects to Find

Bell

Carrot

Button

Sailboat

Toothbrush

Glove

Comb

Bread

Make a Match

Find three pairs of matching rakes.

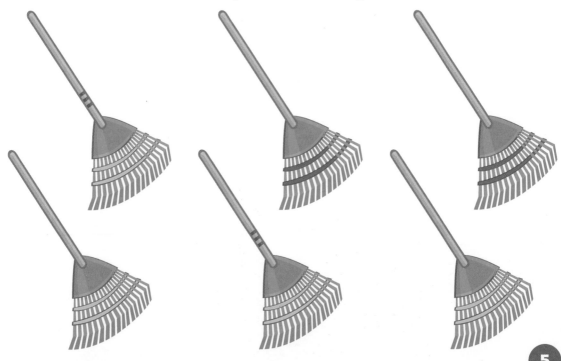

Bare Bones Café

What's on the menu for today?

Objects to Find

Tennis Ball

Boomerang

Cloud

Wedge of Lemon

Whale

Tennis Racket

Ruler

Key

Find Your Way
Which monster ordered which meal?

Pumpkin Carving

Gio and Adriana are almost finished with their jack-o'-lanterns!

Objects to Find

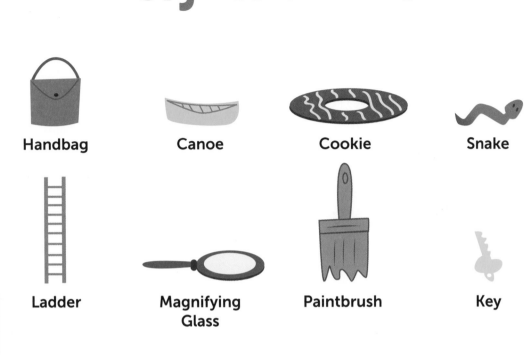

Handbag

Canoe

Cookie

Snake

Ladder

Magnifying Glass

Paintbrush

Key

Imagine and Draw

What would you like to be for Halloween?
Draw a picture of your costume here.

Witch Way?

Where are these witches flying off to?

Objects to Find

Wristwatch

Wok

Whale

Waffle

Wrench

Worm

Whistle

Watering Can

Make a Match
Find 3 pairs of matching brooms.

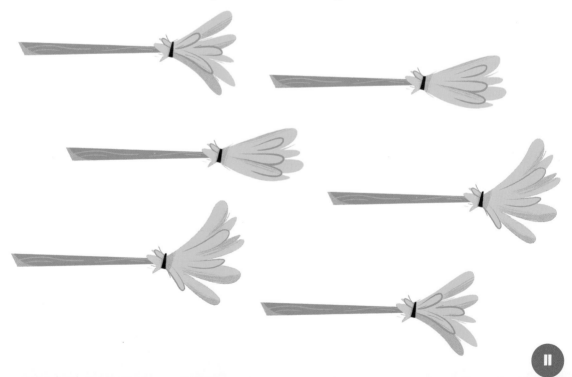

Brilliant Jack-o'-Lantern

This pumpkin is ready for Halloween.

Objects to Find

Umbrella

Toothbrush

Comb

Ruler

Paintbrush

Sailboat

Envelope

Belt

Find Your Way

Help the trick-or-treaters find their candy bags.

Trick or Treat!

These trick-or-treaters are getting lots of candy today.

Objects to Find

Hairbrush

Hot Dog

Horseshoe

Hat

Hoe

Hook

Heart

Hammer

Imagine and Draw

Decorate these pumpkins for Halloween.

All Wrapped Up

Nobody knows who's going to win.

Objects to Find

Slice of Pizza

Envelope

Slice of Bread

Candy Cane

Lollipop

Belt

Sailboat

Pencil

Make a Match

Find three pairs of matching mummies.

Ding Dong!

"Trick or Treat!"

Objects to Find

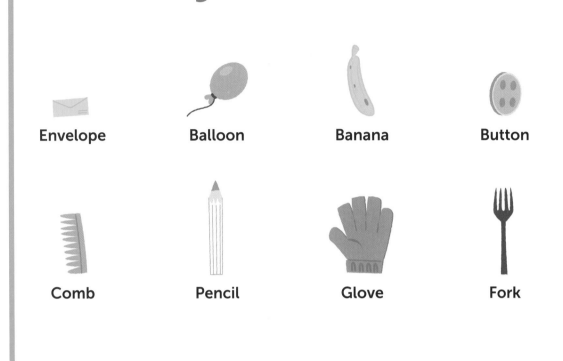

Envelope Balloon Banana Button

Comb Pencil Glove Fork

Find Your Way

Help the trick-or-treaters find the way to the house.

Clownin' Around

Everything is on the menu at this clown restaurant.

Objects to Find

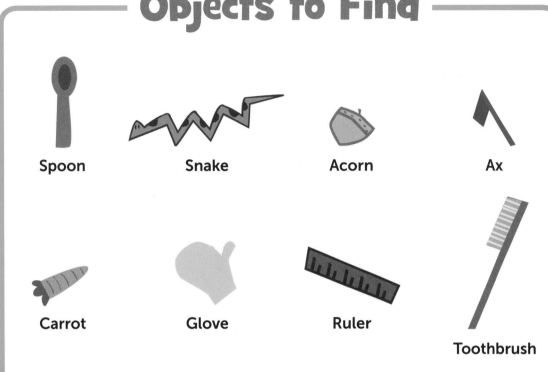

Spoon Snake Acorn Ax

Carrot Glove Ruler

Toothbrush

Imagine and Draw

If you were a clown, what would you look like?
Draw a picture of it here.

Horror Movie

Cover your eyes, this scene is scary!

Objects to Find

 **Golf Club**

 Sock

 Magnifying Glass

 **Butterfly**

 Bell

 **Umbrella**

 Star

 Snail

Make a Match
Find three pairs of matching movies.

Haunted House

What's inside this spooky house?

Objects to Find

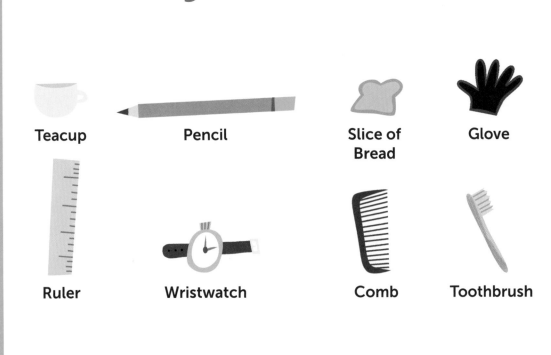

Teacup

Pencil

Slice of Bread

Glove

Ruler

Wristwatch

Comb

Toothbrush

Find Your Way

Which path leads to the black cat's home?

Shopping Bonanza

All shoes are on sale at this popular monster shopping spot.

Objects to Find

Toothbrush

Moon

Pencil

Magnet

Envelope

Slice of Pizza

Crown

Hockey Stick

Imagine and Draw

What kind of shoe do you think a monster would wear?
Draw a picture of it here.

Pumpkin Frenzy

Join the fun pumpkin picking at Perry's popular pumpkin patch.

Objects to Find

Slice of Bread

Ruler

Baseball

Cookie

Umbrella

Kite

Spoon

Straw

Make a Match
Find three pairs of matching owls.

Night Games

Who-o-o will win this game of hide-and-go-seek?

Objects to Find

Canoe

Cheese

Snail

Funnel

Sock

Glove

Seashell

Horseshoe

Find Your Way

Follow the lines to see what hat each squirrel will wear for Halloween.

31

That's the Spirit!

With a spook-tacular performance by the Ghosts, they take the lead!

Objects to Find

Ice-Cream Bar

Slice of Pizza

Eyeglasses

Waffle

Ice-Cream Cone

Slice of Pie

Sailboat

Magnet

Imagine and Draw

If you were on a basketball team, what would your uniform look like?
Draw a picture of it here.

Candy Swap

Who will trade a chocolate bar for a lollipop?

Objects to Find

 Baseball

 Snake

 Hockey Stick

 **Teacup**

 **Kite**

 Candle

 Comb

Slice of Pizza

Make a Match
Find three pairs of matching treat bags.

An A-maize-ing Maze

Don't tell secrets in the maze—the corn has ears.

Objects to Find

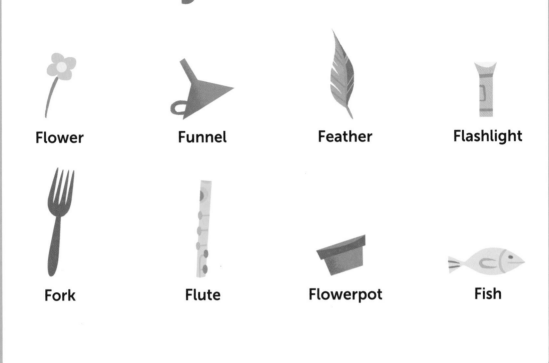

Flower   Funnel   Feather   Flashlight

Fork   Flute   Flowerpot   Fish

Find Your Way

Help Jade find her way through the corn maze.

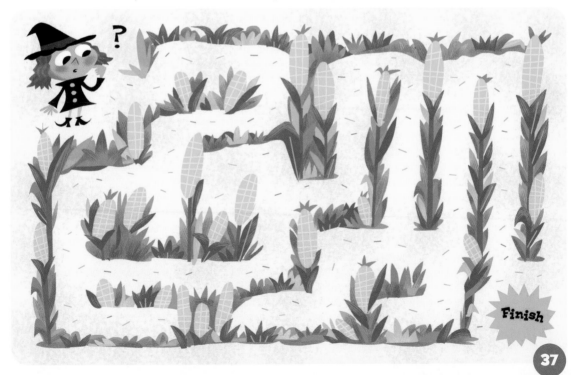

Finish

Vampire Bat Bedtime

The sun is up—time for bed!

Objects to Find

Cheese

Ice-Cream Bar

Party Hat

Toothpaste

Ice-Cream Cone

Pumpkin

Carrot

Ax

Imagine and Draw

What do you think a worm's home would look like?
Draw a picture of it here.

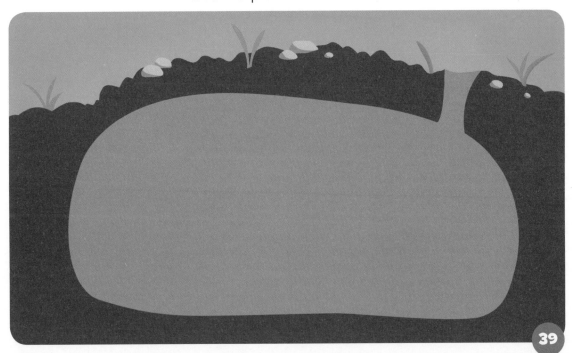

At the Costume Shop

These wolves are almost ready for Halloween.

Objects to Find

Worm

Banana

Canoe

Horseshoe

Hockey Stick

Lollipop

Ruler

Toothbrush

Make a Match

Find three pairs of matching boots.

Boogie Nights

The pack is dancing long into the night at the annual Halloween Bash.

Objects to Find

Slice of Pizza

Comb

Ruler

Moon

Baseball Bat

Ring

Crown

Yo-Yo

Find Your Way

Follow the path to find out who won which prize for dancing.

What a Web!

Sally Spider is an expert at weaving her web.

Objects to Find

 **Pen**

 **Sled**

 Vest

 Egg

 Lemon

 **Jet**

 Bell

 **Tent**

Imagine and Draw

A spider's home is its web. What does your home look like?
Draw a picture of it here.

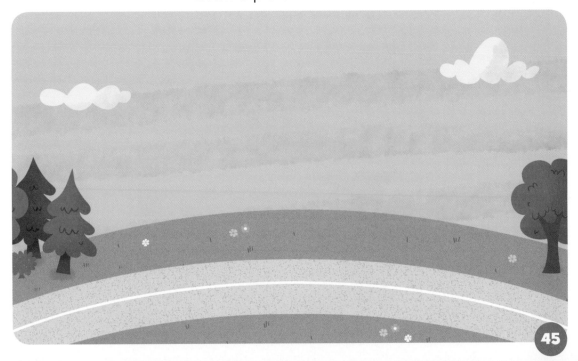

Answers

Page 2

Pages 4-5

Pages 6-7

Page 8

Pages 10-11

Pages 12-13

Page 14

Pages 16-17

Answers

Pages 18–19

Page 20

Pages 22–23

Pages 24–25

Page 26

Pages 28–29

Pages 30–31

Page 32

47

Pages 34-35

Pages 36-37

Page 38

Pages 40-41

Pages 42-43

Page 44

For information about permission to reprint selections from this book,
please contact permissions@highlights.com.

Published by Highlights Press
815 Church Street
Honesdale, Pennsylvania 18431
Printed in Humen Town, Dongguan City, China;
Stickers manufactured in Huizhou, Guangdong, China.
06/2020
ISBN: 978-1-64472-116-2

First edition
Visit our website at Highlights.com.
10 9 8 7 6 5 4 3 2